Praise for *Zaidy's Band*

"With humor, wit, and pathos, Aron Heller tells a largely unknown story of Jewish heroism in the air in the struggle to defeat Nazism. In these times, it is a story that is well worth repeating."

David Jay Bercuson, Professor of History, University of Calgary, author of *The Secret Army*, and Officer, Order of Canada

"Despite the author's formidable journalistic interviewing skills, it was his self-deprecating World War II veteran grandfather Mickey Heller who for years remained his most elusive subject. But with persistence and dogged research, Aron Heller eventually managed to paint a nuanced yet colorful portrait of what motivated his Zaidy and a band of his compatriots to leave their homes in Canada and fight Hitler. Some later volunteered to help Israel's ragtag army repel five Arab armies in that country's 1948 War of Independence. The author also chronicles that service and notably unpacks the mystery of a long-overlooked crew of unsung heroes whose stories have largely been ignored."

Ellin Bessner, author of *Double Threat: Canadian Jews, the Military and World War II*

"In this moving account of his search for his grandfather's World War II past, Aron Heller ponders the gaps in his knowledge about his Zaidy's history. How well do we know our own kin? And what do we know exactly? Piecing together shards of information, a key issue surfaces, all too relevant today: the deep patriotism of minority group members – so deep that it prompts them to take up arms."

Debórah Dwork, author of *Saints and Liars: The Story of Americans Who Saved Refugees from the Nazis*

"Many of us wonder what our grandparents were like in their primes. But few make the effort to find out. In *Zaidy's Band*, Aron Heller goes above and beyond in this difficult mission with a heartfelt tale that is a memoir, a mystery and a history book all in one. The result is a deep appreciation for Mickey Heller and a fascinating glimpse of a forgotten group of comrades who played unlikely roles in defeating the Nazis and shaping the modern Middle East."

Josef Federman, Deputy Middle East News Director, The Associated Press

"The Greatest Generation that defeated fascism in World War II was not limited to one nation. Nor was the specific experience of Jewish soldiers, whose service and sacrifice also meant to rescue their European brethren. In this lucid, informative, and deeply honest book, Aron Heller tells the Canadian version of both of those narratives. Heller may have started with the narrower mission of discovering the wartime experiences of his beloved yet evasive grandfather Mickey, but in the end he paints a broader portrait of valor and purpose by tens of thousands of Canadian Jewish soldiers."

Samuel G. Freedman, author of *Jew vs. Jew* and Professor Emeritus, School of Journalism, Columbia University

"From breadcrumbs of personal information about Mickey Heller, his grandson, Aron Heller, provides us with a feast of history, telling the story of his Zaidy and of Canadian Jews who risked their lives to fly and fight against the Nazi regime in World War II and for the nascent State of Israel in 1948. This book reads like a detective novel, with family insights and international intrigue, as Aron Heller tries to convince his grandfather to disclose personal memories of his World War II experience. We learn that for many who put on a uniform, the 'most impressive feat was to have endured.'"

Rabbi Baruch Frydman-Kohl, Rabbi Emeritus, Beth Tzedec Congregation, Toronto, and Member, Order of Canada

"Aron Heller masterfully brings to life the courage of a small band of Jewish brothers who stood up to Nazi Germany, while at the same time paying moving tribute to his own grandfather."

Yaakov Katz, author of *Shadow Strike* and co-author of *While Israel Slept*

"Beautifully written and illustrated with rare photographs and documents, Aron Heller's book begins as a deeply personal quest to better understand his grandfather, a veteran of the Canadian Armed Forces during World War II. It unfolds into a powerful exploration of forgotten heroes: the Jewish soldiers and officers who fought in the war. With the curiosity and rigor of an investigative journalist, Heller retraces the lives of his grandfather and his comrades – their service, their friendships, and their enduring role in building and sustaining peace. This is history at its finest: rooted in human stories yet illuminating a broader historical narrative."

Anna Shternshis, J. Richard and Dorothy Shiff Chair in Jewish Studies, University of Toronto

ARON HELLER

ZAIDY'S BAND

The Untold Stories of a Jewish Band of Brothers in World War II

New Jewish Press
An imprint of University of Toronto Press
Toronto Buffalo London
utppublishing.com

Printed in Canada

ISBN 978-1-4875-6118-5 (paper)
ISBN 978-1-4875-6120-8 (EPUB)
ISBN 978-1-4875-6119-2 (PDF)

Library and Archives Canada Cataloguing in Publication

Title: Zaidy's band : the untold stories of a Jewish band of brothers in World War II / Aron Heller.
Names: Heller, Aron, author.
Description: Includes bibliographical references and index.
Identifiers: Canadiana (print) 20250265192 | Canadiana (ebook) 20250265257 | ISBN 9781487561185 (paper) | ISBN 9781487561192 (PDF) | ISBN 9781487561208 (EPUB)
Subjects: LCSH: World War, 1939–1945 – Participation, Jewish. | LCSH: World War, 1939–1945 – Participation, Canadian. | LCSH: Jewish soldiers – Canada – Biography. | LCSH: Veterans – Canada – Biography. | LCGFT: Biographies.
Classification: LCC D810.J4 H45 2025 | DDC 940.53089/924071 – dc23

Cover design: (front) Jerrin Heller; (back) Kristjan Buckingham
Cover image: Courtesy of the Heller family.

We wish to acknowledge the land on which the University of Toronto Press operates. This land is the traditional territory of the Wendat, the Anishnaabeg, the Haudenosaunee, the Métis, and the Mississaugas of the Credit First Nation.

University of Toronto Press acknowledges the financial support of the Government of Canada, the Canada Council for the Arts, and the Ontario Arts Council, an agency of the Government of Ontario, for its publishing activities.

Canada Council for the Arts
Conseil des Arts du Canada

Funded by the Government of Canada
Financé par le gouvernement du Canada

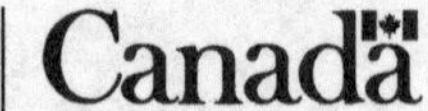

To Zaidy, who took his time telling his story and led me to others.
And to Ima, who always believed in me and would have been so proud to see this book published.

Contents

THE CANADIANS

THE MUSEUM

THE HELLERS

Photos

Preface

In May 2011, with my grandfather – my *Zaidy* – Mickey Heller closing in on his ninetieth birthday, I vowed to conquer a lifetime of frustration by embarking on a mission that had long eluded my extended family – to figure out what happened to Zaidy in World War II.

We knew he had spent two years in Europe as a navigator in the Royal Canadian Air Force. He even posed in uniform at his 1944 wedding. But any further broaching of the subject was strictly taboo. He was already a man of few words, but when it came to that chapter, there were hardly any words at all.

My curiosity burned. I had become suspicious that there was a deep, dark secret to uncover, and I spent years scratching the surface to find out what it was while still trying to respect his desire for privacy.

But now was the time to dig deeper. As a journalist, I found I had a knack for earning the trust of typically shy veterans and Holocaust survivors and producing stories that made them proud. Silence had served them well to get through the daily grind of life, but candor gave them peace as they neared the end of it.

I felt I owed my grandfather the opportunity to leave something behind as well. He deserved another chance to tell his story and I, as his devoted, World War II–obsessed journalist grandson, was just the one to nudge him there.

That's how our more than decade-long journey began. What followed were eight Israel-to-Toronto visits and countless other calls and messages that turned into a detailed journal that interspersed these exchanges with my own interactions with other veterans and Holocaust survivors of his generation.

As the Jerusalem correspondent for the Associated Press, I had a professional mission to log as many of these stories as possible into the archive of human history before it was too late. Now, I was devoted to doing the same in a personal mission about my relative with the closest link to that era.

Hesitantly, Zaidy began to slowly open up, shining a narrow light, if not so much on his own biography than on the monumental shadow that the war cast upon men like him. It was a see-saw dynamic in which he would surprisingly blossom and then suddenly snap shut like a vulnerable flower determined to protect a treasure it kept hidden deep inside.

That delicate dance transformed our relationship, redefined his final years, and, most significantly, spawned dozens of other previously unknown storylines of World War II–era figures. Zaidy introduced me to the long-lost tales of friends such as Somer James and Wilfred Canter. By varying degrees of separation, I came to know throughout this journey so many other colorful characters from that different time and place – all of whom have since passed away. Their catchy monikers – Smoky, Tolka, and the King of the Negev – tell just a sliver of the story.

I set out to unpack the past of my family's patriarch. I imagined a discovery that would help me understand him better, perhaps an epic tale to add to the canon of Jewish wartime heroism. What I've come away with, though, has amounted to something far different yet no less significant. It has offered a rare glimpse into the soul of one of those silent majority of World War II veterans, those who never sought to write their memoirs and preferred instead to be left alone. Still, with the passage of time, Zaidy ultimately did drop some breadcrumbs for his inquisitive grandson, leading to the discovery of long-lost friendships, tragedies, acts of bravery, and reunions.

Piecing these unknown stories together through the connecting tissue that is my grandfather has provided a fresh look at a wide array of Jewish men who partook in the defining moments of their times, namely, the war against Nazism and, shortly after, the battle to establish Israel. My individual journey with Zaidy and his mostly Jewish band of brothers paralleled that of a prospective museum in Israel that sought out the same mission on a grander scale: to unpack the largely untold legacy of the 1.5 million Jewish World War II soldiers.

Like their respective countrymen, these fighters were motivated by patriotism and allegiance to their home nations. But they had an extra driving force: to save their defenseless Jewish brethren in Europe from a Nazi regime bent on their destruction. Some 250,000 Jewish soldiers died for the cause. For those who survived, it was a life-altering event that spurred many veterans to channel their military skills toward the fight for Israeli independence, to guarantee a Jewish homeland as a bulwark against another Holocaust.

It was a moment of moral clarity, when the divide between good and evil was explicit, and their stories unfolded throughout a pivotal era in Jewish history. Their voices, however, are not mere relics of the past. They speak to us today as we endure perhaps the most dangerous wave of antisemitism since then and the most perilous period for the Jewish state as well.

The Nazi genocide of European Jewry inspired these men to take a stand against the Jew-hatred of their time, with the hopeful vision that that war and its consequences would rid their people of the most murderous elements of the ancient threat against them. Each one's individual choices influenced the paths their lives would take, and these same dilemmas of faith, values, belonging, courage, and sacrifice still define the Jewish experience of our times.

All this has come into much clearer focus following the October 7, 2023, atrocities and the far-reaching fallout they have created. A country founded to serve as a haven for Jews endured its single deadliest day since the Holocaust. Suddenly, life in Israel had been transformed into a new reality of sirens, missile attacks, and disruption. The prolonged hostage crisis has torn at the soul of the nation, as have the steady stream of casualties from the war in Gaza. Israel's retaliation delivered massive devastation upon the Palestinians, sparking war crime accusations, international rebuke, and a stunning surge in anti-Israel actions and antisemitism worldwide.

After decades of assuming that both Israel's long-term survival and the continued safety and prosperity of North American Jews were givens, we have now been snapped back to similar insecurities that molded the characters of this book in the 1940s. This is no mere exercise in nostalgia. There is much we can learn from them.

The result of this project is a look at how World War II shaped a generation and deeply affected the lives of so many fighters and their extended families – including my own. The varying routes they took offer a blueprint to those of us who've followed. As I have navigated through the modern-day challenges of what it means to be an Israeli and a Jew, I've often looked back at these stories in search of guidance and inspiration.

The findings of this deeply personal journey have generally boiled down into three separate storylines. The first is a comprehensive account of the largely unknown tale of a Dakota aircraft's fateful flight in Israel's early days and my grandfather's connection to its passengers. The second focuses on my grandfather's wartime friends and comrades and the unique Jewish Canadian contribution to World War II. The third centers on the yearslong effort to establish a museum in Israel dedicated to the wartime service of Jews like my grandfather.

Finally, there is the story of my mysterious grandfather himself and what I have discovered about him, his times, his extended family, and, ultimately, myself.

As it turned out, Zaidy eventually did have something to share after so many years of stubborn silence. I'm proud to present his story and the firsthand testimony of his contemporaries. They are among the last remaining voices from that historic era.

The Zaidy

CHAPTER ONE

Mickey Heller, My Grandfather

Mervin (Mickey) Heller was born in Toronto on November 3, 1921. He was the youngest of seven children of Samuel Heller, an immigrant from Russia, and Lena (née) Davis, whose family arrived in Toronto from Kovno, Lithuania, shortly before her birth in 1884.

They married in 1905. Their first six children were born within eight years of each other. The oldest, Maurice, born in 1906, became a lawyer and moved to Windsor, where he died in a plane crash at the age of twenty-five. In quick succession, next came Lawrence, who worked as a steamfitter; Gordon, who died of mastoid fever at age ten; Jeanette, who went on to become one of the original Radio City Rockettes; Aubrey, who became a professional rower with the Toronto Argonauts before moving west to Edmonton, where he worked in a cigar shop; and finally Joe, who was born in 1914 and later got into the printing business.

Photo 1.1. Mickey Heller
(Courtesy of the Heller family.)

Before Zaidy was born at the old Toronto Western Hospital in Toronto, his father was in business for himself in Paris, Ontario. "I guess he collected bottles and such and then brought them into Toronto to sell. So, they lived out there for a couple of years before my time," he said.

The outbreak of World War I dramatically shifted family dynamics. Struggling to find employment in Toronto, Samuel Heller couldn't support his growing family and, eventually, joining the military made the most financial sense.

But patriotism must have also played a role. Some 5,000 Canadian Jewish men enlisted for World War I at a time when the entire Jewish population was no more than 100,000.[1] Many were like Samuel, first-generation Jews who had fled the rampant pogroms of the Russian Empire.

Samuel signed up and served for five years, some of which were spent overseas in France and England, leaving

Lena to raise six young children on her own. When he finally came back in 1919, he was a different man.

Samuel said nothing about World War I and years later Zaidy confessed: "I'm ashamed I never asked."

The family tried to rebuild after the war and Zaidy arrived on the scene in 1921, seven years after Joe was born and one year after Gordon died. The Hellers continued to struggle to make ends meet and some of Zaidy's older siblings had to quit school early to help financially.

"He couldn't get a job," Zaidy, much later in life, said of his father.[2] "It was the Depression. The government paid for all the kids. It was very difficult."

The family lived in various homes near Bathurst and College Streets in downtown Toronto, on addresses such as Lippincott Street, Manning Avenue, and Robert Street. Zaidy, like his siblings, went to nearby King Edward Public School.

"We rented every time, but my mother always managed to move close to a school," he said.[3]

After school and on Sundays, he went to *cheder* (Hebrew school) for his Jewish education. He was active in the Boy Scouts and enjoyed riding his bicycle around the neighborhoods of his youth, known today as Little Italy and Harbord Village. In 1936, the *Toronto Daily Star* reported that a fourteen-year-old Mickey was taken to Toronto Western Hospital after being knocked off his bicycle. The driver of the car who struck him drove him there and Mickey was thankfully reported "to have suffered nothing but shock."[4]

These were rough and tumble times in a rough and tumble area, a time and place where one had to transition quickly from childhood to manhood.

"It was here that I had many a battle and many broken bones while growing up," wrote Zaidy's brother Joe in an unpublished summary of his life. "But I learned to fend for myself, to protect myself and to earn a dollar during the Depression years."

In his distinct sense of humor, Zaidy too would joke that he had a knack of leaving the house with two dollars and coming back with five.

Their Toronto neighborhood, like many to the south of Bloor Street then, was a mishmash of working-class immigrant families.

"My best friend was an antisemite, but he didn't know it," Zaidy recalled with a wry smile. "He was Irish. Lived right near us in a cottage that was lit by gas. He called me a dirty Jew, not knowing why he called me a dirty Jew. But my mother and his mother were friends. And I was his friend."[5]

Such attitudinal antisemitism was socially acceptable at the time and part of mainstream Canadian society. Slurs, university quotas, prejudice, and social and professional discrimination were par for the course. Jews were typically denied membership at golf courses or sailing clubs. Jewish physicians eventually opened their own hospital – Mount Sinai – because they couldn't get work at others. Antisemitism was prevalent in churches, in newspapers, and at the highest levels of government.

Often it turned physical.

Zaidy was not yet twelve when the infamous Christie Pits Riot[6] erupted nearby on August 16, 1933 – in a defining moment of Canadian antisemitism. One of the worst outbreaks of ethnic violence in Canadian history broke out when Nazi-inspired Canadians from "Swastika Clubs" unfurled the Nazi flag and began chanting "Heil Hitler" at a baseball game between Jewish and Protestant teams. A massive brawl followed with some 10,000 participants, some wielding bats, lead pipes, and other improvised weapons, as Italians and other marginalized immigrants fought alongside Jews against the agitators. The riot inspired Toronto's mayor to prosecute future displays of the swastikas in one of Canada's first policies prohibiting hate speech.

Zaidy's family pinned much of its fortunes on Maurice, hoping that his professional success as a lawyer would lift them out of poverty and allow for younger siblings to also pursue higher education. His sudden death in 1931 was a devastating blow.

"My oldest brother graduated in the Depression, couldn't get a job and moved to Windsor. In 1929, I went down to stay with him during Pesach [Passover]. He lived in a flat. Had an office out in the suburbs there and he left me by myself all day. Back then the drug stores had slot machines," he said mischievously. "So many stories."[7]

Despite the large family, Zaidy often found himself alone at home with his mother. His surviving older siblings had already left the house. And eventually his father did too.

Samuel was largely absent thereafter. He became a political operator for the provincial Conservative Party of Ontario and eventually landed a job at the Liquor Control Board of Ontario. It's unclear how much he supported the family, and Lena, a small, hunchbacked woman, also had to hustle by working at a local grocery store.

She kept a kosher home and was relatively observant. Samuel was not – just one of the forces that drove them apart. Years later, Zaidy would recall that because of their meager means all they had to eat during the week-long Passover holiday was Matzo, eggs, and tea. Despite the struggles, or perhaps because of them, Zaidy and his mother were incredibly close and remained so until her death in 1958.

But for his older siblings who grew up under the cloud of a troubled marriage, it was hardly the warmest of homes. "My family never paid any interest in me, I was not a special person in the family," his sister Jeanette confided in me in 2007. "Nobody ever said that they loved us or told us that we were pretty when we were kids."

Zaidy went to high school at Harbord Collegiate, a heavily Jewish public school (sometimes upward of 90 percent of the student body was Jewish) where he made several friends for life. The school produced illustrious graduates in Canadian politics, medicine, sports, and show business. More than 700 went on to serve in World War II and fifty died, the majority in the Air Force.[8] When Harbord Collegiate celebrated its 125th anniversary in April 2017, the *Globe and Mail* columnist Marcus Gee aptly described the school as "Toronto's famous immigrant launching pad."[9]

But it was at nearby Central Commerce Collegiate Institute where – during a visit to the school – his life changed forever when seventeen-year-old Mickey first laid eyes on fifteen-year-old Eunice Book, a recent émigré whose Jewish family had fled what was then the southeastern Polish

Photo 1.2. Eunice Book in her youth
(Courtesy of the Heller family.)

district of Galicia. He was smitten, saying she reminded him of Hollywood starlet Myrna Loy.

Like others of his generation, Zaidy was profoundly affected by the Holocaust. But he had little personal connection himself. His family had fled Europe decades earlier and was all but settled in Canada by the late nineteenth century. He hated the Nazis, but it wasn't as personal for him as it was for others whose families came to Canada to escape just the type of antisemitism that eventually brought the Nazis to power.

For Mickey's beloved Eunice Book, though, it was another matter. She was born in 1923 in the Galician village of Mosciska, in what was then southeastern Poland and is now Western Ukraine.

The history of Mosciska, alternatively spelled Mostiska or Mostyska, exemplifies the tumultuous history of the region. Jews first settled there in the eighteenth century, somewhere around the 1772 transfer of power from Polish to Austrian rule. After World War I it became part of the Second Polish Republic from 1919 to 1939, when it was seized by the Red Army. Two years later it was captured by the Nazis.

Tired of poverty and the threat of antisemitism, Eunice's family immigrated to Canada in 1929 when she was six years old. It was not an easy transition. Back in Mosciska, her father, Isaac, was a lumber merchant but in Toronto he struggled to find work and toiled as a dealer in a coal yard. The family lived on Major Street, a short street in a Jewish neighborhood west of Spadina Avenue that later would become known as the address for a high number of young Jewish men – at least thirty – who had gone off to war. Half a dozen did not make it home.[10]

Isaac's difficulties drove him to make the unusual choice of moving back to Poland just as the Nazis were rising to power. Back in Mosciska, the family was once again living the rural life, using the outhouse and facing the same threats. Eunice, the youngest of five and the only daughter, said she cried the whole year they were back in Poland.

Her mother, Miriam, one in a long line of opinionated matriarchs, quickly realized the grave mistake they had made and laid down the law. She was taking her daughter back to Canada, with or without her husband. They exchanged threats of divorce but eventually he relented, and the family came back to Toronto for good by 1934.

It was a wise decision. The Jewish community of Mosciska was liquidated on November 28, 1942, when its 2,500 residents were deported to the Belzec death camp. Included among these were my paternal grandmother's entire extended family.[11]

Her older brother Meilech also barely escaped extermination. He didn't initially return with the rest of the family and, by the time he tried to rejoin them, the Canadian authorities rejected him on account of his polio. He sheltered for two years in a hideaway home of a non-Jewish family in Antwerp, Belgium, before he was finally allowed to immigrate after the war. The family that saved him was later recognized as "Righteous Among the Nations," Israel's highest honor for those non-Jews who had risked their lives to save Jews.

Unlike Zaidy, Bubby was never shy about sharing her past. But she too was no fan of nostalgia. When I went on a student delegation to the former Nazi concentration camps in 2000, I tried gleaning more background from her. I asked her if she ever had any interest in traveling to Poland or visiting her hometown again.

"No," she sharply retorted. "There's a reason we left."

After finishing high school in 1939, Mickey immediately sought a variety of odd jobs to chip in financially. In one, he made soap and was paid every two weeks. In another, he recalled earning $7 a week for a sixty-hour workweek. Eventually, he asked for a raise and when that wasn't granted, he opted for Plan B – enlisting in the military.

"We weren't making any money, so I said 'enough,' and I went and joined," he said.

Such supposed petty reasoning mirrored what his father once claimed to have been his driving force in joining up for World War I. But it downplayed the fact that Zaidy didn't merely join, he volunteered for the Royal Canadian Air Force (RCAF). Unlike those in the army, who could generally stay safe in Canada during the early years of the war, only navy and air force volunteers like Zaidy were sent off to the European front from the get-go.

Still just nineteen, he enlisted in March 1941 and thus begun the black hole in his biography, a four-year gap from which he reemerged only in late 1944 when he returned from Europe, married Eunice, and never looked back.

I was born in Boston in 1976 and moved often in my early years because of my father's career as an academic, splitting time between the United States, Canada, and Israel. I moved nine times in my first sixteen years, living in places such as San Diego, California; Ithaca, New York; Ottawa, Ontario; and in Tel Aviv, Herzliya, and the town of Kochav Yair in Israel. We never lived in my parents' native Toronto, yet it still became somewhat of an informal second hometown to me because of the regular summer visits that were usually a whirlwind of bouncing between two sets of grandparents and other extended family members.

Photo 1.3. Mickey and Eunice Heller at their 1944 wedding
(Courtesy of the Heller family.)

The Zionist summer camps of their youth in Canada inspired my parents to eventually lay down roots in Israel, half a world away. There was no Zoom or WhatsApp back then, so communication was fleeting. The result was that my siblings – older sister Miriam and younger brother Daniel – and I never developed the type of close connection with our grandparents that most other Israeli kids had with theirs who lived nearby and were an integral part of their daily lives.

We certainly had fun during our visits together, theirs in Israel and ours in Canada, and there was plenty of love. These intense vacations included sleepovers, pool and beach outings, and a myriad of games and activities. In between, we tried to stay in touch with letters and near-weekly phone calls.

But the truth is that both sets of our grandparents didn't know us that well, and we didn't really know them. In the absence of a deep connection, my grandparents became more like symbols to me, symbols of their generation.

They were characters from this foreign Diaspora land where Jews ate bagels, watched hockey games, and played golf. My siblings and I were becoming Israelis – in my case, sometimes reluctantly – and our English-speaking grandparents with their Old Country mannerisms and Yiddish sayings represented the world my parents had left behind.

Of my four grandparents, my paternal grandfather, Zaidy Mickey, was the least vocal and he'd often defer to his more dominant wife, Eunice, who went by Bubby Mum. Even when my other set of Toronto-based grandparents, Nathan and Zella Freeman, died while I was in high school, it had little impact on the depth of my bond with the surviving grandparents.

It was a relationship that was mostly based on rituals: meals, card games, TV game shows, funny sayings, and jokes.

The distance, both physical and emotional, remained as I grew up, completed my mandatory military service in Israel, became fascinated with World War II history, and began to delve into it in my journalism career. Through it all, my grandfather remained a distant satellite, orbiting around the source of my greatest interest.

It felt like such a shame.

As an avid student of history, I had this insatiable appetite to learn. Here, in my own family, was a live witness to the era I was most intrigued about, and his lips were tightly sealed.

Ever since I was a little kid, I knew my grandfather was a navigator in World War II for the Royal Canadian Air Force, stationed in Europe even before the Americans joined that campaign. But that's all I knew. I was desperate to learn more if not for the sake of curiosity, then as a tool to get closer to a grandfather with whom I didn't initially appear to have much natural chemistry.

For decades, he methodically refused to speak about his wartime experiences. I tried at many intersections to prod him into sharing something about his past. But each time I saw a glimmer of reflection in his eye, it was quickly replaced by that disapproving look that was inherited by other members of our family: a pursing of the lips, a moment of silence, and a piercing glance that said: "This conversation is over, move on to something else."

Reluctantly I did, not wanting to risk the affection of a grandparent I saw far too little of anyway.

I tried backchannel routes. My grandmother was of little use. In her blunt manner, she said it was something he didn't want to talk about, and I should let it go. I tried, but I couldn't.

My father, Mark, who encouraged my curiosity in almost every other way, also suggested I cool the inquiries, perhaps speaking from experience. My mother, Barbi, from whom I inherited my deep interest in people, was my greatest champion and celebrated my early attempts at interviewing and writing. But I was still getting nowhere with Zaidy.

The rumors swirled amid his murky silence. One cousin said he had been hospitalized, perhaps from wounds sustained in battle. Zaidy's loquacious older sister Jeanette provided an alternative explanation: she said he had a serious wartime trauma, something along the lines of heading out on a flight with comrades and returning alone. But that story seemed far-fetched since he was a navigator, not a pilot, and it would seem unlikely he would even know how to fly his Vickers Wellington bomber plane.

There was no way of knowing and, as the years passed, the mystery kept growing.

Zaidy's story was almost a cliché of what has become known as the Greatest Generation. Born into poverty as the youngest of seven children of an immigrant father, my Zaidy went off to war after high school and then came back four years later to marry his sweetheart.

The Canadian government offered benefits to returning veterans, so he took a course in radio at Ryerson College (now Toronto Metropolitan University) and started his business career by opening a radio shop on Eglinton Avenue in midtown Toronto. "One day, it caught on fire and that was the end of the business," he recalled years later.

Then he worked as a traveling clothing salesman for many years, hauling his wares all over Ontario, before finally opening his own manufacturing business in Toronto that specialized in women's blouses.

During his early years on the road, he and Eunice saved up by living with her parents on Nassau Street, near where Zaidy had grown up. Zaidy would typically come back on the weekends and my father, Zaidy's eldest child who was born in 1946, grew up in that Yiddish-speaking home until he was four. Eventually, Mickey and Eunice moved out, had four children, three sons and a daughter, and settled into domestic life on Manor Haven Road near Bathurst Street and Lawrence Avenue.

It was a largely Jewish neighborhood but far from the more southern immigrant neighborhoods of their youth. Instead of the tightly squeezed duplexes or row houses they grew up in, Mickey and Eunice now lived in a backsplit house, with a backyard and a park across the street where the kids could play. They bought the house in 1952 for $21,500 and it quickly became the focal point for family gatherings of Mickey's and Eunice's many siblings, and an informal gathering point for Jewish teenagers

Photo 1.4. Mickey Heller playing his favorite card game of Clubbyish with an eight-year-old Aron in 1984
(Courtesy of the Heller family.)

from all around Canada who arrived for the same Zionist summer camps and youth movements their children attended.

As the kids moved out, my grandparents moved a bit south, to a midtown Toronto condominium on Heath Street. After retiring, Zaidy spent his winters in Florida, playing golf and bridge with fellow Jewish Canadian retirees and regaling his visiting grandchildren with stories, jokes, and Yiddish sayings. We bonded over the intricacies of the card game Clubbyish, over the *bisele* of Yiddish phrases he taught me, and over our shared playful sense of humor.

In short, he lived a typical life, and he seemed to be a typical Zaidy of his generation.

But there was this one chapter of his life that remained perpetually sealed: He would never tell us, or anyone else, what he had endured during the war. In short, he played the stereotypical strong, silent type.

However, I sensed that under that veneer there was something more. He wasn't that strong, and he wasn't that silent. He was never a chatterbox, and he kept information on a need-to-know basis. But on the rare occasions I had quality time with him alone he would open up about many things, about music, about politics, about history – but rarely his own.

When I was young, he liked to drive me around town in his beige Cadillac Sedan DeVille, which we grandchildren came to call the "Zaidy car." I'd tag along as he'd cruise up and down Bathurst Street to stop by the bank or the hardware store or go for a haircut and manicure at his regular barber shop – Sam & Vito's. I thought that long, shiny Cadillac was the coolest car in the world, and I loved playing with the automatic door locks and window buttons. Sometimes Zaidy would let me sit on his lap and press the clicker that opened the underground parking garage. It was in that car that I first heard the crooning voice of Frank Sinatra. Naively, I asked if he was Jewish.

"No, he's Italian," Zaidy casually explained. "It's basically the same thing."

Methodical by nature, Zaidy walked me through his rituals during my Toronto visits, showing me how to properly tuck in bedsheets, iron dress shirts, and use a shoehorn.

Photo 1.5. Mickey and Eunice with Aron at his 1989 Bar Mitzvah in Israel (Courtesy of the Heller family.)

Each chore had to be done "just so." He also liked to offer life lessons, such as encouraging me, a pensive dreamer, to go into business.

"That's where the money is," he'd assert.

"That's also where you lose money," I'd retort.

"You lose and you lose," he responded, before providing his formula for transitioning from poverty to relative affluence. "Eventually you'll make something."

Our outings typically involved a meal at United Bakers in Lawrence Plaza or Yitz's Delicatessen on Eglinton Avenue near Avenue Road. If he was in the mood for a walk, we'd head over together to nearby Spadina Village to grab a pizza or rent a film and sample the free popcorn at the local Blockbuster Video store. Entertainment was a movie or, more often, a repeat visit to the Royal Ontario Museum or Black Creek Pioneer Village, where Zaidy would flaunt his knowledge about Canadian days of yore.

But I was interested in a different period of history, the one he would not touch. In the dusty underground storage room at my grandparents' Toronto condominium, he kept old newspaper clippings he had collected over the years. Long before I even thought of becoming a journalist I was captivated by the yellowing, fraying pages he saved about the attack on Pearl Harbor, the bombing of Hiroshima, the establishment of Israel. But when I asked him where he was during these events, the conversation quickly shifted elsewhere.

I was nourished only by the clues, such as his black-and-white wedding picture in which he posed in his full RCAF uniform and service cap. His clothing choice was just another mystery. Was he required to be in uniform because he was still in service or was it more of a statement of patriotism as the war still raged? When I asked Zaidy, he sheepishly said his uniform was the only suit he owned.

Elsewhere in the apartment, there were other various photos that were buried in random albums: one where he and some RCAF buddies in uniform stood in front of a bomber plane, one where he posed with his navigator wings, another of him in overalls and a jumpsuit, and finally a last one of him (with the thin mustache he would sport for the rest of his life) with more pals in front of a sandbag-fortified house in Europe.

Photo 1.6. Mickey Heller (right) and friends in World War II
(Courtesy of the Heller family.)

There was also a clipping in a photo album from a 1942 announcement in the *Globe and Mail*, Canada's leading national newspaper, detailing how a Sgt. "Mickey" Heller, a former carrier for the paper in the Toronto "D" district, was a sergeant observer in the Royal Canadian Air Force who recently departed for an eastern Canadian base. I also found his RCAF ID enlistment card (number R97329) that said he was nineteen years of age, 5′9″, weighed 140 lbs., had dark brown hair, brown eyes, a mark on the palm of his right hand, and a scar on the index finger of his left hand.

He would never expand upon any of these hints. All he would say is that he joined the Royal Canadian Air Force because all his friends did, he needed an income, and he

ROYAL CANADIAN AIR FORCE

Name HELLER, Mervin R 9 7 3 2 9

Rank W/O2 RCAF

Age 19 Height 5'9" Weight 140

Hair Dark Brown Eyes Brown Hair on face Dark

Marks, scars etc. Mark on palm of right hand. Scar on index finger left hand.

(Signature of holder)

(Signature of issuer)

Place R.C.A.F. Mountain View, Ont. Date August 6, 1941

Card serial number 6 4 3 5 8

Photo 1.7. Mickey Heller's Royal Canadian Air Force enlistment card (Courtesy of the Heller family.)

wanted to get even with Hitler. He bemoaned how his military service took away valuable years of his life and that if he hadn't gone to Europe, he would have gotten married sooner.

When I was drafted into the Israeli Defense Forces at age eighteen, a natural point of reference, he gave me just two pearls of military wisdom: "Never volunteer" and "Keep your feet clean and dry." That was it.

In retrospect, this was probably when I first began to seriously think about my grandfather's World War II experience. Drudging through what felt like my own largely insignificant first year of service, I struggled with the militarism being thrust upon me and questioned the value of giving up my own prime years for a cause I couldn't yet quite conceptualize. For most Israelis, military service is a time-honored rite of passage that is widely celebrated. For me, at least at the beginning, it was a rude awakening.

I was from an immigrant family. My parents had left the Canadian comforts their own parents were so proud to have provided them in favor of what they perceived to be a more meaningful lifestyle in Israel. But my siblings and I were to be the first to experience the full gamut of the Israeli experience.

I didn't have a father or an older brother who had been recruited out of high school in the typical mandatory service stream. So, I hadn't been raised upon the inevitability of being called up for three years of compulsory service. Instead, I dreamed of playing basketball at an American college, and I certainly didn't have the communal spirit or gung-ho mentality of many of my Israeli peers. Besides, we were the generation whose parents naively told us when we were children that by the time we came of age, there might be peace and Israel's mandatory military service may no longer be necessary. In short, I had no real desire to join the army, and I would have much preferred to have spent those formative years doing something else somewhere else.

But I had no choice in the matter. In the words of the famous song, I was "in the army now." I was hungry and tired, lonely and homesick. Through weeks of gloominess, I pointlessly pondered my predicament.

Why was I being harassed and humiliated through basic training? Why was I marooned on a desolate base deep in the West Bank? Why was I being aimlessly shuffled around? Why was I guarding settlements? What was the point of it all?

Amid this emotional turbulence, I yearned for a sense of meaning. Would I have felt any different had I had a clearer sense of the cause? Had I known that my service was making a difference? Had I felt that my struggles were contributing to a greater good?

In those agonizing first few months of basic training, I became a soldier. I learned how to fire a rifle, fight off bullies, and fend for myself. I also got my first glimpse of Israel's continued entrenchment in the West Bank, and its troubling effects, when I locked eyes with a scared Palestinian child as my platoon passed through a hilltop village. And I had my first encounter with death when a commander who was particularly kind to me died in an accident on our last day of training.

It was then I really began to ponder what a World War II service may have been like. It must have been so much more rewarding, I imagined, to have had a clear mission, a clear vision who you were fighting against and what you were fighting for, to know where you fit into the bigger picture.

Perhaps understanding my grandfather's service would not only make me feel closer to him but would also help me get through what up to that point was the most difficult period of my life.

But it was not to be. My Zaidy was not going to be my guide.

Maybe he had a trauma, maybe not. Perhaps his service was uneventful, perhaps not. It was the pursuit of finding out that frustrated me for so long. But he would not budge, and eventually I gave up. A fascination, even obsession, with World War II remained, it just wasn't through the prism of my grandfather's past.

We reverted to our typical, superficial exchanges.

When I came to visit Toronto after my army service, and again throughout my early twenties, Zaidy would often hand me "mad money" for my late-night outings with a cheeky directive to "be good. And if you can't be good, be careful. And if you can't be careful, name it after me." We'd sometimes rendezvous several hours later, when I had returned and he was just getting up to do his early morning exercises.

Once email came along, Zaidy became fond of forwarding silly messages and Borscht Belt–style jokes.

> One day Benjy comes home from school, goes straight to his father, and asks, "What is fornication, Dad?" Zaidy wrote to me in 2009. He gets the answer all Jewish fathers give: "Why don't you ask your mother." So, Benjy goes into the kitchen and asks his mother, "What is fornication, Mom? Dad said you would know." His mother replies, "I'm busy right now, Benjy, why don't you go and ask your Bubby. She will tell you." So, Benjy goes upstairs to his Bubby's room, knocks on her door and shouts, "Please Bubby, what is fornication? No one here seems to know."
>
> Bubby says, "Come inside, Bubelleh." She then takes him to her closet, opens the door, takes out a beautiful full-length pink, beaded evening dress and says, "This, Bubelleh, is foranoccasion."

I tried responding with similar humor to prod him into sharing something about our most elusive topic.

> An old Jewish man is invited to his grandson's class to speak about flying missions over Nazi Germany. The kids gather

in a circle, and he begins. "So, I was in the cockpit, and I had this German fucker on my tail. I looked around and there was another fucker on the left of me and a fucker on the right of me," he said. The children naturally began giggling and the teacher quickly interjected: "Children. The FOKKER was a German airplane and that's what our guest is referring to." The grandfather leered awkwardly at the teacher and barked: "What the hell are you talking about, those fuckers were flying Messerschmitts."

Zaidy chuckled at that joke, but he wouldn't crack.

It was only years later, as a journalist, that I would find great satisfaction in extracting the stories of others of his generation who had stayed quiet for decades.

After graduating from the Columbia University Graduate School of Journalism in New York in 2004, I found myself back in Canada as a reporter for the *Ottawa Citizen* newspaper. It was there that I first delved into Holocaust reporting, leading our coverage of the establishment of International Holocaust Remembrance Day on January 27, 2005, marking the 60th anniversary of the liberation of Auschwitz.

Later that year, I returned to Israel as an Associated Press correspondent in Jerusalem. In fifteen years on the job, I developed a specialized history beat that focused primarily on World War II and the Holocaust. It resulted in dozens of articles chronicling the experiences of elderly veterans and survivors, many of whom confided in me to publish their stories for the first time.

I had made it my career goal to "own" this beat. I sought out survivors anywhere I could, with a mission of meticulously logging their sagas into the archive of human history. The scope of the stories was endless: I interviewed siblings who reunited after sixty-five years of thinking the other was dead. I profiled the man who survived as a child by hiding for several months inside the trunk of a hollow birch tree. I reunited three men who as teenagers stood one after the other in the tattooist's line at Auschwitz and still bore those consecutive numbers on their arms. I chronicled how observant Jews kept the faith even after all they had endured and reported on the mental health center where, for some survivors, it was as if the Holocaust had never ended.

Each of these, and dozens more, have been among the most rewarding stories I have ever written. Zaidy appreciated them too. He made a point of dropping me an email anytime he saw one of my stories appear in his morning paper in Canada.

This became a sort of coded way in which we communicated about the war. It was the language we used to speak about the unspoken. Still, it was telling that despite his repeated refusal to discuss my most curious subject, the articles that he chose to engage with all seemed to revolve around the same topic. It was consistent with the approach-avoidance dynamic we had developed over the years, in which each time I would withdraw, he would initiate a new thread.

Even as he continued to rebuff my wartime inquiries, he had a way of countering with those of his own.

Sometimes it came in the form of him sharing war-related stories he had discovered, such as "The German Jew Who Bombed Berlin" about the improbable journey of Georg Hein, who fled Germany and later became a British pilot named Peter Stevens.[12] Hein bombed his hometown, crash landed, escaped two prisoner of war (POW) camps, was decorated for his bravery, and then became a Cold War spy for MI6 (the UK Secret Intelligence Service) before immigrating to Canada.

But mostly it was my stories about World War II and the Holocaust that piqued Zaidy's interest and seemed to touch a nerve.

In December 2015, for example, he acknowledged a story I wrote about American World War II veteran Roddie Edmonds, who became the first serviceman ever honored as "Righteous Among the Nations" for saving Jews during the war. [13] Zaidy was touched by the account of how Master Sgt. Edmonds, the highest-ranking non-commissioned officer held captive in a German camp, refused to identify and turn over more than 200 Jewish-American soldiers under his command. Even with a pistol aimed at his head, Edmonds defiantly told his Nazi captors: "We are all Jews here."

In February 2016, Zaidy wrote to say that he read my story in the *Globe and Mail* about the passing of Samuel Willenberg.[14] Willenberg was believed to be the last of just sixty-seven known survivors of the famed 1943 revolt at the Treblinka death camp, where more than 875,000 Jews were systematically murdered in a one-year killing spree at the height of World War II. Willenberg's two sisters were murdered at the camp, and he described his own survival as sheer chance. "It wasn't because of God. He wasn't there. He was on vacation," he told me.

In August 2016, Zaidy wrote to say that he read my article published in the *National Post* about a group of Holocaust survivors who attempted to poison 2,200 Nazi SS paramilitary men in an American POW camp after the war.[15] It was the most brazen attempt ever of Jews to avenge their former tormentors and the leader of the plot, Joseph Harmatz, was one of the more intense characters I had ever interviewed.

Slouched in a chair and staring at me intently over his drooped reading glasses, the ninety-one-year-old Harmatz, who still went by his wartime nickname Julek, explained how after surviving the Holocaust he had a burning desire to avenge his dead family. In a hoarse voice just above a whisper, he methodically described how he tried to poison the Nazis with arsenic. The goal, he said, was simple: "Kill Germans ... as many as possible."

His former comrade, ninety-two-year-old Auschwitz survivor Yehuda Maimon, who went by the nickname Poldek, remained equally defiant. "Heaven forbid if after the war we had just gone back to the routine without thinking about paying those bastards back," he said. "It would have been awful not to respond to those animals."

I suppose the tension of the story came across, because Zaidy made a point of saying he read it all the way through. "It was a three-quarter page spread. Most interesting," he wrote.

This required a response, especially since Harmatz had passed away just weeks after my story ran, and I had just finished writing his obituary.[16]

"Having this happen so shortly after interviewing him reinforces my faith in doing these kinds of stories now, before it is too late," I confided in Zaidy in one of my more vulnerable emails. "I know we've discussed it often, and you aren't going anywhere soon, but it's just another reminder of how eager I am to hear any stories you have of the war. I'm always here if you are ready to share."

In a follow-up call, I asked Zaidy if he had gotten my email. He said he had and even read it over several times. A long pause followed, but that was it. We said our goodbyes. There was nothing more to say.

Typically, though, Zaidy would mostly engage about the peripheral. Along with modest praise, he'd often add an additional plea to include more playful Yiddish expressions into my regimented Associated Press stories. This was a running theme between us, and he'd often send me newspaper clippings with examples to encourage me further.

"I believe that every journalist should have one thing that makes them stand out. Perhaps for you it should be the Yiddisha shtick," he suggested in a handwritten note dated August 15, 2017. "I wonder what your readers would think when they'd see articles from Israel with an added Yiddish word thrown in, especially from someone so young."

It was only after I left the Associated Press in 2020 that I managed to fulfill that desire, and I enthusiastically informed him that I sneaked in a mention of *kvelling* and *mensch* into one of my political columns.

It was satisfying to know that I was reaching him some way through my varied reporting. Still, I couldn't understand his steadfast refusal to share more about himself.

I thought I had heard just about the very worst a person could witness: watching one's children being shot before one's eyes, facing gas chambers and crematoria, being left for dead in a pile of bodies. What kind of trauma could my grandfather have endured that would be too much for him to share and for me to absorb?

I found that giving such testimony proved therapeutic for these people as they pondered their mortality. But that same logic didn't appear to apply to my Zaidy. He was hardly impressed with a magazine feature I wrote in 2007 about his sister Jeanette and her freewheeling days as a Radio City Rockette.[17] She spoke about her unconventional life as an unmarried Jewish woman, about her exotic world travels, and about rubbing elbows with the celebrities of her time like Bob Hope, Louis Armstrong, and Red Skelton. She also shared insight on Heller family dynamics in which sharing emotions was frowned upon, about how her extroverted nature was rejected, and how no one gave her the time of day. Nevertheless, I was glad I got some of her story out there, especially since she died the following year.[18]

Even though age had softened him, Zaidy would be a far tougher sell.

His sister Jeanette was desperate to have her story told. All her life, she was ready to tell dramatic tales, but no one in the family showed any interest. By the time I came around and was ready to listen, age had ravaged her memory and her narrative had started to wander. She just couldn't retrieve her stories anymore or tell them with the same clarity. Our relatives were of little help; they either couldn't recall specifics or were never interested enough to

Photo 1.8. Jeanette Heller in the 1930s
(Courtesy of the Heller family.)

begin with. Her friends were all gone, seemingly along with her glorious past.

I vowed not to let that happen with Zaidy. If he had a story, I would get to it.

He'd send emails about his pride in his children and grandchildren, share news stories about Israel and Jewish life in Canada. When I expressed interest in the Freemasons, after reading a Dan Brown book, he sent me some fliers from his group. He was a longtime brother in Palestine Lodge No. 559 of Toronto,[19] and not, as he would often joke, the fraternity of "*Zaidy Laida Shiksa.*"

(To be clear, Zaidy was no skirt chaser, but as a man of his time, he could indulge in the discourse and use terms that could be deemed today as disparaging or derogatory, such as *Shiksa* – a Yiddish slur denoting a non-Jewish woman.)

The lodge was a big part of his social life. He joined in 1953 and was a "Worshipful Master" for fifty-seven years, attending weekly meetings and playing in their bowling league. He said he only went as far as the seventh degree out of the possible thirty-two since he "had to make a living for our growing family."

Its members, mostly Jewish, made up his closest friends and business acquaintances and he wore a black masonic lodge ring on his finger for the rest of his life.

Later, his synagogue became a larger part of his social circle. Though not a particularly observant Jew, he enjoyed attending Saturday morning services, if not so much for the prayers than for the camaraderie. It was a recommendation he passed on to one of his sons, saying "you should join a shul, so you'll have friends when you need them." At his core, Zaidy was a curious man who enjoyed learning, asking questions, telling a good joke or a good story – all traits I seem to have inherited. But when it came to the war, he was like a clamshell and seemed determined to take the details of his war experience with him to the grave.

I think it's a shame to let a good story go untold. In fact, I think there's a certain responsibility involved in passing on meaningful tales, even if they are sometimes difficult to share. Having said that, I also know that you cannot (and should not) force a story out of anyone.

It's a tricky task, even more so when it involves a member of your own family. But I've discovered that in certain cases, without being overly aggressive, a little push is enough to get even the most private person to open up and discover how rewarding an experience that can be for them. Often the best stories are indeed hidden inside such people.

Zaidy would prove to be my most challenging case. I was determined to get to the bottom of it, if for no other reason than my own peace of mind that I tried before it was too late. Over eleven years, I would methodically chip away, trying to glean one detail at a time to complete the puzzle of this mysterious man.

The first step in that journey involved queries to Library and Archives Canada and Veterans Affairs Canada. Current protocols dictated that the records of those who died in battle were open to the public, as were those who had been dead for twenty years. But with living veterans, a written approval was required to release the records. Knowing Zaidy, that was going to be difficult. Not surprisingly, he repeatedly refused to grant me access to his records.

In time, however, I would come to learn much from him if not so much about him. That's because my Zaidy was always much more comfortable speaking about others than about himself.

Photo 1.9. Mickey Heller walking down a Toronto street
(Courtesy of the Heller family.)

The Dakota

CHAPTER TWO

Wilf Canter, the Great Escapist

It was early 2012 when, out of nowhere, Zaidy sent me the following email with specific instructions:

> I wonder if in your spare time you may be able to find out something for me.
>
> I was overseas in 1942 with a fellow from Toronto named Wilf Canter. He was I believe a Sgt. Spitfire Pilot. In the latter part of 1943, after several ops he was shot down over Germany but managed to work his way through France, Spain, and Gibraltar and back to England. He was awarded the D.F.M (Distinguished Flying Medal) and sent me a letter if I could meet him in London at Buckingham Palace where he was to be presented with his medal. As luck would have it, he had gone back to flying, was shot down again and spent one year as a prisoner of war. Released at the end of

the war by that time he had been promoted to an F/L [Flight Lieutenant].

Next thing I heard it was 1948 and he was over in Israel, having volunteered as a pilot. As a newspaperman, do you have any way that you might find out if this is so?

Now that's something that's never happened.

For the first time, Zaidy has come to me with a quasi-wartime story and, even better, an assignment. I'm awash with questions: Why is he interested in this? Why now?

In a subsequent email, Zaidy explained that the Toronto branch of the Jewish War Veterans of Canada had dedicated a war memorial monument on November 11, 2011 (Canadian Remembrance Day), featuring the names of "the Jewish boys who died" in World War II on the front.[1] On the back of the monument there were listed the names of all those who came back and who signed up to be included. "As you can see, this placed Wilf's name in abeyance," he wrote.

The ambitious plan took more than a dozen years to complete and was marred by administrative issues and financial shortfalls. But eventually, an eight-foot-long black marble structure with large granite rocks on both sides was erected.

Zaidy seemed excited. He had signed himself up along with his brother Joe and Bubby's brother, Morris Book, both of whom were conscripted and served domestically. He even included the name of his own father, Samuel Heller, who served in France and England during World War I.

Zaidy wrote that out of a Jewish population of 170,000, some 17,000 enlisted (including some 280 women).

"Ten per cent overall; more than any other group," he wrote proudly.

My later research showed an even more impressive statistic, that about 40 percent of the military-age Jewish male population of Canada served. Roughly 45,000 Canadian service members died (including nearly 450 Jews) in World War II and more than a third of those were in the RCAF, including many men I could only assume served with my grandfather.

Zaidy also purchased the naming rights to two flagpoles at the site in front of the Prosserman Jewish Community Centre on Bathurst Street:[2] They hoisted a Canadian flag in honor of his relatives who had served in World Wars I and II and an Israeli flag in honor of his children and grandchildren (including me) who had served in the Israel Defense Forces over the years.

This rare opportunity was too good to waste. Filled with excitement, I called Toronto. Bubby and Zaidy were spending their first winter there in thirty years, having given up their last Florida condo in West Palm Beach – part of the larger master plan of wrapping up all the loose ends before, well, the end. But Zaidy didn't seem to be in any rush. When I called, Bubby answered. She said he was out, walking to the bank in minus-ten-degree Celsius weather. We spoke long enough for him to return. He said he had gone out to check that "all my money was still there."

Then we got down to business. I had never noticed such interest before. He spoke about being involved in the

Photo 2.1. Inscription on flagpole outside the Prosserman Jewish Community Centre, Toronto (Photo credit: Aron Heller.)

Jewish War Veterans of Canada and the memorial that was unveiled on November 11. And then he began sharing anecdotes – the kind I had been yearning to hear my whole life.

Zaidy became wistful when speaking about Wilf Canter, about how they were close friends before losing touch. He said they sailed across the Atlantic Ocean together in 1942 aboard the RMS *Queen Elizabeth* "along with 30,000 other guys." They were in the RCAF together and Zaidy told of how Wilf managed to dodge death several times in the war before returning to action in the early days of Israel, from where he would never return.

Photo 2.2. A profile photo of Wilfred Canter in uniform (Courtesy of Wayne Gershon.)

"He had quite a life," Zaidy said. "The funniest thing about this guy was that he was a 'crier.' He had balls, but he cried at the drop of a hat."

It was finally happening – Zaidy was opening up. The first piece of the puzzle was going to be Wilf Canter. I put on my journalist hat and got to work. What I discovered blew my mind.

Wilfred Lloyd Canter was born on February 7, 1921 (nine months before Zaidy), near Kyiv, to Eva and Leon Canter. His father died while he was still an infant, and his mother decided shortly after to seek a better life in Canada. He grew up downtown and went to Clinton Street School and the Central Technical High School before enlisting in the RCAF in 1941. The following year he got his wings and went to war, stationed in England after completing his training in Canada.

In April 1943, the Halifax bomber he co-piloted in the RCAF's 408 Squadron was shot down on the way back from a mission over Stuttgart. Canter parachuted into occupied France, breaking a leg when he landed. The only member of the six-man crew to survive and evade capture, he lay in hiding for nine days, kept alive by a local family who took pity on him and gave him food and clothing before passing him on to members of the French Resistance who smuggled him to Paris, then Bordeaux, then over the Pyrenees by foot into Spain. From there he made his way to Gibraltar and then England, where King George VI awarded him a Distinguished Flying Medal at Buckingham Palace.

"A veteran of many sorties against numerous enemy targets, he has carried out his duties faithfully and co-operated efficiently with other aircrews," read the citation. "In an air operation, Flight-Lieutenant Canter displayed courage and tenacity of a high order."[3]

After less than a month of home leave in Toronto, he deemed himself fit for duty and returned to England to resume his bombing missions, including one in which his plane took fire but returned safely to base.

In April 1944, he was not as lucky. Canter was shot down again, on a bombing run for the 433 Squadron over Dusseldorf, and was captured by the Germans. After a lengthy Gestapo interrogation, he was detained for nine months in Stalag Luft III, the notorious German POW camp from which eighty British and Allied air officers escaped on

March 24, 1944, by crawling through a 360-foot-long tunnel that they had dug out. Over the next few days, German guards recaptured all but three of the escapees. An enraged Hitler ordered their execution, and fifty Commonwealth officers in the camp were shot dead by Gestapo death squads. Their bodies were cremated and buried in a corner of the camp in an attempted cover up.[4]

The dramatic episode became a defining World War II event and inspired the classic 1963 war film *The Great Escape*, starring Steve McQueen, James Garner, Charles Bronson, and Richard Attenborough. The film notoriously played loose with some of the escape's most pertinent details. One of these was that despite the Anglo-American-centric Hollywood depiction, major plotters of the escape were, in fact, Canadian.

According to Canter's Israeli military biography, he participated in that famed prison break and was in line to break out when they were exposed.[5] But the chronology of his official Canadian wartime record indicates he arrived at that camp at least a month after the escape. Either way, his adventures were far from over.

As the Allies were closing in on Germany, the camp's remaining war prisoners were force-marched westward.[6] Canter escaped and managed to connect with a British unit. He was briefly recaptured by a German officer, but resistance forces shot the German dead, freeing Canter again and handing him the officer's Luger pistol, which he kept as a memento.

"To this day, I don't know how I got out of there alive," he later told his mother.[7]

But he didn't tell her much. Most of what she learned was from his friends and from the International Red Cross. She went months without knowing if he was dead or alive.

Finally, Canter returned home to Canada, having logged 2,500 wartime flight hours.

The paths the two friends took after the war diverged dramatically. Zaidy came back to his awaiting fiancée, intent on starting a family and a business – and mostly forgetting about the war and moving on.

By contrast, that domestic life wasn't in the cards for Wilf Canter. After several fitful years during which he failed to find his calling, he was drawn back to battle, this time to the war taking place in Israel, arriving on August 5, 1948, with other volunteers. He was one of just five Jewish Canadian pilots with World War II experience who served in the young Israeli Air Force. Canter, who in Israel went by his Hebrew name, Zeev, joined 103 Squadron at Ramat David Airbase near Haifa and primarily flew Dakota planes on bombing and supply missions.

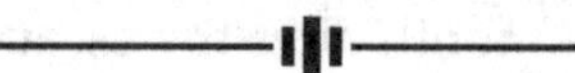

What led Canter to Israel in 1948 had a lot to do with the kind of life and service he'd had up to that point, and a psychology that could likely be traced back to his early childhood. Canter's recently widowed mother became quite ill and incapacitated on the journey to Canada, leaving five-year-old Wilf and his eight-year-old sister Sophie to mostly fend for themselves aboard the ship. While Sophie felt the trauma of separation, for young Wilf it was an adventure, instilling in him an early sense of independence and self-assuredness that carried through to his wartime experience.

Despite his dramatic time in wartime Europe, Canter told little of what truly transpired. His mother only learned about the torture and Gestapo interrogations years later. A handwritten note in her name provided the military with most of the biographical information that became known about him for the following seventy years.

"After all the torture and hardship he endured, he couldn't talk about it with me and he couldn't find comfort," wrote his mother, Eva. "I suppose his soul was just too wounded after all he saw and suffered."

Eva Canter passed away in 1989. Sophie, his sister, died in 2016 at the age of ninety-seven, handing off any reminders of Canter to her youngest son, Wayne Gershon. At Sophie's funeral, Gershon placed Canter's Distinguished Flying Medal in the casket with her so a part of her little brother would remain with her for eternity.

Gershon told me he rarely asked his grandmother about Wilf, as the pain of losing her only son lingered for the rest of her life. He said his mother was also scant with details, mostly describing the warm feelings she had as an older sister rather than any insight on Canter's wartime experience or his brief time in Israel. But Gershon did inherit the only physical remnants from an uncle who had died two years before his own birth.

According to the official military record Gershon sent me, Canter embarked from Canada on August 21, 1942, and arrived in Britain eleven days later, on September 1. It was during this journey that Zaidy said they bonded. Typically, Zaidy would not expand much about their interactions.

Photo 2.3. Wilfred Canter
(Courtesy of Wayne Gershon.)

"There were thousands of guys on that boat, and we did most of the talking while waiting in line for hours to get a meal," he said.

The record confirmed the dates of Canter's tumultuous journey and his service as a pilot in Squadrons 408 and 433. It appeared that part of the confusion over his role in "The Great Escape" derives from his mother's recollections and a press clipping from a 1947 edition of the *Vancouver Sun* newspaper in which Canter is pictured with other former prisoners reviewing maps of Stalag Luft III and pointing to the tunnels used in the escape. Tunneling continued after that attempt and it appears that Canter may have been planning to join that effort. Either way, he must have been familiar with details of the famed escape having arrived so shortly after it took place.

The package of items Gershon shared with me also included Flight Lt. Lloyd Wilfred Canter's official discharge papers, his war record, his war service badge, prisoner of war information, and more. He was listed at 5-foot-10, with a medium build, blue eyes, and brown hair. Military ID J17845 was finally a real person on paper, with a new photo to go along with the only known one to date of his handsome face stoically looking aside.

I also got the diary he kept as a prisoner of war in the Stalag Luft III POW camp, near the town of Sagan, 100 miles southeast of Berlin. He was provided a "wartime log for British prisoners," in which the POWs were encouraged to keep notes, draw sketches, and preserve mementos of their time in captivity. It is the only known firsthand account of Wilf Canter.

Canter's diary contains no reference to "The Great Escape" – and naturally it doesn't mention his Jewish faith, or that of other notable Jewish prisoners such as British pilots Peter Stevens and Robert Sanford "Lucky" Tuck, which could have proven fatal if discovered by his Nazi captors.

But the diary does provide some unique glimpses. He drew sketches of the camp, its layout and illustrations of sentry boxes. His sketch of the "North Compound" included a baseball diamond, a basketball court, and a cricket pitch that were supposed to keep captives busy since, officially at least, the Geneva Conventions prevented Germany from putting captive officers to work. A boxing match that the prisoners put on in the "East Compound" served as both spectacle for the prisoners themselves and a distraction for German sentries as others began plotting "The Great Escape."[8]

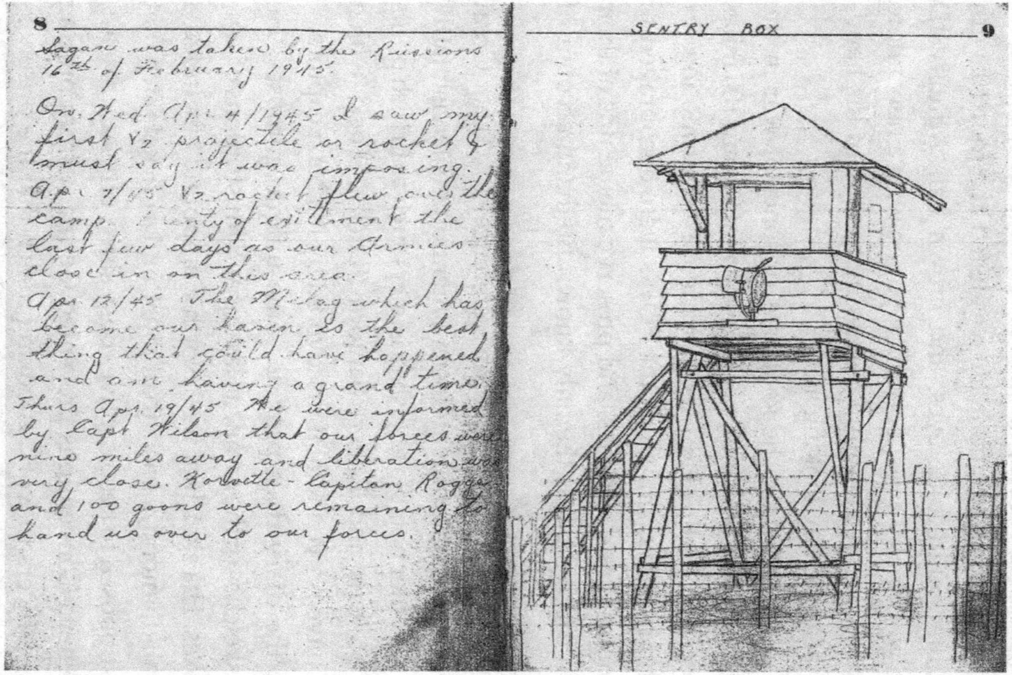

8

Sagan was taken by the Russians 16th of February 1945.

On Wed. Apr. 4/1945 I saw my first V2 projectile or rocket & must say it was imposing.
Ap. 7/45 V2 rocket flew over the camp. Plenty of exitement the last few days as our Armies close in on this area.
Ap. 12/45 The Milag which has become our haven is the best thing that could have happened and am having a grand time.
Thurs Ap. 19/45 We were informed by Capt Wilson that our forces were nine miles away and liberation was very close. Korvette-Capitan Rogge and 100 goons were remaining to hand us over to our forces.

SENTRY BOX 9

Photo 2.4. Pages from Wilfred Canter's diary in captivity at Stalag Luft III
(Courtesy of Wayne Gershon.)

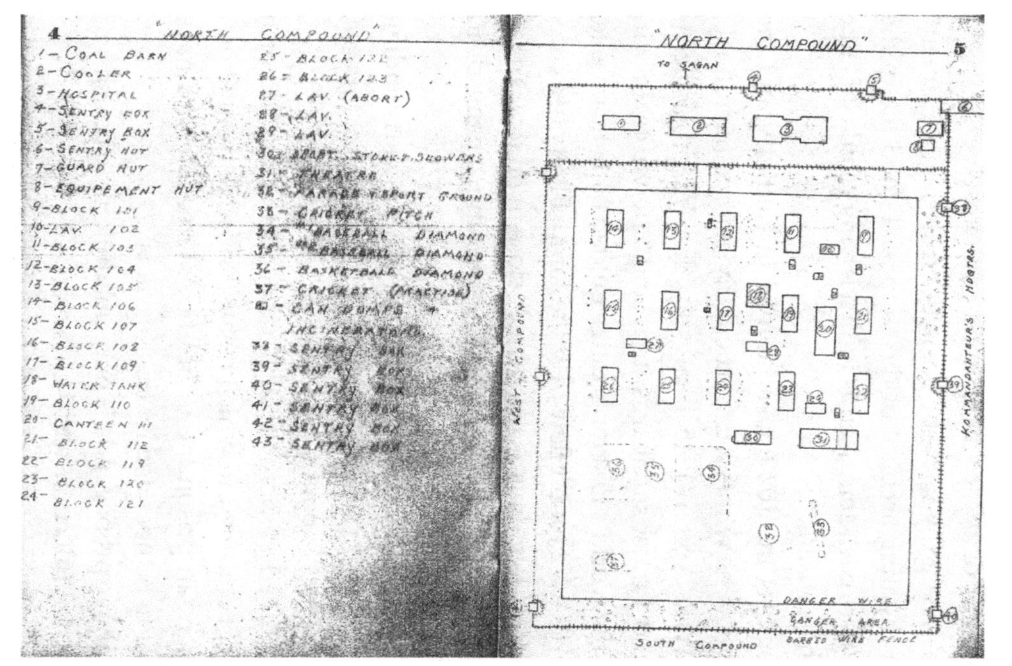

Photo 2.5. A sketch of the Stalag Luft III compound from Wilfred Canter's diary in captivity
(Courtesy of Wayne Gershon.)

With impeccable handwriting, Canter composed poems and described the daily routines, the food they ate (rations of barley and jam), the activities in which they partook (such as sports and theater), and the conversations among the prisoners, or *kriegies*, as they called themselves.

There's a lengthy sarcastic poem titled "Kriegies Lament" that is a rhyming account of the supposed good life in the camp, before each stanza ends with a jarring rebuke of "like bloody hell we are."

Canter lists the 102 books he read in captivity and the major events he witnessed, particularly close to liberation.

"On Wed. Apr. 4/1945 I saw my first V2 projectile or rocket and I must say it was imposing," he wrote, of witnessing the world's first long-range guided ballistic missile. "Apr. 4/45, a V2 rocket flew over the camp. Plenty of excitement the last few days as our armies close in on this area."

After liberation, he described witnessing "many dead goons lying about in the woods. It is a horrible sight." Meanwhile, the kriegies were living off the surrounding land, where there were "countless chicken, geese, turkeys, lambs and pigs" about.

He included an account of Nazi claims in the Swedish newspaper *Aftenpost* in which it says British personnel preferred German prison life to Bolshevist freedom and have asked not to be liberated by the Russians.

"The above propaganda is pure unadulterated bullsh – t," he wrote, the full curse word crossed out.

He noted the dates on which he got his parcels from the Red Cross and listed the diseases contracted in the camp. He included extracts from POW letters with some of the funniest notes they received from loved ones, including what can only be assumed to be wives or girlfriends. "I hope you will not return passion-dead," one reads. "I don't doubt that you will really feel queer when you meet someone of the opposite sex," reads another. "I'm so glad you got shot down before flying got dangerous," another note said.

The diary claimed that German meteorologists said the winter of 1944 was the coldest in 100 years and that five German planes were shot out of the air on March 7, 1945.

The best parts were the random observations and wartime stories circulating about, including that of the miraculous survival of British tail gunner Nicholas Stephen Alkemade.

"RAF Sgt. Alkemade fell 18,000 ft. without a parachute and lived. This has been corroborated by the Germans," he wrote. "Ken Edwards won the sweepstakes of 1500 marks on June 1944 in Sagan. Scottish F/Sgt/ Mac, former British boxer, was blown out of air at 22,000 ft. and lived. Confirmed by the Germans who found him without chute."

Canter and Zaidy exchanged letters throughout their time in Europe and Canter invited my grandfather to the ceremony in London where he received his Distinguished Flying Medal, but my grandfather responded that he sadly couldn't go.

Zaidy's last handwritten letter to Canter on Salvation Army stationery was a matter-of-fact exchange between two old friends. But the letter, sent in 1944, never arrived at its destination. It was returned and on the tattered envelope – that my grandfather saved in his desk drawer for the next seventy years – was a stamp that read "present location not known" and large red capital letters that read "MISSING." Unbeknownst to Zaidy, Canter had already been shot down by the Germans and taken prisoner.

After the war, Canter was shipped home, but he never reconnected with my grandfather, and he struggled to find his way.

Wayne Gershon confirmed what I had suspected: Canter was depressed and struggled to find purpose. He did odd jobs as a draftsman but was frustrated by his lack of employment options, comparing his plight to that of his grandfather who couldn't be a pharmacist in Ukraine because he was Jewish. Mostly, though, he longed to fly again, and he only fully emerged from his funk when he heard, through word of mouth in the Jewish community, that there were aviation opportunities in the new State of Israel. When he departed, Canter left behind a girlfriend named Leah whom both his sister and mother liked very much.

"I think it was personal for Wilf to double down and go to Israel," Gershon said. "He recognized the cause. I didn't get the impression that he relished battle just for its own sake."

In 1948, as Israel prepared to declare itself a sovereign nation, the fledgling state sought foreign assistance to fight the Arab nations that moved against it. Thousands of mostly Jewish volunteers from around the world with combat experience made their way to Israel – often in clandestine fashion, to avoid running into trouble with their own governments.

Canter arrived in Israel on August 5, 1948, and immediately joined a newly minted air force that had few aviators with any significant operational experience. He was placed in 103 Squadron and flew in bombing raids and in supply missions to outposts that were besieged behind enemy lines.

"He was trained to fly a plane in any condition," said 103 Squadron commander Daniel Rozin, according to an account about the origins of the Israeli Air Force. "Character wise, he was quiet, focused, and unflappable. He was incredibly friendly and well-liked by his comrades."[9]

Late on the night of October 24, Canter and four other crewmen, two of them Canadian, took off in their rickety Douglas C-47 Dakota transport from Tel Aviv's Sde Dov Airport to deliver supplies to the isolated Negev outpost of Sdom, which was encircled by Egyptian forces.

After a delay because of foggy conditions, the plane took off smoothly. Just minutes into the flight, though, the right engine began to overheat and spit out flames. Canter redirected for an emergency landing at the Tel Nof Airbase, but the engine exploded within sight of the airfield, breaking off the right wing and sending the Dakota spiraling to the ground at 23:55. It burst into a ball of fire on impact, killing everyone on board, in one of the first fatal aerial transport accidents in Israeli history.

At 1:15, Rozin was awoken with the news. He immediately called headquarters and after consulting with the air force chief of air operations he flew to the scene, where at 3:40 he identified the bodies amid the smoldering remains of the Dakota. Firefighters who arrived on the scene found debris and "burned body parts" scattered for miles.[10]

"I'd never seen such devastation. There was nothing left of the plane," Rozin, who had logged 60 flight hours of his own on that Dakota, wrote in his report.[11]

An investigation could not determine the exact cause of the crash, but the negligence was obvious. The Dakota was 100 hours overdue for servicing and criminally overworked.

"After the crash there was outrage in the squadron," Eddy Kaplansky, a volunteer pilot from Montreal, wrote years later. "Because it was clear that the horrible technical condition of the plane led to the deadly crash. On the one hand there were no replacement engines but on the other hand there was lots of pressure to keep going on more missions."

The squadron's chief mechanic, Abe Nurick, had begged to have the Dakota's engines replaced and a nagging oil leak fixed. He had also repeatedly warned against flying without proper fire extinguishers on board. But on the eve of the fateful flight, he was granted a rare forty-eight-hour leave and the flight took off without his consent.[12] The crew had neither fire extinguishers on board nor emergency parachutes and IDs, as required.

"He was horrified because he said if he had been on duty as chief mechanic, he would have checked the logbooks and he would never have allowed that plane to take off," recalled Nurick's friend Shmuel Amid, a radio signals technician in 103 Squadron.

Living in a retirement home within walking distance of my home in Kfar Saba, the British-born Amid attested to the makeshift nature of the times, recalling how the Dakotas were often converted into bomber planes and how he would moonlight as a "bomb chucker" in response to notices posted seeking volunteers for the improvised missions.

"I was the fuse puller," he said with a grin, as he recounted the surreal scene of passing live bombs hand-to-hand inside a shaky plane before hurling them out of an open hatch in the floor. When the bombs ran out, he said they reverted to tossing empty beer bottles.

"When the bottles fell, they used to make a terrifying screeching noise," a then-ninety-six-year-old Amid told me in 2019. "The idea was psychological. When bombs fell you couldn't hear them but with these things screeching down, we hoped it would put the fear of God into them. And if they happened to land on someone, then well and good."[13]

Paul Orringer, an American pilot with 103 Squadron who witnessed the crash, said he had encountered "backfiring" in his previous flights in the Dakota, and he and Canter briefly refused to fly it. Only after squadron commander Rozin assuaged their concerns did Orringer complete a mission on October 23 – the night before it crashed.

"The plane was defective, old and unsafe to fly," Orringer said, according to an account in an internal air force publication about 103 Squadron.[14] "The only reason Canter flew it is because I did the night before and told him it was OK."

Orringer said because of the Dakota's faulty state, crew members were supposed to wear parachutes but, in effect, very few did. None on the October 24 flight had any on.

"It was far less romantic than one would like to imagine," explained Tal Landman, the commemoration coordinator of 103 Squadron. "These planes had no seatbelts, no essential equipment, and they didn't get proper mechanical servicing. They were like flying taxi cabs, hunks of metal in the sky."

Despite its clunky reputation, there was only one other fatal Dakota crash in Israeli Air Force history when a pilot dangerously flew low with one in July 1980. The fleet was permanently retired in January 2001.

But that October 1948 crash was devastating.

The following day, flight orders were clarified so that flights had to have parachutes for each of those departing, under penalty of court martial. The crash led to safety concerns generally being taken more seriously. More flights were canceled, and pilots more often refused to take off if they felt unsafe.[15]

Following the accident, military headquarters also ordered that no additional passengers be flown without special air force authorization. But this instruction seems to have been immediately flouted, as a different Dakota filled with personnel without such approvals departed days later for the funerals of the fallen airmen.

Wilfred Canter was twenty-seven when he died.

By that time, my grandfather was already a struggling young salesman and father of one in Toronto. He only learned of Canter's death years later and didn't delve into the details until enlisting my help decades later to tell his friend's story.

"He came from the Old Country, you know," Zaidy told me. "What a life. What a *shanda* [Yiddish for shame]."

On August 13, 2012, on my way back to Jerusalem from a reporting assignment in coastal Herzliya about an elderly

Holocaust survivor, I decided on a whim to veer off the highway and head south to Rehovot. It was time to track down Wilf Canter's gravesite in central Israel.

A fifteen-minute drive later, I found the military cemetery off a main road in Rehovot. It was empty. I entered the grounds alone and, aside from the distant sound of whizzing cars, all was silent. Off in the distance, cranes were working on a new apartment building. Inside, I sensed the tranquility such cemeteries often conjure.

It was a typical Israeli military cemetery, rows upon rows of simple, uniform rectangular plots covered by tiny, manicured garden beds and headstones with each soldier's basic information engraved. I found the grave nestled between two others with identical dates of death – Michael Weimers and William Fisher – men I could only assume at the time were his comrades in the fatal plane crash. Against this eerie silence, I placed a small pebble on Canter's headstone and mouthed aloud: "Zaidy says hi."

The brief, solitary pilgrimage left me wondering if anyone else had ever paid his grave a visit over the past sixty-five years and made me question how many other men like him were out there – even in just this cemetery – that lived such short, dramatic lives but left little behind.

I dutifully reported all my findings to Zaidy and excitedly awaited his response. This was the breakthrough I'd been waiting for all my life. I couldn't wait to learn more. What else could Zaidy share about this remarkable man?

Zaidy appreciated all the legwork I did to complete Canter's biography, but once the report was delivered, the task was done. There was no follow-up, just a terse, single-sentence response acknowledging my service.

"Thank you very much. That is great information. I now know where to go for action," he wrote.

It was classic Zaidy – he was shutting down again.

"My pleasure, Zaidy," I replied. "He really sounds like quite a guy. Where did you serve together? What more do you remember about him?"

As expected, there was no further response.

CHAPTER THREE

Fred Stevenson, the Devoted Wingman

With my passion project stalled, Zaidy and I retreated to our typical correspondences, exchanging emails and phone calls in between my three visits to Toronto over the next six years. The Wilf Canter story had gone cold and had nearly drifted from memory when, out of the blue, came a cold call in 2018 from a woman named Efrat Gal who said she was seeking information about him.

Motivated by her own lost relative, an uncle who died in the 1956 Sinai Campaign and whose fate she only learned about much later, she had taken on a passion project of her own – to track down the next of kin of all the fallen airmen from 103 Squadron for a vast memorial project at the Nevatim Air Force Base in southern Israel. Contacting the native-born Israelis was the first step, but things got trickier when it came to the foreign volunteers who arrived in 1948 and never put down roots in Israel.

With help from her husband, Gideon, a former private investigator, they had somehow touched base with various families around the world. Wilf Canter, it appeared, was their final target, the last fallen airman from 103 Squadron who had no known descendants and whose biography remained incomplete.

To my astonishment, they had tracked down relations for nearly all the crew of Canter's fateful final flight. Gideon's sleuthing had led him to Zaidy, who had published an appreciation of his old friend in *The Canadian Jewish News* that was largely based on the research I provided him.

That's how the Gals got in touch with me. They wanted to pick my brain and have me contribute my findings, which I gladly did. But they did more than that. They sparked in me a renewed passion to explore the history of this remarkable man, and his crewmates, particularly in lieu of my failure to do so with my own grandfather.

Re-energized, I realized there was a story here after all, if not about Zaidy, then about his friend Wilf Canter and those like him. The result would be several articles about the Wilf Canter-piloted Dakota aircraft, the forgotten men in it, and their overlooked service as foreign volunteers in the early days of Israel.

In Efrat Gal, I found a woman dedicated beyond belief. Barely five feet tall, with thick-rimmed black glasses and short, spiky, silver-dyed hair, Efrat had fully immersed herself in the Nevatim commemoration project, which had become for her a fanatical mission derived from her own traumatic past.

When she was three, her father, Schmuel Schlesinger, mysteriously fled Israel and disappeared for decades. Later, after Efrat was already a young mother of two little girls, her husband was grievously wounded in the 1982 Lebanon War. Caring for what she called that war's most seriously injured soldier became her full-time occupation. During his long years of incapacitation, she discovered he had been unfaithful before his injury and divorced him while still caring for him and his elderly parents until their deaths. Only years later, once she had remarried and had another child, did she discover the impetus for her biological father abandoning her in the first place. It turned out that he had a younger brother, Uri Schlesinger, who had been a pilot who crashed to his death in the 1956 Sinai Campaign. That drove his devastated mother, who had come to pre-state Israel on the *Exodus* passenger steamship after her husband was murdered in a Nazi death camp, to flee Israel for Australia and convince her lone remaining son to come with her.

Learning that, in addition to all her other woes, she also had an uncle she never knew existed inspired Efrat to search for the comfort of other bereaved families. Discovering that so many hadn't been properly commemorated and that others like herself knew little about the sacrifices of their own relatives, gave her a new purpose that she had since doggedly pursued.

"For so many years, we knew nothing about my uncle and there was no one to visit his grave," she explained. "The thought that there were others out there who didn't know, or that the military was looking for but couldn't find their bereaved families, made me uneasy. I decided then and there that I wouldn't have it. I'd turn the world over to find them."

Efrat and her husband, Gideon, became the operational arm of Tal Landman, a burly one-man team of encyclopedic knowledge about Israeli Air Force history. His three-year mandatory service as the commemoration and heritage coordinator of Nevatim, which featured a unique in-base memorial, turned into twenty years of devoted reserve duty. The task of maintaining contact with the base's bereaved families had often overtaken his civilian day job as a drama teacher at an elementary school in central Israel. For him, it was a moral imperative to commemorate the base's more than 110 fallen airmen and to find any documents, belongings, and personal connections for those who had been forgotten by history.

"I believe that no one deserves to die twice. No one deserves to fall in the abyss of obliviousness," he explained. "These people gave their lives for the country, and we can't have a situation where no one knows that they ever existed."

The Gals gave him the kind of firepower in his field the military never could and together they tracked down a dozen families of long-forgotten soldiers, filling out their biographies and bringing them into the air force's tight-knit circle of bereaved families. With Landman's scope limited to Israel, the Gals took the mission overseas. They found families, arranged for them to be flown to Israel to visit gravesites, and even hosted them in their own home. Along the way, they changed the lives of many who didn't even know they belonged to a larger community: people like the descendants of Fred Stevenson – Wilf Canter's devoted co-pilot on the fateful Dakota flight.

Fred Stevenson was born in Flint, Michigan, on March 6, 1919, to Ann and Ilf, Protestants with Icelandic roots. When Fred was ten, the family moved to Saskatchewan, Canada, where his father worked in agriculture. Fred split his youth between Regina and Eston. He played baseball, sang, and dabbled in wood carving.

He enlisted in 1941, leaving a wife and infant behind, and served in the RCAF for five years, including as a transport pilot. He flew over Europe, logging about 1,600 flight hours on various aircraft. A relative said part of his mission was providing air cover for Canadian ships carrying troops and supplies across the Atlantic Ocean on their voyage to Europe. A photograph of Stevenson from this period shows a smooth, baby-faced portrait with Nordic features and a service cap tilted on one side of his head.

He returned home to work as a farmer in Saskatchewan before moving to Vancouver to be closer to his young daughter. Unlike his Jewish comrades, his reasons for volunteering to fly in Israel were less straightforward. But he was no mercenary, and it seemed his Christian faith and personal situation were driving forces.

By 1948, he was adrift, separated from his wife and looking for a cause. According to an account in the *Israelite Press*, a Yiddish-English language Jewish weekly in Western Canada, Stevenson one day picked up a phone book, dialed the

Photo 3.1. Fred Stevenson
(Courtesy of Tal Landman.)

number of a Jewish-sounding name and told the unsuspecting man on the other end of the call that he wanted to volunteer for the war in Israel. The man he randomly reached, a local Jewish lawyer, made the arrangements and off Stevenson went. He became one of more than ninety non-Jewish, World War II veteran airmen who volunteered for the war, making up more than 15 percent of the aerial fighting force.[1]

Stevenson landed in Israel on an October day at 4 p.m. and four hours later was already airborne on his first mission. His comrades described him as an adventurous, happy-go-lucky kind of guy, who went by the nickname "Stevie" and was the perfect wingman to his new friend, Wilf Canter.

His only child, a girl named Sharone, was told little about him by her mother, who had remarried. But Sharone's grandmother told her in generalities about a gentle man who loved to dance and sing and had a good sense of humor. She doubted the account of him calling a Jewish lawyer to volunteer; she had heard that a friend had tipped him off about the war in Israel, sparking his interest.

"He simply found a way to help out a country, which included being able to fly for that country and doing what he thought and felt was a good cause," a seventy-seven-year-old Sharone Deschenes told me in 2018. "Believe me when I say that he knew the score about going over there as he asked my grandparents to raise me because he would not be coming back."

Her few memories of him include him swinging her around, singing songs, and buying her a gray elephant with a red bow on one of his visits with her. "He bought me a red coat for winter. I was so excited and thought it was the most beautiful coat I had ever seen," she recalled in a phone call from her home in Strathmore, Alberta, near Calgary.

Stevenson's last visit with his daughter was in the spring of 1948, when she was visiting her grandparents in the small town of Wartime, Saskatchewan. He bought her a blue bicycle. "It might as well have been a new car, all of us were beside ourselves," she said.

It was then that he informed the adults he was thinking of going to fight for the Israeli cause. "I didn't know at the time that that would be the last time I ever saw him," Deschenes said.

She remembered coming home from school for lunch one day that October. As she walked in, the radio was playing "English Country Garden," which always played at noon. Her mother and stepfather sat her down and said her father had been killed flying a plane in Israel and would not be coming home. "I didn't even know he had gone to a place called Israel," she said.

Fred Stevenson was buried in the Christian cemetery in Jaffa three days after his death at the age of twenty-nine. At the family's request, he was transferred in 1951 to a Protestant plot in the military cemetery in Haifa, at the foot of Mount Carmel overlooking the Mediterranean Sea, alongside other non-Jewish casualties of the 1948 war.[2] His daughter visited the grave in 1994, with her husband, Ray, and again in 2018, with her daughter, Corinne, marking Israel's 70th anniversary.

"I guess he felt like I do that everyone is entitled to their independence," Deschenes said. "He did what was in his heart and I'm proud of him."

Photo 3.2. Fred Stevenson
(Photo credit: Aron Heller.)

CHAPTER FOUR

Willie Fisher, the Zionist Navigator

The third member of the Dakota crew was, like my grandfather, a Jewish Canadian navigator in Bomber Command during World War II. But unlike my grandfather, Willie Fisher had friends and relatives who openly shared vivid details about his life and service.

Most significant among them was his nephew, Wilf Mandel, who coincidentally shared the unusual first name of the pilot on Fisher's final flight.

Mandel, who was two when Fisher died in Israel, grew up on the tales of his fallen uncle. But that did not necessarily translate into a family affinity for Israel. Mandel told me that his grandmother, Fisher's mother, held Israel responsible for her son's death and that any interest he later developed in the Jewish state had to be kept on the down low. So, he had to sneak out to attend meetings of the Habonim youth group and quietly joined a student Zionist organization. When the Six-Day War broke out in 1967, he considered volunteering. His mother quickly quashed the idea, saying she had already lost a brother to Israel and couldn't face the risk of also losing a son.

Only after his parents died did Mandel begin researching more thoroughly about his uncle Willie. He contacted various organizations, visited his uncle's gravesite in Israel, spoke to local schools in Canada, and addressed a Jewish community memorial event in Fisher's hometown of Winnipeg.

Mandel also made a habit each year of writing a letter to the editor published in *The Canadian Jewish News* to keep the memory of the Dakota crew alive. One year, he got an interesting inquiry in response to his mention of Wilf Canter. Turns out my Zaidy, who's often more comfortable discussing his past in the company of strangers, reached out to tell him about his connection to the pilot. Mandel, who also lived in Toronto, told me that my Zaidy sounded lonely, so he paid him a courtesy visit.

It was one of these posts in *The Canadian Jewish News* that Gideon Gal eventually tracked down, setting off the journey that led him to Mandel and other relatives of the Dakota victims until only Wilfred Canter was left. That's how the Gals found my grandfather and, eventually, me.

And that's how I also began researching the life of Willie Fisher, who discovered the allure – and the adversities – of Israel long before my family ever did.

William-Wolfe Fisher was born on August 28, 1923, in Proskurov (now Khmelnitsky), Ukraine, two months after the death of his father[1] and less than four years after the infamous Proskurov pogrom in which at least 1,500 Jews were killed in a single day. The remaining Fisher family – his mother, Freda, and three older siblings, Max, Sonia, and Maurice – remained with next to nothing. Impoverished, Freda took a small amount of jewellery she had hidden and used it to move to Canada, where she had a wealthier extended family in Winnipeg who helped her get by for several years. The family lived in a two-bedroom apartment on Burrows Avenue and the little boy the family called Velvel became known as either Bill or, mostly, Willie. The kids went to school and got a Jewish education before heading to work to help the family get through the Depression. Young Willie was known as a "mama's boy," staying close to home to help his widowed mother.

His best friend from childhood, Leon Tessler, described him as a fearless free spirit who would take a dare to do almost anything and who excelled at sports, especially in the high jump, in which he won several medals at Luxton High School. He said Fisher was a gifted artist who taught his friends shadow drawing, but who also partook in pranks like shooting his water gun at passing cars on the street. With a few other Jewish boys, they formed a club that met regularly at Fisher's home.

"He was truly a great friend who never had a bad word to say about other people. He always looked on the bright side of things," a then-ninety-four-year-old Tessler told me over the phone from Toronto in 2018. "In our formative years he was always interested in the stars and the constellations. I guess that's how he became a navigator and when he

Photo 4.1. Willie Fisher
(Courtesy of Wilf Mandel.)

joined the air force that was his dream. He always dreamed of flying and following the stars."[2]

Fisher enlisted in 1942, straight out of high school, and served three years as a navigator in a Lancaster bomber, flying missions over Germany and France until the war's end in 1945. He survived twenty-eight bombing missions and returned to Winnipeg, where he first worked in his uncle's shirt factory before opening his own small nut shop.

Tessler, who served in the Royal Canadian Corps of Signals during World War II and wasn't deployed to Europe, said Fisher (like Zaidy) spoke little about his wartime service, wanting to leave it in the past.

"He was never a braggart, and he never spoke about his exploits," Tessler said, noting a similar dynamic with his other friends. "If they had been in battle, they never talked about it. They never talked about it, and we never pushed them because we took it for granted that they had had a hard enough time as it is."

Fisher visited Tessler and his wife in Toronto in 1948 as he was making his way to Ottawa, en route to Israel, informing his longtime friend of his big decision to move to Israel. "Willie never worried about himself, he had no fear," Tessler said. "But he wasn't looking for adventure. He was an ideologue. He was looking to help out any way he could."

Fisher traveled to Israel by way of England and Switzerland; he used the assumed name "Mordechai Mandel," for fear of running into trouble with Canadian authorities and risk losing his citizenship. By volunteering, many fighters were violating the terms of their passports and potentially other laws and were subject to severe punishment if prosecuted.

In Israel, Fisher immersed himself deeply in aviation, learning new systems. His 1948 wartime logbook shows bombing missions over Beersheba and deeper south into Egypt. Unlike most of the fellow volunteers who planned to return home after the war, Fisher was of the mind to stay and had begun studying Hebrew before he died.

In a letter to Tessler, he shared some of his observations about the new country, wowed by how Jewish men took on manual labor jobs in the Holy Land that he had seldom seen Jews do before. "The weather is absolutely wonderful, if not a bit on the hot side," he wrote. "How they manage to get anything out of sandy soil is beyond me. It was Moses who led us out to this Promised Land. I say he led us to the wrong place. It should have been California."

He described his trips to Haifa, Jerusalem, and various *kibbutzim*, noting that the agricultural life of the communal farms was not for him. "The free love is about the only agreeable thing that most Americans find there. Not many Western people could bring themselves to set up living in that style," he wrote. "We have here Western cities with a very Oriental flavor. And as for the traffic, you've never seen anything like it. Just standing and watching I feel like closing my eyes and screaming. A driver could go absolutely mad. The sidewalks are considered fair territory for all manner of vehicles, and they use them often."

He went on to describe the type of chaos that would be familiar to North American newcomers to Israel, both then and now.

"The army here is rotten with politics and it really is shocking. You get the feeling that we have a situation like the South American republics where they have a revolution a day and so on," he said. "They have many hot heads here."[3]

Still, he found himself drawn.

Allan Chapnick, another Canadian volunteer, knew Fisher from Winnipeg and bumped into him once in an army mess hall in Israel. But he was on a six-week, halftrack boot patrol in southern Israel at the time of the crash and only learned about it upon his return to Beersheba.

"They were many casualties and it's seventy years later so it's hard to remember anybody. I can tell you who were the guys that were on my halftrack though," the then-ninety-year-old told me by phone from Winnipeg in 2018. "It [the Dakota crash] was just another incident, that's all it was. I didn't even know it was Canadians."[4]

In September, Fisher sent a letter to his mother in Yiddish from Tel Aviv. "To my beloved Ma. I can write to you that I am fine. I hope you are all well, too. I am waiting for a letter that I hope will arrive soon. What is happening with you?"

He apparently got a response, since on October 24, 1948, the eve of his fateful flight, he sent a telegram via Canadian Pacific that stated simply: "Received your mail. All well." It was the last anyone heard from him.

Firefighters who arrived on the scene of the crash found debris and body parts scattered for miles. Fisher was identified by the ID tag found among his clothing.

He was twenty-five when he died.

"Israel was in trouble," said Wilf Mandel, Fisher's nephew. "They had no fliers, and there was a need, and he felt that he could help with that need."

Much of what Mandel learned about his uncle's service in Israel came from Eddy Kaplansky, a Montreal pilot and fellow Canadian volunteer who meticulously collected information on the foreign fliers and put it in a 128-page book called *The First Fliers* that was published in 1993.

In conversation with Mandel, Kaplansky bemoaned how the Dakota accident was avoidable, summarizing succinctly: "We pushed those planes too hard."

According to Kaplansky, Fisher was his navigator on a couple of night reconnaissance flights into enemy territory during "Operation Taskit" in late September and early October 1948. The purpose of the five-night reconnaissance mission was to map the deployment of enemy forces west of the Jordan by dropping pyrotechnics over targeted areas as operators monitored various frequencies for enemy signal activity.[5]

As a result, Kaplansky said he and Fisher quickly grew close.

"I respected him as an excellent navigator and reliable crew member, and we became fast friends," Kaplansky, who witnessed the crash, wrote to Mandel in 2000, five years before his death.

The account mirrored what Mandel long believed.

"My uncle had no fear of anything. He would try anything. He was very adventurous. He was easy to like," Mandel said in a video played at an event at the Nevatim Air Force Base marking Israel's 70th Memorial Day in 2018. "They all went because they felt they could 'do something right.'"

In conversation with me, though, Mandel acknowledged that there was likely something deeper driving these men. The experience of war had done something to their psyche, particularly those in Bomber Command, where the life expectancy of a new crew member was no more than six months.

Figures from the Bomber Command Museum of Canada in Nanton, Alberta, helped bring the full scope of such a perilous service into clearer focus. Of the 120,000 men who served in Bomber Command, 55,573 were killed – more than 45 percent – including some 10,250 Canadians. The museum called it a loss rate comparable only to the worst slaughter of the trenches in World War I. Only the Nazi U-boat force suffered a higher World War II casualty rate. According to the museum's website, Bomber Command suffered more losses on a single night than did Fighter Command during the entire Battle of Britain.[6]

The early years were particularly brutal. Bomber Command's major achievements were still years away, but it still took devastating losses, so much that on any given night more of its fliers were killed in the air than were Germans on the ground.[7]

Between March 1943 and February 1944, for instance, the period when my grandfather and Fisher were deployed, members of crews that ran a full tour of thirty bombing operations had a grim 16 percent survival rate, according to the Bomber Command Museum.[8] The Canadians and the Royal Air Force flew their missions at night. Their aircraft had no belly gunners and were at the mercy of Luftwaffe fighters that attacked from below. Whenever they lifted off on a mission, they departed with the knowledge that this sortie could easily be their last.

Given these ghastly figures, it's more understandable why Zaidy, an already intensely private man, would choose to keep his experience to himself. Mandel said his father used to say Fisher had "survived" World War II. I suppose it must have felt that way and produced a similar psychology to that of the many Holocaust survivors I've interviewed, replete with the trauma of war, the anguish over comrades who fell, and the guilt over surviving yourself.

Both Fisher and my grandfather served as the all-important observer (or navigator) in bomber planes. Until 1942, the navigator was also responsible for aiming and releasing the bombs and he served alongside two pilots and a wireless operator. When the heavy bombers were introduced, a flight engineer replaced the second pilot, and the other crew members were given single, more specialized roles. The navigator's primary responsibility remained keeping the aircraft on course, reaching the target and then getting back to base safely. It required a high level of concentration for virtually the entire flight, which could last up to seven hours.[9]

Such a service deeply affected those who survived. Perhaps my grandfather's stubborn compartmentalization of World War II is what helped him avoid the seductions of war that appear to have lured Canter, Stevenson, and Fisher back. My grandfather kept quiet and moved on to live a long, fulfilling life. The others were seemingly drawn back in to fight for Israel and ended up buried in a foreign land, thousands of miles from home.

Zaidy, unsurprisingly, offered scarce new details. Mandel reported that Zaidy was cagey with him as well when they met in Toronto.

"It's unbelievable that most of the survivors didn't suffer some form of PTSD [post-traumatic stress disorder], yet they kept flying," he wrote to me after they met. "I understood completely when your grandfather would only say he was lucky to come back alive."

Mandel's insight makes perfect sense. Zaidy's reluctance to discuss the war could easily be the result of what most veterans likely experienced – some undiagnosed form of PTSD, what back then they merely called "shell shock" or, even worse, "lack of moral fiber" – a devastating designation of shame on those who couldn't carry out their air missions.

The best way to get over that, men of Zaidy's generation likely concluded, was not to talk about it at all.

CHAPTER FIVE

Leon Lightman, the Idealistic Airman

Wilfred Canter, Fred Stevenson, and William Fisher were among the 123 foreign volunteers who died in the battle for Israel's establishment in 1948. These included eleven out of some 300 Canadians who volunteered.

The outsized influence of the 4,800 volunteers from fifty-nine countries[1] has been largely overlooked in the collective consciousness of modern-day Israel, where wartime heroism has mostly been the domain of the prickly Sabras (native-born Israelis) who went on to lead its military and government.

But Israeli statesmen and historians have keenly noted that without *Machal*, the Hebrew acronym for "Volunteers from Abroad," Israel would have been unlikely to overcome its long odds in the war. No less an authority than David Ben-Gurion called them the Jewish Diaspora's greatest contribution to Israel.

My Zaidy had no interest in joining their ranks. World War II was more than enough for him. He was perfectly content remaining in Canada and supporting Israel from afar. But he did send his children to a variety of Canadian Zionist summer camps and youth movements, inspiring his two oldest sons to volunteer in Israel and eventually make Aliyah (immigrate to Israel). As a result, Zaidy made over a dozen trips to Israel over the course of forty years to visit his children and grandchildren, sometimes staying for as long as two months at a time. He joined local bridge clubs and mason lodges and connected with old friends. He was also the first person I remember who brought my attention to Machal and shared his pride in the long-unnoticed contribution of his fellow Canadians.

En route to work one morning in 2018, I took a quick detour off the main Tel Aviv-Jerusalem highway at the Shaar Haguy exit to visit the Machal memorial honoring these foreign volunteers. I'd driven by the exit sign hundreds of times, but the recent discovery of these men drew me there on this day. A white stone memorial with the engraved names of the fallen volunteers was located near a forested picnic ground with an Israeli flag at half-staff. It stood just by the start of the Burma Road that paved the way to besieged Jerusalem in 1948. On this scorching weekday morning, it was completely empty.

"You came to us when we needed you most during those dark and uncertain days in our War of Independence," then-Prime Minister Yitzhak Rabin said at the dedication ceremony of the monument, on Memorial Day, April 25, 1993. "My generation will never forget what you have done, how much you made it possible for us to achieve what has been achieved."[2]

These Jewish and non-Jewish volunteers, particularly those with vast World War II combat experience, indeed played a decisive role in Israel's battle for independence.

One of those was George "Buzz" Beurling, a Royal Canadian Air Force pilot who was among the most famous World War II aces. Beurling, who was not Jewish, had shot down over thirty enemy German planes in the war. He perished when the Norseman plane he was preparing to fly to Israel mysteriously burst into flames and crashed at a small airport near Rome in May 1948.

But I was more drawn to the names of other Canadians memorialized at the site. Wilf Canter was there, as were the other Canadians who crashed with him in the Dakota on October 24, 1948: co-pilot Fred Stevenson and navigator Willie Fisher.

Also memorialized there was a fourth member of their doomed Dakota flight: British radio operator Leon Lightman.

Jerome Leon Lightman was born in London to Avraham and Miriam on June 9, 1923. From a young age, he showed a keen interest in both Zionism and aviation.

As a teenager, he joined the Habonim youth movement and dreamed of building a pioneering society in the Holy Land. After graduating from high school, he studied agriculture and became involved in the Jewish groups that planned to settle the land of Israel. He was one of the founders of the Shmaryahu "Garin," a group made up of young Brits and refugees from central Europe who planned to immigrate to Palestine and settle in kibbutzim in the Upper Galilee. It was during those three years that he was said to have exhibited excellence in instructing and organizing. He became known as both demanding of himself and of others as well as a jokester who claimed creative rights over various silly expressions.[3]

This is also where he formed some of his closest friendships and tried to overcome the heartache of his first love. His friend Eric Arenberg wrote about Lightman falling madly in love with a girl named Louise from a fellow Jewish group. She did not return his love, and Lightman joined Shmaryahu in part to get over her. It only partially worked: the two friends would stay up late at night, lamenting lost love and imagining their future in the Jewish state.

But before he could settle in pre-state Israel, there was a war to be won. In 1943, Lightman mobilized into the Royal Air Force and trained as a radio and radar operator. As with the Canadians Canter, Stevenson, and Fisher, the casualty rate was high, and many survivors emerged from the war as broken men. Lightman seemingly appeared to come out unscathed. He spoke little of the experience, cryptically telling his friends that "you had to be lucky to survive."

During the war, Lightman had a non-Jewish girlfriend who, Arenberg wrote, loved him dearly. Upon Lightman's discharge, he returned to Shmaryahu, where he worked in agriculture and as a medic while he prepared to move to Palestine. The girlfriend once visited with him, and there were those there who questioned whether Lightman could return to agricultural life, given the glamor associated with RAF men. But he did. Eventually he and the girlfriend split, and he made his way to Palestine alone, where his passions for Zionism and aviation finally melded together.

He helped with early weapons smuggling, settled in the Galilee, and, together with his English mates, founded Kibbutz Kfar Hanassi. Lightman joined the Israeli Air Force on May 14, 1948, the same day Ben-Gurion declared independence and the same day his fellow British kibbutz friend Meir Reines joined the navy.

"When the war broke out, he saw it as his duty to be among the first to take to the skies," Reines recalled in a eulogy in 1957, a copy of which his daughter provided. "Full of confidence in his abilities, he was eager for the mission: to meet the enemy in the air and destroy it."[4]

Lightman served for five months before he crashed to death at age twenty-five.

Lightman, whose Hebrew name in Israel was Aryeh-Yehuda,[5] was first buried in Rehovot along with his crewmates. In 1950, his remains were transferred, upon the request of his close friends from Habonim and Kfar Hanassi, to the military cemetery in Rosh Pina, near his newfound home in Israel.

For decades, a group of close friends made the pilgrimage twice a year to participate in a ceremony honoring him at the serene cemetery overlooking the Sea of Galilee.

At a reunion several years ago, a group of these six nonagenarians recalled a friendly person who liked music and was a skilled first-aid medic. But they also said he tended to keep to himself, describing him as a "lone wolf" or "mystery man." They described Lightman as a deep thinker who was cheerful, well-liked, and had a sharp sense of humor, while also having a serious side that was prone to spells of depression. One said that prior to his death, Lightman had "disappeared" and was barely seen in the community.

"He was a gentle soul, a romantic; a sensitive and vulnerable young man with four main goals in life: to make Aliyah, to become a pilot, to study medicine, and to find real love," kibbutz friend Rachel Avidor recalled at a remembrance ceremony in Kfar Hanassi many years later.

"Leon, we who knew you and fulfilled your dreams sit here today either bald or pot-bellied or with graying hair, surrounded by our children and grandchildren and you have stayed forever young, a beautiful young man who is still in our thoughts," she added.[6]

Avidor described Lightman as tall, thin, and blue-eyed, and that with his boyish mustache, he looked "more like a British officer than a Zionist and pioneer."

Reines, who served in the British Royal Navy, said Lightman looked and sounded like a British aristocrat, and that his accent and sensibility more than once got them out of trouble with the British authorities in Palestine. Reines recalled how once after Jewish underground fighters raided a British freight train to steal weapons, Lightman stayed behind while the others fled.

"When the British showed up, Leon just chatted with the police officer and said what he said in his aristocratic accent and they let him go," a 100-year-old Reines recalled in 2024.[7]

Reines, who at the time had a great-grandson serving in the Israeli military in Gaza, said that Lightman was deeply

Photo 5.1. Leon Lightman
(Courtesy of Tal Landman.)

affected by his World War II service. "These guys would go out on missions, and every flight could have been their last," he said.

Lightman's last flight came on October 24, 1948. Firefighters who arrived on the scene of the crash identified him by a passport picture he was carrying in his clothing.

"I was devastated. The news came upon me like thunder on a clear day," said Reines. "I just couldn't believe that after emerging without a scratch from all his dangerous missions in World War II something like this could happen to him here in Israel on a routine flight."

But Lightman's old British friend Eric Arenberg said that he also saw symbolism in that tragic end.

"Leon loved planes, he dreamt of planes, and he found his death in a plane," he recounted. "Being the romantic that he was, I don't think he would have chosen to end his life any other way."

Photo 5.2. Leon Lightman's gravesite
(Photo credit: Aron Heller.)

CHAPTER SIX

Michael Weimers, the King of the Negev

With the assistance of Efrat Gal and Tal Landman, I had managed to piece together the life stories of these four men who, like my grandfather, had survived their tumultuous years as World War II airmen.

Canter, Stevenson, Fisher, and Lightman were all around the same age as Zaidy and learning of their wartime pasts helped me get a better sense of what his may have looked like. Fisher's experiences, as a Jewish Canadian navigator in Bomber Command, offered a particularly potential parallel to Zaidy's. But there was no Wilf Mandel-type in my family, no one who had done any research into my grandfather or could share any insight on his wartime years.

Where it was clear that my grandfather's path diverged from the others was after the war. He went home to Canada having apparently internalized the lesson he later repeatedly imparted to his various grandchildren upon their military enlistment in Israel: "Never volunteer." It was part of his overall philosophy of staying in the pack, keeping your head down, and not looking for trouble.

The others did exactly the opposite, joining Machal and heading to Israel where they found their deaths in a tragic accident at a critical point in the country's fight for independence.

But there was a fifth passenger on the Douglas C-47 Dakota transport plane that fateful night of October 24, 1948. He was different from the rest of the crew in more ways than one. And his story was truly legendary.

Michael Weimers was a strikingly handsome, English-educated immigrant from Germany who earned the moniker "King of the Negev" because of the airlifts he orchestrated

Photo 6.1. Michael Weimers (Courtesy of Noa Schendar and the Weimers family.)

to besieged Jewish communities in the south. His efforts to erect vital airfields ultimately helped liberate Israel's vast Negev desert at a key turning point in the 1948 war.

He was a pioneering meteorologist and air force officer who in his day enjoyed the admiration of his peers. But for some reason his legacy suddenly disappeared upon his death to the point that it has since become quite difficult to piece his extraordinary life together.

Weimers was not a World War II veteran. He was neither a foreign volunteer nor a member of 103 Squadron like the others. In fact, he wasn't even supposed to be on board. He hitched a ride on the fated Dakota moments before takeoff, heading toward a separate mission near the besieged Negev community of Sdom, at the southern tip of the Dead Sea.

The four foreigners who died alongside him had no local advocates for their commemoration, but they were included in monuments and other annual memorial ceremonies honoring the Machal casualties from overseas. Weimers was not.

Because of his murky status, and a puzzling lack of outreach from any surviving members of his extended family, there remained a loophole: Weimers wasn't formally commemorated at any military facility, and he remained conspicuously absent from even the air force's own vast memorial project. As far as the air force was concerned, he had essentially vanished.

Tal Landman, it appeared, was as uncomfortable as I was about this glaring omission and that Weimers's stunning biography has been shrouded in decades of anonymity.

Landman's mission, after all, was to seek out the so-called "orphaned fallen soldiers" who hadn't been formally commemorated.

However, Landman's main domain was 103 Squadron and the other units that were represented at the remembrance hall he established in 2008 at the Nevatim Air Force Base. That's why Weimers was the odd man out – he didn't belong to the squadron. However, Weimers wasn't recognized anywhere else either, leaving him as one of just twenty-six "orphaned fallen soldiers" among the 1,520 casualties in the history of the Israeli Air Force.[1] He belonged nowhere.

Landman, a longtime reserve air force non-commissioned officer, was not about to let a technicality get in his way. Once he became aware of the slight, he set out to rectify it. He began lobbying the Nevatim Air Force Base personnel for Weimers's inclusion and, in parallel, began digging up Weimers's file and searching for any relatives.

A lengthy paper trail led to an interview in the early 2000s in an obscure newsletter of a non-profit called the Association of Israelis of Central European Origin, in which a certain Yoav Tsur described his upbringing in Germany. In the interview, he disclosed that his original family name was Weimersheimer and that he had a younger brother who died in the 1948 war for whom his youngest son was named.

A phone directory search led to Landman placing a late-night phone call in February 2021 to a stunned Michael Tsur, who suddenly discovered that the Israeli Air Force was looking for the next of kin of his namesake and long-lost uncle who had died more than seventy-two years earlier.

Two months later, on April 9, I found myself in a stately home in an upscale neighborhood of the coastal city of Herzliya for an emotional family reunion.

Together with Landman, other air force officials, and Efrat and Gideon Gal, we met more than twenty members of Weimers's extended family across four generations who until recently had no idea that anyone besides them had any knowledge of Michael Weimers.

Weimers's now-deceased siblings – older brother Yoav Tsur, and older sister Michal Yaffe – each had four children of their own, and their children and grandchildren were just as curious as we were to learn more about their mysterious great-uncle.

Tsur's daughter, Noa Schendar, came armed with pictures, scrapbooks, and documents. Others shared stories about this long-gone mystery man and his unlikely journey from Germany, through England, and eventually to Israel where he played a key, yet long-overlooked, role in the 1948 War of Independence.

One of the more significant guests at the meeting was Weimers's now ninety-three-year-old sister-in-law, Yehudit Milo, who had firsthand memories of the man. She told me she recalled Weimers as very handsome, gentle, and polite. Once, he had asked her out to a movie and was a perfect gentleman.

But she also described an awkward man who had trouble connecting with others and, she said, that had he lived today he would likely be diagnosed with a learning disability or placed somewhere along the autism spectrum.

The sudden discovery of this long-forgotten family and their archive of materials helped me wrap up the Dakota project by assembling the most captivating life story of them all.

Ernst-Moritz Weimersheimer, the future Michael Weimers, was born in Harlingen, Germany, on April 3, 1920, to a secular Jewish family. His father, Moritz, was a doctor who died four months before his son's birth – an odd recurring trait he shared with Dakota crewmates Wilf Canter and Willie Fisher, whose fathers also died before they were born or shortly after – and he grew up in a youth village run by his widowed mother, Klare, and her sister, renowned educator Anna Essinger.

The youth village was a special establishment, focusing on a free and eclectic learning environment in nature and drawing children from all over Germany, including those of diplomats and actors and those with special needs. Inspired by his surroundings, Ernst-Moritz became a vegetarian at a young age and developed an intense, lifelong interest in music, animals, the outdoors, and meteorology. It was a place where his gentle, dreamy nature flourished alongside his two older siblings, even as the family struggled financially in the inflation-ridden Germany of the 1920s.

When the Nazis came to power in 1933, the institution faced immediate sanctions and was ordered to fly a Nazi flag atop the youth village in honor of Hitler's birthday.[2] The shocked sisters refused and decided instead to uproot, and Anna relocated the school to England, along with sixty-six children, while Klare searched for a more permanent home.

Klare found her way to Palestine, where in 1935 she negotiated with Zionist leader Henrietta Szold about moving her youth village there. She eventually bought a plot near Pardes Hanna, about halfway between Tel Aviv and Haifa, and then returned to Germany to shut down her school property. With the Nazis confiscating much of the land as part of their anti-Jewish purge, she ended up selling what she had for just a third of its true value.

Ernst-Moritz, meanwhile, went with his aunt Anna and spent his early, awkward teenage years in England, where he became a Boy Scout, began studying agriculture, and became fluent in English. He had no permanent home and struggled to make friends throughout his education near Kent at the New Herrlingen Country Home School that his aunt had established.

Inspired by her exposure to American Quakers, Anna served as a hands-on school principal known as a strict disciplinarian but also as a beloved figure affectionately known as "Tante Anna" (Aunt Anna), or TA for short.[3] Even more significantly, her progressive school later became a destination for thousands of Jewish students who fled Germany before the war began, thus sparing them the atrocities to come.

In a report on April 10, 1934, marking Ernst-Moritz's first half year there, his group teacher Adolf Prag graded his development as "favorable," noting that while he had fallen behind in English, German, and history, he was serious and reliable.

"At times he is still dreamy and childish," the teacher wrote. "His interests are entirely practical, and he takes his duties very seriously, often neglecting his schoolwork on account of them."[4]

A later letter summarizing his education and signed by his aunt hints at a possible diagnosis of dyslexia, which afflicted other family members. Moreover, it offers deeper insight into these formative years and provides a glimpse

Photo 6.2. Michael Weimers with his mother in 1929
(Courtesy of Noa Schendar and the Weimers family.)

into the kinds of qualities that defined his later contribution to Israel.

"He developed very slowly and was not systemic in his schoolwork. He was, however, very much interested in everything connected with nature – sun, moon and stars, animals, flowers and grasses – and acquired knowledge of these things in an unusual way," his aunt wrote.[5]

"He was not worldly wise, but his character was above reproach. He never lied, and he was reliable and trustworthy in big and little things alike."

In 1936, at age sixteen, he joined his mother in Palestine, changed his first name to Michael, and shortened his last name to Weimers (sometimes spelled Wymers). Socially,

Photo 6.3. Michael Weimers (bottom left) and his siblings in 1932 (Courtesy of Noa Schendar and the Weimers family.)

he struggled. He had difficulty adjusting to the local schools and eventually dropped out to seek employment. He briefly worked in the fields before his amateur interest in meteorology caught the attention of Rudolf (Reuven) Feige, an aviation pioneer and founder of Israel's meteorological service. Fiege hired Weimers as a meteorological scout at the airports in Lod, Ramle, and Haifa. More consequentially, the fellow German refugee became a mentor and father figure to Weimers in his new home.

Weimers's family friend Zohar Vilbush recalled a bright-eyed, pale-skinned, and rosy-cheeked kid nicknamed "Brody" who stuck out from his fellow peers and had trouble connecting at first with the local Zionists. He struggled with Hebrew and mostly kept to himself, choosing to spend his free time with Feige at the airports, where he would often listen to music and play his flute. With his mother busy with her school and his brother and sister immersed in local life, he became a bit of a loner. Still, he was gentle and patient as Vilbush would speak for hours about the romantic aura of life in pre-state Israel.

"He listened and he absorbed, but he didn't 'feel' this type of life. He couldn't find his way to it," Vilbush recalled in a post-mortem letter, discovered among the documents Noa Schendar provided me in 2022.

When war broke out in Europe, Weimers attempted to join the British RAF and sought out contacts in England to vouch for his character. A 1940 letter from the local department of civil aviation to an RAF recruiting officer states that Weimers is "a reliable meteorological officer of good character. His experience includes upper air observations, and he has some knowledge of wireless telegraphy, electrical wiring and carpentry."

In a subsequent handwritten letter to his mother in 1942, though, Weimers says he "did not get any definite reply from the RAF."

He ultimately opted to stay with the Palestine Meteorological Service until 1944. Upon his release, his supervisor reported that "he did a lot of extra work, constructed and installed instruments and introduced upper air observations on his own initiative. He was an excellent observer, and I must say that I am very sorry to lose a man like him."

But it was time for Weimers to move on and take a more active role in laying the foundations of the Jewish state. He completed several professional courses, including welding, and attempted to join Kibbutz Alonim in the north. But with his Anglo sensibilities and eccentricities – some locals suspected he was a spy after he unspooled wiring across the kibbutz for meteorological testing – he failed to fit in and was rejected. So, he gave it another shot in the south, descending upon Revivim – the first Jewish kibbutz established in the Negev.

Kibbutz member Yoel de-Malach recalled in his memoir how an attractive blond man with green-blue eyes arrived by foot with just a backpack and sat down in the communal dining room where he began eating. He then announced his intention to stay.

"My name in Michael Weimers," he declared. "I'm almost a pilot, almost an engineer and I have a lot of experience with meteorology. If you don't want me, I will leave."[6]

In Revivim, Weimers fell in love with the barren Negev landscape. He began working to establish a meteorological center that measured temperatures three times a day and researched the phenomenon of artificial rain. He was completely devoted to the task. Thanks to his connections to top meteorologists, Weimers was able to procure sophisticated equipment from various sources, including those that the British had left behind when they abandoned Lod airport.

At first the locals were suspicious of the European oddball, but it was the women who, charmed by his dashing appearance, successfully lobbied for him to be accepted as a member.

Though Weimers didn't appear to reciprocate amorously, he became friends with the women and also found favor with the rest of the community, becoming renowned for his technical skills, such as ably wiring connections and fixing irons, typewriters, and other appliances. He figured out how to capture radio signals by balancing an antenna in his mouth, and he famously assembled the radio receiver that allowed kibbutz members to hear David Ben-Gurion declare Israel's independence on May 14, 1948.[7]

Two weeks later, his mentor Feige was killed by a Jordanian shell that slammed into a meteorological center in Jerusalem.

The outbreak of war steeled Weimers's decision to enlist. He believed the best way to help link his beloved Negev to the central heartland was to serve in the burgeoning nation's nascent air force.

"I'm going – the air force needs me," he proclaimed, according to the account of de-Malach, a botanist and agricultural researcher.[8] But as in other chapters of his life, Weimers wouldn't be taking a direct route there either.

Israel's newly formed military also didn't quite know what to make of the strange outsider with English and German mannerisms. But the Wild West atmosphere of the times suited Weimers perfectly. Rather than being formally drafted, he did the "Israeli thing" (i.e., taking initiative rather than waiting for instructions) and created facts on the ground. He simply showed up and got to work. According to de-Malach's memoir, Weimers zigzagged on foot within sight of Egyptian outposts across the sandy terrain in search of hard, dense land. When he found it, he declared: "I will build an airport!"[9]

And he did, clearing out a landing ground adjacent to his Negev kibbutz for light aircraft arrivals.

"It seems unrealistic today, but that was the mindset in '48," explained Uri Dromi, a former navigator and editor of the air force magazine. "The air force was in its infancy. It was haphazard and disorganized. The focus was on building a staff at headquarters and erecting major bases. No one paid attention to the periphery. If someone like him showed up with initiative and ability to execute, the higher ups just took what they could get."[10]

Though not a pilot, Weimers still stumbled into air action, where his creative thinking came in handy. On one of his sorties aboard a Piper aircraft, an Egyptian aircraft appeared and began to circle. The light skinned Weimers with his European features confidently saluted the Egyptian pilot who apparently mistook the Israeli for a United Nations pilot and let him go.

On another mission, Weimers's plane came under attack from anti-aircraft fire. With no ammunition to respond, Weimers began dropping empty bottles to the ground. Their loud shattering apparently did enough to deter those firing to cease and take cover.[11]

When Weimers transitioned to military service, the meteorological station he had set up in Revivim was forced to shut down. But he still made sure to care for his adopted home with repeated supply runs.

With his air force connections and the modest landing pad he helped to establish, Weimers was a frequent flier who arrived bearing much-needed food and clothing. Because of his unique access, he became a key conduit for the besieged residents and was known to arrive bearing modest gifts like battery-powered radios and ice cream – amenities otherwise unavailable in the south. Gestures such as these helped carve out his persona, and his nickname, as the "King of the Negev."

Weimers shuttled frequently between the Negev and air force bases in the heartland, repeatedly lobbying officials for more assistance.

"He was an extraordinary person," then 101-year-old Dan Tolkovsky, a former commander of the Israeli Air Force, told me in 2021. "Very determined, with a particular goal of creating a purposeful connection with the Negev."[12]

On July 3, Weimers wrote to headquarters saying that "the responsibilities at the airfield in Revivim are growing by the day" and members of the kibbutz are no longer able to "provide all the necessary services."[13]

He appealed for a jeep with a trailer and for a deputy commander to assist him in running the airfield and overseeing flight control since he was mostly preoccupied with other operational activities.

Though he wasn't formally air force personnel, and it often remained unclear under whose approval he was acting, his requests were usually granted, and he somehow became the air force's de facto resource for all things related to the Negev. His fluency in English, from his years in Britain, must have also made him an ideal liaison to the foreign volunteer airmen with whom he ultimately shared a final flight. But it was the crucial airfields he established, and the airlifts they enabled, that were to become his true legacy.

It was a pivotal turning point in Israel's fight for survival. After ten days of intense fighting, on July 18, 1948, the warring parties agreed to the second, and last, temporary ceasefire of the 1948 war. The ensuing three months would prove to be the decisive window during which Israel would rearm and regroup before coming back for the final phase of fighting that would drive it to victory the following year.

But there was a major problem. At the break of fighting, the Egyptians controlled the road from Ashkelon to Beit Guvrin, cutting off the isolated villages of the Negev desert from any land connection to the rest of the Jewish-controlled areas. The frontline outposts were choked of vital supplies. Efforts to transport convoys failed and the light aircraft that landed in makeshift fields were far from sufficient.

The Negev was to make up most of Israel's land mass and was central to Prime Minister Ben-Gurion's dream of "making the desert bloom." Without it, there was no Israel.

On August 18, Ben-Gurion convened the military's top brass to discuss the crisis. The prognosis was dire: the soldiers and residents caught behind enemy lines had enough food to last them just a week. For the Negev to survive, 2,000 tons of food, fuel, and equipment was urgently needed. For that to happen, suitable landing grounds were needed for emergency airlifts.[14]

It fell to the newly established air force to find a solution. And the air force, as usual, turned to its mysterious go-to guy in the Negev to figure something out. The man had no official job and no defined assignment. He was a fixer, and most people didn't even know his full name. But if something had to get done in the desolate southern frontier lands of young Israel, the man for the job was a shadowy figure known simply as Michael, King of the Negev.

By the time the second cease-fire kicked in, Weimers's reputation was well established. To the locals, he was "the king" who delivered goods during difficult times. To the air force, however, he was even more essential – a unique guru of the barren, remote lands. So, when the air force started carrying out Ben-Gurion's order, Weimers was immediately called into action.[15]

Within days, he helped convert a modest airfield between Ruchama and Shoval into a 1,100-meter-long and 40-meter-wide dusty road landing strip that could handle aircraft weighing up to 30 tons.

On August 23, at 18:00 hours, the first such airlift arrived, raising so much dust that the airfield and, in fact, the entire operation, bore its name: Mivtza Avak – Operation Dust Bowl. Over the next month, some 200 flights landed at the Avak I airfield. It became more than just a supply route. To some 2,200 soldiers, it was also their only way out for a reprieve, a good meal, and a hot shower.[16]

Soon the frequency of flights increased to about ten a night. In a letter dated September 8, Weimers dispatched a list of his needs for the overworked airfield: a generator, four kilometers of electrical wire, tents, beds, blankets, thermoses, and cash.

With fighting set to resume on October 15 and Israel preparing for Operation Yoav – the crucial eight-day campaign in the Negev that would ultimately liberate Beersheba – the emphasis shifted to military supplies. Ben-Gurion was determined to recapture the Negev and the order came down to construct another airfield farther south. Here Weimers's role was even more critical as he located the strip and laid the foundations for the second airfield – Avak II – near Imra, or present-day Kibbutz Urim.

Weimers vouched for the 1,600-meter strip and sought approval to operate it from General Tolkovsky, then the air force's chief of operations.[17] The approval arrived on September 14 to begin construction based on Weimers's recommendation. Weimers arrived at the field on October 9 to line up the petrol-filled tins along the landing strip that he would light up upon hearing the engines approaching for nighttime arrivals. The following night, the first planes indeed began arriving.

Such precautions were needed, since the conditions at Avak II were even harsher than at Avak I. The field was within Egyptian artillery range and the planes were loaded with fuel, weapons, explosives, and ammunition. However, the Israeli forces managed to deflect the Egyptian attacks, and the airfield proved decisive in the week-long Israeli offensive that turned the tide of the southern front.

The continued airlifts allowed the military to swap out its exhausted forces in the Negev and replenish them with fresh troops from the center and north. Overall, some 2,500 tons of food, fuel, and military supplies were flown to the Negev and more than 5,000 people were transported back and forth before the operation was completed on October 21, 1948.[18]

"What Michael did single-handedly is amazing," said Dromi, who chronicled much of Weimers's exploits in air force history literature. "He was a man with remarkable resourcefulness and an ability to improvise something out of nothing."[19]

Friends and family who came across Weimers at this time say it was his finest hour. His eyes would twinkle when he spoke about the Negev and about his role in the campaign. He seemed to have found his calling. His old friend Vilbush said Weimers was transformed.

"I found a ripe young man, tanned from the rays of sunshine who had been absorbed by the land. It was Michael, not much was left of 'Brody,'" she wrote in 1949, referring to his old nickname. "I think he finally found that balance. He gave the most of his knowledge, of his talent and ultimately of himself to the war effort."[20]

Despite his dizzying array of activity, Weimers largely remained an untethered freelancer who unilaterally took on responsibilities that were formalized only in retrospect, a Forrest Gump of sorts who kept uncannily showing up at key moments.

In fact, only on October 14 did the air force's head of operations finally dispatch a written statement to the head of the southern front stating that Weimers "serves as the air force representative" regarding the airfields.[21]

With the Negev essentially liberated, Weimers's attention turned to Sdom, the ancient Jewish settlement near the Dead Sea that remained besieged. The task was to oversee the paving of a new runway for an airfield, since the current landing strips were susceptible to flooding and hazardous for the frequent flights that arrived to deliver supplies to the more than 350 soldiers stationed there, according to air force history literature.[22]

On October 1, Weimers reported that the engineers in Sdom had found an appropriate landing path, and on October 19 he informed the air force that he had given the order to start paving it. He was heading to inspect the progress when he boarded the doomed Dakota flight on the night of October 24.

The mission began with the four Machal officers boarding the Dakota at Ramat David Airbase near Haifa. They were joined by a joyrider and his dog who disembarked at the Sde Dov military airport in Tel Aviv, where the supplies were loaded for Sdom. Weimers signed the delivery papers and then drank a cup of tea at the canteen before hopping aboard the aircraft to join the others.

Crews dispatched to the scene of the crash identified Weimers by the "three to four-day" stubble on his face. Unlike the others, who were clean shaven, Weimers had recently begun growing a beard.[23]

Upon his death, twenty-eight-year-old Michael Weimers, military ID 81338, was promoted to the rank of lieutenant. He was the ninth, and final, war casualty of Kibbutz Revivim out of its thirty members. He was buried at the military cemetery in Rehovot in a joint bloc alongside two of the Canadian volunteers who crashed with him: pilot Wilfred Canter and navigator Willie Fisher.

"Only after he died did we fully realize who this man was and how vast were his talents," wrote his kibbutz mate de-Malach.[24]

"He was a special sort of character. Just very positive," added Tolkovsky, the former air force chief. "Just a very nice man. Energetic, humble and constantly running about dealing with things about the Negev."[25]

The early days of Israel were a time of mythmaking. The bloody 1948 War of Independence marked not just the birth of a nation. It also spawned the creation of Zionist legends that would form the ethos of a national narrative of long-displaced Jews taking their destiny in their hands and reclaiming their ancestral homeland.

It was the war that introduced Yitzhak Rabin, the ginger-haired Sabra who broke through the siege of Jerusalem, and Ariel (Arik) Sharon, the burly fighter who supposedly drank his own blood to survive a gunshot wound in the battle of Latrun.

Of the war's 6,000 casualties (a full 1 percent of the Jewish population of the time), many would become the martyrs the country championed as its iconic founding generation. These were larger-than-life figures who paid the ultimate price so that Israel could come into existence.

These were people like ace pilot Modi Alon, a World War II vet and commander of Israel's first fighter squadron and hero of its first aerial assault, who crashed to death after a bombing mission. And David "Mickey" Marcus, the West Point graduate and US Army colonel who became Israel's first modern general and was accidentally shot dead by a local sentry.

The types of figures most memorialized were those with captivating life stories and idiosyncratic personalities who made a genuine contribution to the war effort. Their personas often reflected a prototype of the era and tended to include an endearing nickname and, ultimately, a mysterious death.

So, it's curious that someone who checked all these boxes not only escaped frequent mention but also nearly evaporated entirely from the annals of Israeli history.

After Weimers's death, the war pressed on and he, like the others, was forgotten. There was nothing glamorous about the overloaded, rickety plane long overdue for servicing that crashed while delivering flour, coffee, and soap to besieged Israelis when heroic military sacrifices were happening all around.

When the fighting ultimately subsided and Israel finally began to tell its story, there weren't many around to tell Weimers's.

Eventually, the airfield in Sdom was named after him,[26] and his name appeared on a few long-forgotten war monuments scattered across the country. In 1978, Kibbutz Revivim renamed the meteorological center he founded in his honor. The kibbutz also casually mentions him as one of its fallen at its annual Memorial Day remembrance service.

The only known media reference to Weimers's wartime contribution appears to have come in 1964, when an Israeli radio trivia show did a segment on Weimers and his role in Operation Dust Bowl. In a letter to the show's producers on May 29, 1964, his sister, Michal Yaffe, noted how happy he was in the final months of his life. She said he was consumed by his service and would arrive exhausted for brief stays with her, during which he could sleep for twenty-four hours straight.

Among the other new material to emerge in Landman's search was the testimony of Yoav Tsur's wife, Shulamit, who recalled Weimers's last visit with them during the first cease-fire of the 1948 war. She said he arrived for the circumcision ceremony of their first-born son bearing gifts such as cigarettes and a jerry can of petrol that could be swapped for great value. Their next son, Michael, was named after him.[27]

Michael Tsur, born fifteen years after Weimers's death, said that on the rare moments his father would painfully open up about his late brother, he would remark to his son about the similarities between the two of them, how both were determined men of action who overcame obstacles.

"He would say things like, 'That's something only my brother Michael would have said,'" Tsur recalled. "My father didn't say much but he missed his brother. And my name, and these similarities, helped us grow closer. It gave me great pride to carry that name."

Generally, though, the family was detached, helping explain some of Weimers's lack of recognition. Yes, the Israeli military was less scrupulous in those days about honoring its dead and keeping in close contact with their survivors. But it seems that Weimers's family also had little interest in delving into the past.

"They were a '*Yekke*' family who didn't indulge in emotions," explained Weimers's niece Noa Schendar, using the term for Jews of German-speaking origin. "They didn't invest in his memory and didn't discuss it. They weren't religious and ascribed no significance to Jewish traditions. It wasn't in their culture. As far as they were concerned, what happened with Michael happened and they moved on."

Schendar, who inherited the family archive from her aunt Michal, said it was typical of the family's inability to cope with emotions. When she discovered Landman's outreach she was overcome with a deep sense of regret.

"How could Michael be considered an 'orphaned fallen soldier?'" she asked. "We have a large family. We just didn't know."

In retrospect, however, she says there is symbolism in how it all played out.

"All his life he was an outsider, someone that people didn't quite understand or know how to handle," she said. "It's fitting that he would remain so in death."

More than seventy years after his passing, Weimers is now officially recognized at the Nevatim Air Force Base for his crucial role as the liaison between the air force and

Negev villagers. Several folders of material detail his life and career and honor him for "establishing the landing pads that provided for besieged residents and laying the foundations for the landing of 103 Squadron's Dakotas."

His siblings' descendants have since visited the site and have been included in various air force alumni events. The story of Michael Weimers is one the family now celebrates and shares.

On Israel's Memorial Day, in the spring of 2021, Michael Tsur made the pilgrimage to his uncle's gravesite in Rehovot. There he felt a sense of guilt over all the lost years in which Weimers was forgotten.

"I asked for forgiveness," Tsur told me. "This was a very special and unique man who we didn't know anything about, and we made no effort to find out about either. But now there is a feeling that we are righting that wrong."[28]

CHAPTER SEVEN

The Dakota Revisited

A year later, in early May 2022, I made my own pilgrimage to the military cemetery in Rehovot. Ten years had passed since my previous visit.

It was Yom HaZikaron, Israel's annual Memorial Day, and marking the occasion was the publication of my long-awaited story about Michael Weimers in *Tablet* magazine.[1] The feedback had been wonderful, particularly from the family itself and from my like-minded peers Tal Landman and Efrat Gal. It had been seventy-four years, and now it felt like this latest publication had truly resurrected the memory of Michael Weimers and his crewmates.

Brought together by fate, these five fatalities were among the rag-tag outfit of foreigners without whom Israel would not have won its independence. Together they made up the palette of early Israel's desperate fight for survival. With meager means and small acts of heroism, each member of this disparate group of young men with varied backgrounds and life stories played a part in the rebirth of the Jewish nation.

And for me, discovering and publishing their stories more than compensated for not having had a similar breakthrough with my grandfather.

The visit to the cemetery was far different this time. The previous visit, in 2012, was solitary. I was there alone. It was quiet. It was personal. On this day, it was part of a national commemoration. The cemetery was packed with thousands of mourners gathered tightly around the 438 graves of fallen Israeli soldiers. It was all hustle and bustle as soldiers chatted and grieving mothers wept over the gravesites.

But when the Memorial Day siren wailed at 11:00 a.m., all went silent, and everything came to a standstill as it did everywhere else in Israel at that instant. I'd experienced that moment so many times in so many different circumstances: with classmates at schools, with fellow soldiers on military bases, with the country's top leadership at the national cemetery in Jerusalem, alongside other drivers who had stopped along the side of the highway, or just alone at home. Each locale added its own unique experience.

But looking down at the graves of Michael Weimers, Wilfred Canter, and William Fisher before me generated its own kind of emotion. The graves were adorned with purple flowers and memorial candles. Flags with personalized dedications were planted into the flower beds that covered them. Ceramic hearts designed by local school children were placed on the headstones.

I'd always had an ambivalent approach toward these somber national days in Israel. Of course, I appreciated their significance in the national narrative and, no doubt, realized the meaning for bereaved families to have the entire nation join them in their grief for just one day. But on the other hand, I always struggled with what felt like a "forced emotion" of the masses and a tendency, especially among those military-aged, to hyper externalize their connection to the dead, no matter how authentic.

These feelings were likely the result of my family being immigrants. As in many others facets of Israeli life, we weren't entirely immersed in all the nation's rites of passage.

Unlike many Israeli families we, thankfully, had not lost any close relatives in Israel's wars or in decades of terror attacks against it. But over time, as it is in this country, it grows closer to you. Nearly everyone in Israel at least knows someone who has been afflicted firsthand. I too had encountered the deaths of army peers, siblings of friends and neighbors, and even close acquaintances. But it still felt relatively distant, not enough to warrant the kind of outpouring of grief I saw so frequently around me.

I'd been to many funerals, was even in the honor guard of one. I found myself informing my closest army pal about the death of his best friend, Yiftach Shlapobersky, in the 1997 helicopter disaster in which seventy-three soldiers died in a mid-air collision on their way to deployment in southern Lebanon. It was a pivotal event that ultimately spurred Israel's withdrawal from southern Lebanon three years later. Still, I managed to keep a sense of detachment.

Perhaps the most direct impact I experienced was the 1995 death of Ilai Dagan, a close classmate of mine from sixth through ninth grade in the central Israeli town of Kochav Yair. We bonded over our shared love of basketball and remained friendly for years after, until he was killed in a suicide bombing attack when we were both in the military. Not yet knowing his fate, I arrived on the scene of the carnage shortly after as part of my military police duty to remove the belongings of the dead and to keep the order amid an angry mob of Jewish protesters who hurled insults at Prime Minister Yitzhak Rabin as he inspected the scene. I found myself carrying off backpacks with charred pieces of flesh stuck to them, trying not to gag from the horrendous stench.

That hit me hard. But I could never quite figure out if Ilai and I were close enough friends for me to have long visits with his family or to regularly attend his annual remembrance service with the rest of our classmates. I often did but was self-conscious about highlighting our connection when others seemed far more devastated at such events. I made my peace with this dissonance years later in the best way I knew how – by writing a first-person tribute marking a decade since his death that was published in a Canadian newspaper.[2]

But today, in this cemetery, with Canter and the other foreign casualties and my connection to them through my grandfather, I finally felt like I belonged. They were the ultimate outsiders, and I suppose it took an outsider like me to get at the gist of their story. This was where I needed to be on this day.

Their young faces flashed before my eyes as I observed the piercing two-minute siren and the subsequent ceremony in which the mayor of Rehovot, a government cabinet minister, and other officials spoke and lay wreaths.

Beside me I met a stranger who had also come to pay his respects to Willie Fisher. His name was Shmulik, and he said his parents were friends of a nephew of the late navigator. I also got to know a visitor to the neighboring plot, Gershon Dobinboim, who bore the same name as his uncle who had died the same day in 1948 as the three airmen in the Dakota and was now buried next to them.

Most significant, though, was meeting the half-dozen air force officers and soldiers dispatched to watch over these gravesites. The military makes sure that not a single fallen soldier's grave is unattended on Yom HaZikaron, dispatching active service members to stand by the plots of those who don't have next of kin to commemorate them.

As it were, the soldiers there from 103 Squadron had learned about Canter, Fisher, and Weimers from a previous story I had written about them, and which was featured in their memorial hall in Nevatim. So, on this Israeli Memorial Day, I improbably found myself fielding questions from young soldiers about the lives of these long-forgotten casualties who suddenly appeared forgotten no more.

Photo 7.1. From left to right, the graves of Fisher, Canter, and Weimers in the Rehovot Cemetery
(Photo credit: Aron Heller.)

The Canadians

CHAPTER EIGHT

Somer James, the Reluctant War Hero

Despite the wide age gap, it was telling that I'd managed to forge some significant relationships with members of the Greatest Generation over a shared interest in World War II. Unfortunately, my grandfather had not been one of them.

We'd never had enough solo quality time together to build that kind of connection. Even in those rare one-on-one times, he wasn't the greatest conversationalist, and it was always clear which topic was out of bounds.

Still, anytime I crossed the path of someone whose life experiences could have potentially paralleled his, it always made me wonder.

In many ways, I feel like I was born in the wrong era. I'm sure I've been influenced by popular movies and TV shows – *Band of Brothers, Saving Private Ryan, Schindler's List* – but for some reason I could always see myself in that time: covering World War II, witnessing the early days of Israel, being part of the birth of TV news.

Part of the draw to the characters of that generation likely also had to do with demeanor, with the way they seemed to cope with the adversity of their times. With all my Generation X ambivalence and insecurities, I couldn't help but admire these men and women who seemed to instinctively know what needed to be done – and then did it.

This innate instinct quickly translated into my journalism career.

When I was a reporter for the *Ottawa Citizen* in 2005, I anchored our coverage of the inauguration of International Holocaust Remembrance Day. It sparked my journalistic passion for documenting as many survivor stories as I could in the coming years.

But it was an obituary the paper assigned me to write a few months later that really got me thinking about Zaidy.

World War II veteran Bob Melcalfe died in April 2005 at the age of ninety. From research and interviews with his family, I found out that the English-born Metcalfe saw six years of action. His wartime resume read like a highlight reel of the war itself – he was wounded in France, evacuated from Dunkirk under fire, survived the Battle of Britain, and had his ship chased by the Bismarck en route to North Africa, where he served under General Bernard Montgomery. He then took part in the invasion of Sicily, which took him up the Italian boot, where he met and married his wife: a physical therapist at a Canadian military hospital.

His daughter, Sue, told me that from his time in Africa, he developed a great respect for the German General Erwin

Rommel, the Desert Fox. Later in life, she said he even corresponded with the general's son, Manfred Rommel, the mayor of Stuttgart.

"He lived life with few regrets," she told me. "He taught us what it really meant to be a serviceman, in every sense of the word."[1]

Ten years before he died, Metcalfe finally put his adventures down in writing, publishing *No Time for Dreams: A Soldier's Six-Year Journey through WWII.*

In the obituary, I noted that Metcalfe's legacy would continue to live on in each of our pockets every day. "He's the tall soldier with a beret depicted on the back right side of the Canadian $10 bill, under the title 'in the service of peace,'" I wrote.[2]

Sue gave me a copy of her father's book with a dedication that read: "Dad would have been tickled with your article 'tribute.'"

It was one of those truly rewarding moments I've had as a journalist. Still, I couldn't help but think: What if my own grandfather had such a story? What was it he was withholding? How could I feel such kinship to a man I never met, when my own grandfather could be harboring something similar?

It was the first time in my professional life where I really delved into a wartime story that could have mirrored that of my grandfather's, and it made me long to find out more and hopefully produce something for him to leave behind as well. That was the backdrop, and the inspiration, when I finally went in for my first direct pitch to Zaidy.

"You don't like talking about the war that much, do you?" I asked Zaidy in 2011, during my first trip to Toronto on this mission.

"What's there to talk about?" he replied flatly. "A lot of guys went over, not a lot came back."

But I pressed on, and he slowly started talking about his World War II veteran friend Sammy Greisman who lived in London and had sent him an old calendar that featured a different RAF plane each month. Leafing through the photos seemed to rekindle his memory. The names – Vickers-Armstrong Wellington twin-engine bomber, Lancaster, Spitfire, Hawker Hurricane – rolled off his tongue.

"Actually, the Hawker Hurricane did more damage than the Spitfire, but the Spitfire got the publicity," he explained.

He then pointed toward a picture of an American Boeing B-17.

"You see they had something we didn't have in the Lancaster," he said. "Now what happened is we [the RAF] had rear gunners here and a front gunner and a top gunner but didn't have a bottom gunner and the Germans used to come up from under and 'boom' that was that."

"The Americans flew in the daytime; the RAF flew at night. And they [the Americans] flew en masse together, and they had five or six gunners in each plane and lots of fire power, so the Germans couldn't get close to them. The RAF had a terrible time."

"You know, the aircrew lost 50 percent. Fifty percent of the guys didn't come back, and they were all twenty, twenty-one," he said, his voice trailing off.

This single exchange was the most he had ever shared with me about World War II. It's probably more than he'd ever shared with anyone else in our family.

"So, you must have had some close calls?" I egged him on.

"Ah, come see some pictures – that's what you want to see," he replied, in a classic Zaidy diversion tactic.

We looked at old pictures and newspaper clippings in an album and quickly digressed into talking about family history and other odd stories.

He showed me an old telegram he sent to my grandmother referencing the ring he had sent home asking her hand in marriage. It was sent from "#R97329, flight sergeant Hellar" – his last name misspelled.

"I remember that number ... by the time I got home I was a warrant officer," he said.

Only much later did I realize that this was unusual, since navigators were often eventually given officer ranks (though some Jews were denied this honor and suspected antisemitism as the cause). Either way, that was as deep as Zaidy was willing to go on this trip down memory lane. It was time to play cards, get ready for dinner. Just before he shut the album, he took one last glimpse at an old black-and-white photo of himself with some old friends.

"They are all gone," he said. "Everybody is gone there."

It would be another year before Zaidy started to talk about one of these old friends, a classmate of his named Somer

James who sought to avoid military service because he was against killing.

"So, he went to the merchant marines instead, which was even worse," Zaidy said with a grin, using another name for the Merchant Navy.

Zaidy explained that James once found himself on a cargo ship docked in southern Italy that was carrying high explosives when the Germans attacked. The explosions damaged James's ship and set fire to the dock.

James volunteered to save the ship, jumping onto the burning dock to release the mooring lines so his ship could escape the flames. And then he did it again for other crafts.

"He was the only one who got two medals in one day," Zaidy said proudly.

Milling around Zaidy's meticulous home office in late August 2012, during my next visit to Toronto, I found an essay on his computer screen about James's heroics.

When they were teenagers, Zaidy said he and James went to Goel Tzedec synagogue's Sunday school and on Saturday mornings they would walk there to attend junior services together.

"On Sundays we would sometimes get a lift, sometimes take a streetcar, sometimes walk," Zaidy recalled in 2021. "But on *Shabbos* we'd all walk. It wasn't because we were religious. We didn't have the money."

Later, they went to high school together at Harbord Collegiate.

Zaidy said James was "an ordinary Canadian seaman who accomplished an extraordinary feat on November 5, 1943," earning two medals for bravery for singlehandedly saving his ship. The medals are displayed in the Canadian War Museum in Ottawa.

From my own research, I managed to piece together a fuller biography of a man who embodied a triumphant Canadian narrative in a type of service that has been long overlooked.

Somer James was born on December 24, 1921, to Hyman and Gussie James, the middle child squeezed between two sisters. They were a typical Orthodox Jewish family that was upended by the death of his father from a brain tumor when Somer was just eleven years old.

When war broke out, he wasn't even eighteen years old, and he was conflicted. As a pacifist, he was against the war and did not want to take up arms. But he did want to serve his nation and his people in the fight against Nazism, so much so that despite being described as a bookworm he quit school early to get involved. The compromise he found was to join the Merchant Navy, where he thought he could avoid the killing.

The Merchant Navy has often been regarded as the "forgotten 4th service," even though it entailed a very dangerous job and was crucial to the war effort. Its men and women didn't have parades or badges. Most didn't even have uniforms. They sailed in slow, poorly defended vessels that carried essential cargo and troops and were open to enemy attacks. Conditions were harsh, pay was poor and tens of thousands were killed.[3] Of the 185,000 who served, almost a fifth died, with as many as 24,000 of them having no grave besides the deep cold seas. Some 12,000 Canadians were part of this vital service on freighters, tankers, and ships that kept the Allies fighting. Perhaps no more than ninety of them were Jewish.[4] It would be decades before Canada would officially recognize these people as war veterans.

But for James, it was the only way to serve.

He left Toronto in 1939, underage, and went to Montreal to get on the first ship he could find. The Canadian Merchant Navy did not exist yet, so he first found work as a stevedore before joining various ships that were transporting supplies to Europe even before the main battles began.

"It was civilian activity. That aspect appealed to me because I wouldn't have to shoot anyone or go through any military training," an elderly James said in video testimony that his family filmed toward the end of his life.

Based primarily out of Cardiff, on the coast of Wales, James served on more than a dozen freighters, and he would sail across the seas bordering Europe and North Africa, shipping cargo of coal, wheat, and ammunition.

He wasn't doing it for the money.

In 1941, the year he officially joined the Merchant Navy, the average monthly pay rate for a seaman was $55, compared with $123 for a sailor in the Royal Canadian Navy. Until later in the war, a merchant seaman who was forced to abandon ship even had his pay stopped.

But tapping into an entrepreneurial spirit, James did fine. Cigarettes and tobacco were the primary means of exchange at sea, and as a non-smoker, James traded his rations for other goods and currency that supplemented his income.

He sent some of the money home to his mother and kept the rest in a wallet that he sewed into a waterproof canvas that lasted him through the war.

In England, James met Jean Smith when she came to meet his train at Denham station in London after being introduced through a cousin. They married in 1945 and moved to Canada. Since James wasn't officially in the military, his new wife received no free passage or government assistance. She therefore made a point of correcting anyone who would refer to her as a "war bride."

The couple settled in Winnipeg to start a new life, and they had four children. James was briefly a partner in a theater poster business, but for most of his working life, he was a noted coin expert and stamp dealer.

Starting as a numismatist and philatelist, he later also moved on to collecting paper money. An authority in the fields, he opened the Regency Coin and Stamp Company and ran it till his retirement in 1998. He wrote several books on coins, stamps, and tokens.

A lifelong distance swimmer, he was most at home in the water. He was later also active in various charitable societies in Winnipeg such as the DASCH Society, which aids adults with developmental delays. An annual award in his name is still given to a volunteer board member.

He spoke little of his wartime service and thought little about his two medals until much later in life when he offered them to the Canadian War Museum in Ottawa, which has placed them on permanent exhibit along with James's story.

He died of Parkinson's disease on January 17, 2005, at the age of eighty-three, and was survived by his wife of fifty-nine years, Jean, his daughters Heather and Wendy, his sons David and Keith, and eight grandchildren.

"He took his responsibilities seriously, was a hard worker and an active volunteer and also a devoted family man who loved his kids," said his daughter, Wendy James. "He was calm, he didn't suffer fools gladly and he called it like he saw it. Mostly, he was very morally inclined and felt that people should do their duty, keep their promises, and not call attention to themselves."[5]

Those qualities help explain why his wartime service only began to be recognized much later in his life, when his children began showing an interest of their own.

Ultimately, his life's defining moment remained his heroics on November 5, 1943, when he found himself aboard the SS *Empire Lightning*, a ship in Italy that was loaded with high explosives and moored next to a munitions depot when German bombers attacked. With fires raging on the dock, he jumped ashore and wrestled the ship free from its moorings so it could move to safety.[6]

In his video testimony, James simply said he volunteered because nobody else did.

"I went ashore with a good strong jacket on and a sandwich in my pocket and the naval officer proceeded to shout from the deck which way to go," he explained. "It was dawn when I went out there and I was there all morning. It was exhausting."[7]

The ship's British commanding officer called James's hours-long escapade of loosening the massive ropes perhaps the most amazing feat he witnessed during the entire war.

Years later, when asked by his youngest son, Keith, as to why he volunteered for the dangerous mission, James provided a simple response: "I did not want to die."

Photo 8.1. Somer James in an identification card photograph (Courtesy of Wendy James.)

Keith said his father's athleticism, resiliency, sharp mind, and attention to detail were what made him well-suited for the demanding and altruistic task.[8]

"His bravery and participation in WWII changed and formed his life in the most dramatic ways," Keith wrote. "We Jameses are always reminded of his gift of bravery and courage."

For his actions, Somer James received a British Empire Medal and the Lloyd's War Medal for Bravery at Sea.[9]

And this is how the events of November 5, 1943, transpired, according to the essay I discovered on Zaidy's computer screen and which he had published in *The Canadian Jewish News* on October 18, 2012, to commemorate his old friend:

> The sun was just rising over Torre Aningiatria, a port south-east of Naples, Italy, when German bombers descended on allied shipping. The port was of strategic importance because the Allies could unload massive quantities of

supplies and equipment they needed to drive the Germans out of Italy.

Somer James's ship offered choice prey. Loaded with ammunition, the *Empire Lightning* was moored to a dock piled high with octane fuel when bombs began to find their targets. One struck the fuel, setting it ablaze and threatening both the *Lightning* and other freighters moored fore and aft. The ship could be saved only by a careful combination of dropping some of its lines and doubling others, so it could be maneuvered away from the fire.

The captain called for volunteers. Amid the pandemonium, only Somer James, who was not yet twenty-two years old, stepped up. He donned a heavy jacket and lifebelt and went on deck alone. With the captain shouting instructions down at him from the bridge, with fire raging alongside and with high explosive beneath his feet, he ran the length of the ship.

From one mooring point to another, he did his best to handle the massive hemp lines alone. The entire operation lasted about three hours, but in the end, he managed to get the ship out of harm's way, its sides scorched by fire.

Yet, he didn't stop at that. Once the *Lightning* was secured, he helped move a number of barges loaded with dangerous cargo that had also caught fire.

The action later won him both the British Empire Medal and the Lloyd's Medal for bravery, an unusual double honor. While twenty-nine other Canadian merchant sailors won the British Empire Medal for bravery during World War II, and some won the Lloyd Medal, none received both awards for the same event.

A soft-spoken pacifist with sparkling blue eyes, he was an academic at heart. Largely self-taught, he completed only

Grade 11 at Harbord Collegiate, yet he was deeply intellectual and visited the library often. When war broke out, he was adamantly opposed to armed conflict and could not bear the thought of pulling a trigger on anyone. Instead, in 1940, this pensive Jewish teenager from Toronto took a train ride to Montreal to see whether he could join the Merchant Navy. It would determine his fate for the next five years. He found a Greek steamer, the first of twelve ships he served aboard in the Battle of the Atlantic.

It was the war's longest theater of war and the costliest. One in seven people died in the line of duty, their ships and their valuable cargo sent to the bottom by the German U-boats and surface raiders and sometimes because of collisions while in convoy. Of the 12,000 Canadians who served, more than 1,600 lost their lives.

For the dangers, the job suited Somer. "It saved me from certain actions," he once said. "I did not want to get involved with killing people, shooting them with guns from far away, and getting involved with anything like that."[10]

Only later did I discover that this version relied almost exclusively on James's obituary in the *Globe and Mail*.[11] Still, the account struck me not just because of its sensitivity and how well-written it was, but because it offered some parallels to a grandfather whom I had never heard express himself this way, certainly not about himself.

As I reread the text, I realized that many of the things written about James could also easily be applied to Zaidy. He too was an "academic at heart" who never had the opportunity to pursue higher education and who took great pride in his children's advanced degrees. He too was "largely self-taught," taking private French lessons, completing a course on using the internet late in life, and keeping a detailed record of the hundreds of non-fiction books he had read to fill the gap in learning he felt he had. He too was "pensive" and, like Somer, he probably "couldn't bear the thought of pulling a trigger on anyone."

In his old age, Zaidy was exposing a slice of himself I had never seen before. I doubt anyone, other than perhaps Bubby, had seen it either.

CHAPTER NINE

Alfred Brenner, the Man in the Flying Suitcase

It was a routine reporting assignment. I was dispatched to a security conference in May 2015 to listen to panels of experts discuss Israel's looming security threats. It was only when I was done and began walking back to my parked car outside the Armored Corps' Memorial Site in Latrun in central Israel that the day took a momentous turn.

By sheer chance, I stumbled upon a closed-off construction site with a simple sign hanging on a surrounding fence informing me that this was to become the location of the future official museum for Jewish soldiers in World War II.

I'd never heard of such a thing. So, I started wandering around the premises. I found a relatively newly built, yet apparently abandoned, cavernous structure in front of a row of historic tanks from wars past.

The reporter in me took over. I started making calls and soon discovered that plans for such a museum had been in the works for over a decade but had gotten caught up in a bureaucratic stalemate with no end in sight.

It seemed like such a shame that this had yet to materialize. It struck me as a sacred mission, a complementary establishment to the Yad Vashem Holocaust Museum. This was a place that could honor those who served and fought and not just those who suffered and perished. This could be a place to educate others about the men and women of my grandfather's generation.

I knew firsthand how these veterans were aging, how each day more were passing away. It would be so meaningful to have something like this emerge while there were still some veterans alive to appreciate it.

Amazingly, with all my reporting on the Holocaust, its victims and survivors, and the heroism of the Jewish partisans and resistance fighters in the Warsaw Ghetto, I had never done a feature on the 1.5 million Jewish soldiers who fought for the Allies in World War II, of which more than 250,000 died in battle.

The 70th anniversary of Victory in Europe Day (VE Day) seemed like the perfect news peg to pursue it.

Aside from my professional interest, there was also personal motivation. Finally, there was some comfort that whatever I discovered about Zaidy, no matter how small, belonged in the context of something larger.

My upcoming story, and this whole venture, offered an opportunity to rekindle my inquiries under the guise of something bigger than him.

Knowing how Zaidy had always been more forthcoming about the stories of others, I decided to pursue the friend angle first. Perhaps he had names, details, and photos he could share? Maybe there were other fellow veterans like Somer James and Wilf Canter that he wished would be better recognized? He'd been cold to previous inquiries, but he loved history and museums and had a lot of pride about the Canadian contribution to World War II. I had a hunch he'd be more receptive this time around.

So, I dug into the research and then I fired off an email informing him of my findings and seeking his contribution. The material included a link to a collection of comic-like brochures I discovered online that the Canadian Jewish Congress issued in 1944 seeking to highlight the "Jewish War Heroes."[1]

The "hero" that most caught my attention was Flying Officer Alfred Brenner, a Canadian pilot who was credited with destroying a 5,000-ton German merchant ship on February 18, 1943, near the Frisian Islands, located off the coast of the Netherlands.[2]

"We got that one, Alf. She's sinking," read the dialogue in the comic.

"Yes. And they got us too," Brenner replied. "Can't keep her up much longer."

I figured Zaidy may find the brochure interesting. Little did I know that he and Brenner shared a connection that ran much deeper.

Brenner's was a truly remarkable tale. His three-man crew were on a sortie off the Dutch coast when they came across a convoy of twelve Nazi merchant ships accompanied by five destroyers.

Merchant ships were basically floating warehouses that transported artillery, ammunition, and other war materials that were needed for battle. Both the Allied powers (Great Britain, US, and Soviet Union) and the Axis powers (Germany, Italy, and Japan) did all they could to protect their ships since they were the lifeline for the fighting troops on the front. They did not hesitate to destroy those belonging to their enemy.

Brenner and his crew zeroed in on one of these prime targets. He plunged till he was almost at water level and then dropped his torpedoes.

Brenner and his two crewmates scored a direct hit on a 5,000-ton merchant ship, which burst into flames. Then came the return fire.

Brenner had taken out the freighter, but his own Hampden bomber was shot up so badly that he would have to crash land.

"All hell broke loose. Every ship in the convoy began firing at us," Brenner later told the Canadian Press.[3]

The Hampden was known as the "flying suitcase" because of its cramped cockpit and was considered one of the more dangerous war planes to fly. In fact, by 1942, it had already been removed from most war theaters because it was considered unsafe.

Brenner's plane was badly damaged. The rudder, the port engine and the wing tips had been hit by the flak from the Nazi destroyers. Brenner also felt an immense flash of heat from a shell that penetrated the fuselage through the bomb bays, striking the armor behind his pilot seat.

Brenner climbed up to 2,000 feet, from which point the radio operator was able to send an SOS, before Brenner descended and settled the bomber into the cold waters of the North Sea, thirty miles from Great Yarmouth in England.

The plane sank quickly. But before it did, the crew members were able to inflate a rescue dinghy and escape. However, paddles, flares, sailing masts, and rations went down with the aircraft.

Brenner and his crew used their now-useless flashlights, with dead batteries removed, to bail water from the dinghy as they floated in dangerous waters. Miraculously, one crew member had managed to save the pigeon container, and the pigeons were dispatched back to Bomber Command with coordinates.[4]

Not knowing their fate, the crew members held off from drinking their only fresh quart of water. For meals, they allowed themselves one energy tablet from a first aid kit that they managed to salvage.

Two days later they were spotted by a rescue unit and were picked up near the English coast after drifting for forty-three hours in the North Sea.

The rescue plane skimmed into the water after dropping a smoke flare to guide its way and Brenner and his crewmates were able to grab the rescue float as all the men were pulled on board.

The captain of the rescue flight reported that the men were surprisingly well after such long exposure to the elements. And despite not having had any water in two days, the three men seemed mostly interested in confirming that the merchant ship they'd torpedoed was a confirmed hit.

For these exploits, Brenner was honored with the Distinguished Flying Cross. King George VI presented the award to him on September 10, 1943, at Buckingham Palace. The dispatch to the medal read in part: "Throughout his [Brenner's] tour of operations, this officer has displayed the greatest keenness and devotion to duty."

Brenner was one of nearly 200 Canadian Jewish servicemen who were decorated for heroism in battle. His actions were deemed so heroic that, in 2020, then-Canadian Prime Minister Justin Trudeau chose to highlight them at the start of his address to parliament marking the beginning of Veterans' Week.

"In the face of danger, Alfred and his crew chose to be brave," Trudeau said. "They chose to put their own lives on the line for the greater good."[5]

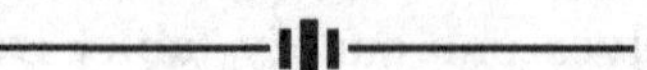

Responding to my detailed report, Zaidy wrote back and casually informed me that Brenner was, in fact, his second cousin.

"Our grandmothers were sisters. But he was from a well-to-do family and went to a private school, so they gave me his hand-me-downs," Zaidy said. "He was older than me and I used to get his grown-out clothes. All I ever wanted was a sweater, but we didn't have any money, and I never had one. The private school he went to did not allow sweaters, only suits. So that's how I ended up being the best-dressed kid in my school wearing a three-piece suit."

Photo 9.1 Alfred Brenner (Courtesy of Historica Canada, https://www.historicacanada.ca/.)

The happenstance made me wonder what other kinds of colorful nuggets like these Zaidy had stashed away from those days. What more was there to discover?

I mean Brenner was a genuine war hero, straight out of central casting. He was essentially the Canadian version of the flyboys depicted in *Masters of the Air*, the Apple TV+ war drama miniseries about the 100th Bomb Group in the Eighth Air Force. In particular, Brenner reminded me of Robert "Rosie" Rosenthal, the highly decorated Jewish B-17 commander who flew fifty-two bombing missions and was shot down twice.

It was another reminder of how Zaidy may not have been a primary actor in the war theater, but he was a bit player on the set. Like the title of Jerzy Kosiński's famous novel, Zaidy's significance seemed to be merely "being there." Or, to use another literary analogy, I never thought he would be the "Great Gatsby," but I still hoped he could be the Nick Carraway who introduced the central characters.

Photo 9.2 Alfred Brenner (left) and a fellow airman, England, 1944
(Courtesy of Historica Canada, https://www.historicacanada.ca/.)

Photo 9.3 Alfred Brenner in 1943 and 2010
(Courtesy of Historica Canada, https://www.historicacanada.ca/.)

Photo 9.4 Alfred Brenner's Distinguished Flying Cross
(Courtesy of Historica Canada, https://www.historicacanada.ca/.)

CHAPTER TEN

Zaidy's Band of Brothers, the Jewish Canadian Soldiers

The discovery of the museum plans led me to publish a story for the Associated Press about Israel finally starting to honor the long overlooked Jewish World War II veterans. It generated a lot of interest and reached far and wide, as it was republished in the *New York Times*, the *Washington Post*, *Stars and Stripes*, and dozens of other publications. All the English-language papers in Israel picked it up and many people approached me asking how they could contribute and include the stories of their loved ones too.

It was one of those deeply satisfying stories that gave me great pride and reminded me why I got into this business in the first place. But at the end of the day, if I was being honest with myself, I really did it for an audience of one.

I hoped that seeing others sharing their stories and realizing the potential of a museum devoted to people like him would finally snap Zaidy out of his decades-long silence.

It was time for me to up the ante and engage more directly; to muster the courage and ask him head-on what he did in the war.

"I didn't do much," he responded, in typical fashion, during a visit to Toronto in 2015.

"I fought in the battle of Piccadilly Circus, though. Have you heard of that one?" he chuckled. "That's where you met all the girls."

I couldn't tell if he was being modest or just joking about the truth: that his service was so uneventful that there was nothing to report. Either way, Zaidy wasn't dodging anymore. He was more than happy to talk about the war, just not about his actual part in it.

Canada's role in World War II has often been overlooked in favor of the more celebrated American and British campaigns, but it was nonetheless substantial.

Overall, some 1.1 million Canadians served in World War II (including more than 50,000 women), and about 45,000 were killed and 55,000 were wounded.[1] They fought in every battlefield and were particularly renowned for their crucial roles in the August 19, 1942, raid on the French coastal resort town of Dieppe (in which more than 900 servicemen were killed in the nine bloodiest hours of Canadian military history[2]). They also played a large part in the Battle of Ortona in Italy in late 1943, in Operation Overlord on June 6, 1944, and in the liberation of Holland in 1945.

The Royal Canadian Air Force played an especially key part in the allied victory. Overall, the RCAF reached its peak strength of 215,000 in January 1944, while Zaidy was still deployed. By the end of the war, the RCAF would be the fourth largest Allied air force.[3]

The Canadian airmen took part in the Battle of Britain, and in battles in Malta, the Western Desert, and northwestern Europe. Its transport airplanes also operated in Ceylon and Burma, in addition to coastal defense missions at home.

But the Canadians' main contribution was in bombing operations. Altogether, they executed one-eighth of all missions of the entire British Bomber Command.[4]

That's also where Canada's Jews found most of their action. Of the 450 Jewish Canadian World War II casualties, more than half – some 250 – were from the air force. Of the 85 Jewish Canadian POWs, 49 were airmen like Wilf Canter.[5]

Both the air force and the navy had policies that could effectively bar people who were not British subjects and not of white European Christian descent, particularly officers. But this was far more enforced in the navy, where fewer than 600 Jews served. That made up just 0.53 percent of the nearly 97,000 members of the service, and just 3.5 percent of the overall Jewish enlistment.[6]

There were plenty of reports of antisemitism at sea and the army barracks. These could range from anti-Jewish jokes and racist talk to actual fistfights.[7]

In contrast, the nearly 6,000 Jews who volunteered for the RCAF represented a more impressive statistic and they made up 2.61 percent of the RCAF fighting force. They too had to overcome initial antisemitic quotes and the discriminatory tropes of the times. But sometimes these prejudices worked in their favor, particularly for the navigators like Zaidy. It was assumed that the educated Jewish airmen would prove particularly valuable in navigation, thanks to their perceived math excellence.

Even so, Zaidy said it took him two years to become a navigator.

"The air force at first didn't want any Jewish boys, but then they ran out of *goyim*," he said with a smile in 2022, using the Yiddish term for non-Jews.[8]

"The trouble was that the Canadian government didn't like to take people of our ilk because they didn't think that we were good citizens."

He too couldn't escape the scourge of the times.

"I had one case of antisemitism. I couldn't get in an aircrew, so I went in as a stenographer," Zaidy said in 2019. "I had one guy from Bowmanville [an Ontario town near Oshawa]. He was the only guy that I encountered antisemitism with. It was one incident, but it went past."[9]

He would not say more, but these attitudes reflected what was also happening on the home front.

With Zaidy off at war, his sister Jeanette returned from New York to Toronto in 1941 to care for their mother for the next three years. She also experienced the anti-Jewish sentiment of the time.

An editorial published on January 11, 1944, in the *Globe and Mail* against antisemitism in Toronto cited the experiences of a certain "J.H.," whose application to a figure-skating club had been denied because she was Jewish.

"[They] told me it had been rejected, and, what's more, said that that was why these clubs had been formed: so as to keep the Jews out," Jeanette wrote in the editorial. "Night after night I have danced at canteens and entertainments for the boys in the service – without pay, of course – and worked all day at the office. Probably some of those boys are sons and brothers of members of this same skating club."

Such slights were also commonplace toward the Jewish soldiers fighting against the Nazis in Europe.

At the peak of its strength, the No. 6 Group to which Zaidy belonged consisted of fourteen heavy bomber squadrons. Its operations included raids on German U-boat bases in France and night bombing raids of industrial complexes and urban centers in Germany. The No. 6 Group flew more than 40,000 operational sorties and more than 800 aircraft were lost. More than 10,000 airmen did not make it back.[10]

Where Zaidy fit into all of this remained unclear, and he wouldn't share any more clues to help solve the mystery. But when it came to his friends, he proudly went on about their heroics. And it turned out that Somer James and Alfred Brenner weren't the only ones who had exceptional wartime stories. One way or another, Zaidy and I stumbled upon a slew of close Canadian acquaintances who played major roles during that pivotal period.

It was sometime in 1944 when my penny-poor grandfather apparently won 30 pounds in a craps game in England. It was a fair sum of money at the time, and he used the proceedings to help buy a $150 engagement ring for his beloved Eunice.

However, as a non-commissioned officer (NCO), he did not have the privilege of sending packages back to Canada. So, he prevailed upon his Torontonian officer friend, Albert Glazer, to send the package back for him.

It arrived in Toronto, and shortly before my grandfather was shipped back to Canada, he received a telegram from

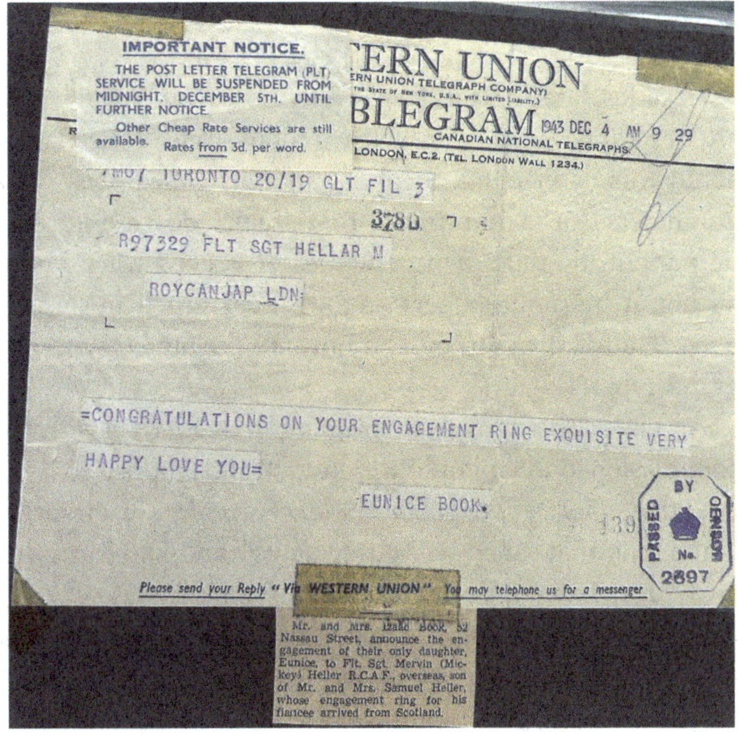

IMPORTANT NOTICE.
THE POST LETTER TELEGRAM (PLT) SERVICE WILL BE SUSPENDED FROM MIDNIGHT, DECEMBER 5TH. UNTIL FURTHER NOTICE.
Other Cheap Rate Services are still available. Rates from 3d. per word.

[WEST]ERN UNION
[WEST]ERN UNION TELEGRAPH COMPANY)
[CA]BLEGRAM 1943 DEC 4 AM 9 29
CANADIAN NATIONAL TELEGRAPHS
LONDON, E.C.2. (TEL. LONDON WALL 1234.)

TORONTO 20/19 GLT FIL 3
378D.
R97329 FLT SGT HELLAR M
ROYCANJAP LDN=

=CONGRATULATIONS ON YOUR ENGAGEMENT RING EXQUISITE VERY HAPPY LOVE YOU=
EUNICE BOOK.

PASSED BY CENSOR No. 2897

Please send your Reply "Via WESTERN UNION" You may telephone us for a messenger

Mr. and Mrs. Izaac Book, 52 Nassau Street, announce the engagement of their only daughter, Eunice, to Flt. Sgt. Mervin (Mickey) Heller R.C.A.F., overseas, son of Mr. and Mrs. Samuel Heller, whose engagement ring for his fiancee arrived from Scotland.

Photo 10.1. Telegram from Eunice Book to Mickey Heller accepting his marriage proposal
(Courtesy of the Heller family.)

Eunice acknowledging receipt of the "exquisite" ring and coyly congratulating him on his engagement. (She'd later joke she had no choice but to accept, saying it was her contribution to the war effort. "I couldn't send him a Dear John letter," she'd quip. "He was fighting for our country.")

Thus, Glazer, who won a Distinguished Flying Cross for his work with radar on board RAF planes and Royal British Navy vessels during the Siege of Malta in 1942, played a central role in what would turn into a seventy-two-year marriage.

Decades later, Glazer's son Stephen would reach out after reading one of my articles to fill in some of the blanks about this connection. Stephen, an avid genealogist who volunteers for a non-profit that tracks down information about the unknown casualties of Israel's wars, knew all about his father's service and, over lunch in Jerusalem, detailed his journey and how it overlapped with my grandfather's.

An electrical engineer by training, the elder Glazer was commissioned as a pilot officer in 1940 and shipped to England the following year aboard the SS *Georgic*, a fast transatlantic liner that sailed without a convoy and had to zigzag away from lurking German U-boats along the way.

"The only other episode that took place on the ship was when one of the officers who was too drunk to know what he was doing, upon feeling cold lit a small bonfire in his cabin to keep warm," Glazer wrote in an unpublished 1997 autobiography.

Glazer landed in Liverpool in March 1941 and then trained on airborne radar and was posted at 612 Squadron in Wick, on the northern tip of Scotland, where he made a few operational flights over the North Atlantic on anti-U-boat patrols and convoy escorts. On one of these flights, he crashed in the North Sea and floated in a rubber dinghy until he was rescued.

Glazer landed on the isolated island of Malta in October 1941 at the peak of the siege, just after the Germans landed in Sicily and North Africa. It was the only British base between Gibraltar in the west and Alexandria in the east. He began flying as a radar mechanic on Wellingtons in routine night searches for axis convoys, trying to deliver supplies across the Mediterranean Sea from Italy to North Africa, and he took part in bombing operations in Sicily, Italy, and North Africa, one of which destroyed a 10,000-ton enemy vessel. In all, he flew seventy-two missions over the Mediterranean and was also in charge of airborne radar on the island.

Glazer served about a year in Malta and throughout the siege of the island as it underwent more than 2,200 raids. "In one raid, we were bombed by 400 aircraft for 72 consecutive hours," he recalled years later.

It was during that stretch that he encountered his narrowest escape. "I was showing a friend around, trying to be brave, when a bomb landed close. I pushed my friend into a shelter and followed," he recalled.[11]

Oddly, he never came across the famed "Falcon of Malta," George "Buzz" Beurling. Years later, though, he did share with his son tales he had heard about the "crazy" daredevil.

"Malta was truly isolated – the nearest British bases were nearly 1,000 miles away," Glazer wrote. "The enemy was much closer. On a clear day, it was just possible to discern the outline of the hills of Sicily no more than 60 miles away."

Overall, he had some 500 hours in operational flying.

"In the course of a large number of sorties, this officer has performed excellent work as observer; the majority of them have been executed at night in all kinds of weather," read his citation. "His courage and devotion to duty are worthy of the highest praise."[12]

Glazer returned to England on August 28, 1942, where he spent most of the rest of the war, befriending my grandfather, Somer James, Alfred Brenner, and the rest of the Jewish boys from Canada. In London, he was best man at the wedding of his fellow military friend Barney Danson, the future Canadian cabinet minister who, as an infantryman, was badly wounded and lost his sight in one eye in Normandy. Glazer detailed his service in a written summary in 1997 and he died in 2004.

Stephen eagerly wanted to question Zaidy as well, feeling that his father's legacy would help him get more out of him than an immediate family member. But he too failed to glean anything beyond the memories of his youth and the names of shared acquaintances. Regarding his own service, Zaidy stayed mum.

Visiting Toronto in early 2017, I met another Jewish war veteran in Zaidy's upscale assisted-living facility. And this one was far less bashful than my grandfather.

Gerry Rosenberg, then ninety-four, was quick to share the highlights of his past: six years in the Royal Canadian Navy from 1940–6, including deployment on the outer layer of the D-Day invasion. Later he was a foreign volunteer in Israel's War of Independence. He showed me his Israeli ID card and told me that the first Hebrew word he learned was *esh*, "fire."

Later reading revealed that Rosenberg had lots of other stories too. [13] As one of the few Jews in the navy, Rosenberg, born in Hamilton, Ontario, endured harassment during his training. He said that after one man in particular kept agitating him, "[I] hit him as hard as I could and threw him across the room." They eventually became close friends.

Rosenberg was on board the corvette HMCS *Battleford* in 1942, serving in the ship's communications room, when his convoy approached a group of German submarines lying in wait between Iceland and the Azores.

In the early hours of December 27, 1942, the Germans fired torpedoes that sank three freighters and damaged a fourth. The *Battleford* and other Canadian warships counter-attacked. Official reports said the German subs included a combined crew of forty-six and that there were no survivors.

Rosenberg took credit for some of that statistic, saying that in fact eight German sailors had survived the initial blast and that he and another Jewish sailor decided to exact some revenge of their own.

"We knew that the Germans were pretty ruthless, even for survivors at sea. They used to machine-gun the life-boats," he said, in testimony to The Memory Project, a volunteer speakers bureau that arranges for veterans to share their stories. "We picked them up on one side, tore their life jackets off, and threw them over on the other side."

When I informed Zaidy about my new acquaintance, he instantly recognized that the chatty Rosenberg was my kind of guy.

"You start talking to him, he'll never let you go," Zaidy said with a smile. "He's had quite a life, and he's more than happy to tell you about it."

It was a year later, however, when I pressed for more information about Wilf Canter and his comrades, that Zaidy mentioned how Gerry Rosenberg also claimed to have seen Canter's plane crash in flames while he was a Machal volunteer. Now, there was a lead. Finally, I had found a live witness to the 1948 crash that I had been relentlessly researching, and I knew that good old Gerry was just the one to tell me all about it.

But then Zaidy quickly quashed my excitement.

"Gerry's gone," he said flatly.

A year is a long time at a retirement home for the elderly.

It was my first article about Zaidy, published in 2019 in the "At War" section of the *New York Times Magazine*, that established yet another connection.[14] The cover photo of the article featured my grandfather, in flight gear, standing in front of a bomber plane and alongside three other aviators.

A random reader named Bruce Oren instantly recognized one of those men in the image as his now ninety-seven-year-old father, Ralph. We exchanged messages and Bruce said his father had trained in Belleville, Ontario, where he assumed the picture of them together must have been taken.

"My dad trained as a navigator bombardier and ended up in a Pathfinder working the radar on the lead plane of bomber squadrons over Germany. He transferred to the U.S. Air Corps, Eighth Air Force, in 1942, where he earned the Distinguished Flying Cross, among other medals," he wrote. "My father is also a Jewish veteran and rarely talked about his experience flying aboard the B-17s. On his Flying Fortress, a radar dome took the place of the belly gun, so he was also vulnerable to enemy planes coming from below."

I excitedly informed Zaidy of the newfound connection. He said he remembered Oren well and would be happy to

Photo 10.2. Mickey Heller (on the far left), Ralph Oren (second from right), and friends in front of a bomber plane
(Courtesy of the Heller family.)

reconnect. Bruce and I discussed arranging a video chat between them – more than seventy-five years after the picture was taken. But that proved too difficult because of Oren's deteriorating hearing and eyesight. Still, we found a way for them to reach each other after all these years. Bruce corresponded directly with Zaidy and sent him a heartfelt note with a link to a video he had shot in which Ralph Oren recalled meeting Zaidy in New York in the late 1940s. He also thought Zaidy had joined him for a visit with relatives in Manchester, England, when they were overseas together.

In the short video clip, shot on June 6 at a rehabilitation center, Ralph Oren also recalled fondly how Pathfinders were all known as "Mickeys" in Bomber Command, as it was code for their on-plane radar systems.

"They didn't want the Germans to know that we had radar, so I wasn't a 'radar operator,' I was a 'Mickey operator,'" he said.

We still hoped to figure out a way for them to see each other face to face. Sadly, Ralph Oren, who flew in the lead B-17 in thirty bombing missions over Germany for the Eighth Air Force, died on July 6, 2019, exactly one month later.

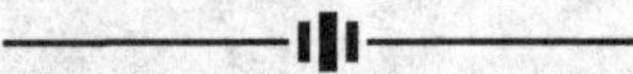

Many of Zaidy's high school classmates from Harbord Collegiate also went off to war, including Lou Somers,[15] a track star who was a year ahead of Zaidy. He crashed to his death in 1943 on a bombing mission over Germany. The Canadian Jewish Congress had honored him with a cartoon brochure, like that of Brenner's, highlighting his heroics as a pilot in the famous Lions Squadron. In one sortie, for example, Somers's plane was struck twenty times before he managed to steer it toward a safe landing.

But it was another Harbord Collegiate friend with whom Zaidy had an even closer connection.

Lorne Winer joined the Canadian artillery and served oversees for five years. He trained for the D-Day landings and, after crossing the English Channel, he fought his way through Normandy and into Belgium and the Netherlands.[16]

Winer said he became inured to death and suffering after seeing so many corpses strewn on the battlefield.

"For whatever reason, it made no impact on me, I don't know why," he told the *Toronto Star* in 2015. "From that day to the end of the war, there was no personality. Nothing. They were dead and I was alive and that was my feeling throughout."[17]

But after the war, he suffered through years of PTSD and shared his harrowing stories about the smell of corpses in Normandy, about his fear of German mortars called "Moaning Minnies," and about the mosquitoes that plagued him in his slit trench after the breakout from Juno Beach in July 1944.[19] Later, while attending a memorial service for Allied Jewish soldiers who had been killed in Normandy, he first came across Holocaust survivors whom he said "looked like wraiths, ghosts standing against the wall."[19]

In 2016, France rewarded him with its highest honor, the Legion d'honneur, for helping liberate their country.

But what Zaidy remembered about Winer was that before they both enlisted, they had worked together on manual jobs

Photo 10.3. Mickey Heller (standing on the left) with Lorne Winer (standing on the right) and friends in London
(Courtesy of Scott Masters.)

such as making soap and wrapping packages in Toronto. He said they didn't have anything to do with each other in the war. But then I found a picture of Winer posing in uniform in London in 1943 and alongside him was none other than my grandfather.

While Zaidy had no recollection of that, Winer did. At 104, he told me over the phone in 2022 that he knew my Zaidy casually and that picture was taken when they bumped into each other outside the Balfour Services Club in London, south of Regent's Park, which became a regular meeting point for Canadian Jewish personnel during the war.

"The Jewish boys would all sit by the fountain and catch up," Winer said. "I really lost track of him after that and all I can remember is that he opened a little ice cream store when he came back to Canada. That's all I can remember. My regret is that I can't be more helpful. I know how important it is to fill all this in." (Zaidy indeed briefly opened a local Dairy Queen franchise in Toronto in the 1950s.)

Winer agreed with my assessment that veterans often go through long periods where they don't want to talk about the war and then, when they are finally ready, their memory won't allow them to do it anymore.

He died in May 2023, at the age of 105.

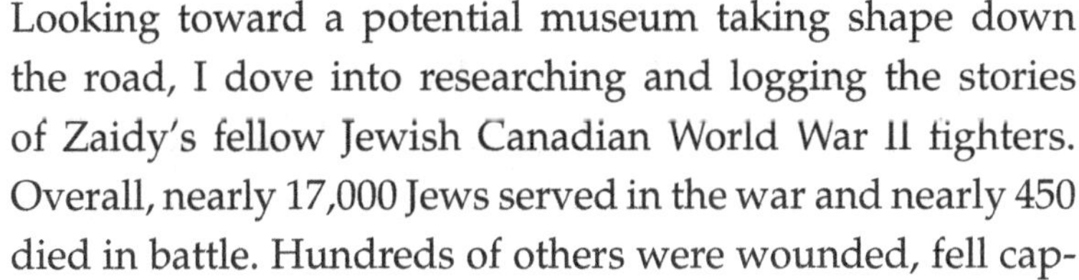

Looking toward a potential museum taking shape down the road, I dove into researching and logging the stories of Zaidy's fellow Jewish Canadian World War II fighters. Overall, nearly 17,000 Jews served in the war and nearly 450 died in battle. Hundreds of others were wounded, fell captive, or earned prestigious citations. These Jews took part in all of Canada's major battles.[20]

I discovered so many who left a legacy and who could feature prominently in the halls of a future museum.[21] Their service likely had very little to do with my grandfather's, but just learning about their contributions helped me feel closer to his past.

There was fighter pilot Sydney Shulemson of Montreal, the most highly decorated Canadian Jewish serviceman in World War II, who was awarded both a Distinguished Service Order and a Distinguished Flying Cross.[22] Shulemson shot down a German flying boat over the North Sea on his first mission of the war. All told, he was credited with sinking at least a dozen enemy ships. He later worked undercover for the Haganah (Israel's main pre-state paramilitary force), helping to recruit some of the 300 Canadians who eventually joined Machal for Israel's War of Independence.

There was infantry officer Benjamin Dunkelman of Toronto, who landed on Juno Beach on D-Day, fought through France, Belgium, and the Netherlands and earned a Distinguished Service Order for his bravery during the final allied assault on Germany.[23] His citation said he destroyed two enemy machine guns and killed ten enemy soldiers "with his pistol and his bare hands" during the battle to capture the Balberger Forest near the Rhine. Despite being an experienced sailor, he was rejected for service by a Royal Canadian Navy known to discriminate against Jews. He later joined Machal and commanded Israel's legendary 7th Armor Brigade that captured the Upper Galilee in the 1948 war.

There was engineering officer Albert Hanson of Alberta, who served in the Royal Canadian Engineers during the Normandy invasion, led mine-clearing operations, and was responsible for access track construction for the forward armored units. He was badly wounded in France and awarded the Military Cross.[24]

There was US-born Wing Commander William Weiser, who moved to Canada to join the war effort and flew two tours over North Africa and Europe. In May 1943, his plane was shot down while returning from a bombing mission over Germany and he was severely wounded. He earned a Distinguished Flying Cross and was named a member of the Order of the British Empire for his war efforts.[25]

There were Leo and David Heaps of Winnipeg, the only pair of Jewish Canadian brothers to both win the Royal Military Cross. Leo parachuted in the famed, and doomed, 1944 Operation Market Garden, was captured by the Germans, escaped, and joined the Dutch underground in rescuing other prisoners of war. David and his artillery unit were credited with knocking out seven German Panther tanks the following year.[26]

There was Gordon Steinberg, a Toronto-born pilot who proudly displayed his heritage by painting a Star of David insignia on the nose of his Hawker Hurricane fighter plane. He completed ninety-two operational flights in Africa before he was shot down near Alexandria, Egypt.[27]

Finally, there was Rabbi Samuel Cass, the Toronto-born Jewish chaplain who held a Hanukkah party for Jewish orphans in Antwerp, led Shabbat services for survivors of the Westerbork transit camp, and later led a Passover Seder and the first battlefield prayer for Jewish troops on German soil.[28]

Zaidy's service appeared to be nowhere nearly as significant as these men's. But knowing that he belonged in their company in this museum was an honor in and of itself.

The Museum

CHAPTER ELEVEN

Zvi Kan-Tor, the General on a Mission

Delving into the prospect of a museum devoted specifically to the Jewish soldiers of World War II was very rewarding since it provided the intellectual backdrop to my personal quest to learn about Zaidy's military past.

This was where his story belonged, where any meaningful relics he may possess could find a home.

I started fantasizing about how he could fit in. Depending on what I discovered, perhaps this future museum could include a mention of his service? If he wouldn't share his full story with me, perhaps he'd be more willing to do so with others?

Wandering through the barren concrete structure that would house the future museum, I could almost imagine his picture and a short bio on the wall.

In the meantime, I filled out a brief profile of him on the prospective museum's website.[1] This was the external instrument through which I had hoped he would reconnect to his World War II experience.

But when I suggested it in 2017, he once again demurred. "I'm just happy if they leave me alone," he concluded.

I thought I was a serious World War II history buff. Then I met Zvi Kan-Tor.

He'd been the driving force behind the development of the museum when I first met him in 2015. For more than a decade, he'd been curating material, fundraising around the world, and navigating through the legendary cumbersome Israeli bureaucracy in a passion project that had been perpetually delayed. He'd developed an encyclopedic knowledge of all things Jewish in World War II and had amassed swaths of materials, testimonies, and artifacts for a future museum. But there remained a real fear the ambitious project may never take shape, and Kan-Tor had often found himself alone in keeping up the good fight.

A retired brigadier general of the Israeli Armor Corps, he had the gruffness of a career military man but also the curiosity of an academic. He had commanded three brigades, and his claim to fame was being among the first tanks to cross the Suez Canal in the 1973 Yom Kippur War under the command of Ariel Sharon.

But he told me that he came to the World War II project not out of his vast military know-how but rather from ignorance about Jewish military history. He wanted to learn more since not much had been shared with him about the contributions of those Jews who had been long overlooked in Israel.

Israel's annual Holocaust Remembrance Day is officially called Holocaust and Heroism Remembrance Day. It's a nod toward not only the victims but also the resistance fighters. In Israel's early days, when Holocaust survivors were often ignored, even ridiculed, for their perceived lack of defiance, characters like Warsaw Ghetto Uprising commander Mordechai Anielewicz and parachuting partisan Hannah Szenes were who the young state chose to champion.

The Jewish war veterans who returned to their home countries were not part of the early Zionist narrative. That honor belonged to the partisans and the plucky resistance fighters in the Warsaw Ghetto Uprising who better fit the country's scrappy pioneering spirit.

Following the 1961 trial of Holocaust mastermind Adolf Eichmann, there was an awakening to the scope and magnitude of the Holocaust and the experiences of its victims still living in Israel. It ushered in a shift in public perception and Remembrance Day began to morph into a more somber recognition of the genocide with a focus on victimhood. That manifested itself into a shorthand for the day that has since commonly been referred to simply as Holocaust Day.

The mass immigration of Soviet Jews in the 1990s marked the next turning point, when the term "veteran" made Aliyah as well and entered the everyday vernacular. Every year, elderly Russian speakers would strut out on Victory Day with their medals pinned on old uniforms, to the astonishment of Sabra Israelis who knew little to nothing about their service. It was one such veteran who first approached

Kan-Tor and convinced him to take on the project of a museum for just such people.

Of the 1.5 million Jewish fighters in World War II, Kan-Tor's research found that nearly 500,000 were Soviet Jews and some 550,000 were American Jews. In some cases, they were among the first to liberate the Nazi death camps, offering an encouraging word of Yiddish to the dazed, emaciated prisoners. Their sacrifice was little known in Israel and abroad, and there was barely any commemoration for the 250,000 Jews who died fighting for the Allies (200,000 of whom were from the Soviet Red Army, according to Kan-Tor).

"World War II in our collective memory has been sealed by a single word: Holocaust," Kan-Tor told me in 2015, seated in a makeshift office in a caravan filled with World War II books that sat alongside the construction site. "We've heard about the victimhood – let's tell this side too. This is the missing piece. Maybe we can finally tell the full wartime story of the Jewish people."

At Israel's official ceremony in 2015 to mark seventy years since Victory Day in Europe, both Prime Minister Benjamin Netanyahu and President Reuven Rivlin acknowledged that the contributions of Jewish veterans had been overlooked for far too long. They said financing would be found to complete the construction of the planned museum, which had been bogged down in bureaucracy for more than a decade.

"We stand here as representatives of a people who gave their best sons in the battleground. While their brothers were being led to destruction, the Jewish warriors stood on the front lines," Rivlin said at the ceremony. "Do our children know this? Do our grandchildren know that the Jewish people fought in the killing fields of Europe?"

Kan-Tor's mission meshed with my own, as I set out to meet and interview World War II veterans who openly shared with me the kind of memories that I had waited a lifetime to hear from my own grandfather.

Brooklyn-born Dan Nadel enlisted in the US Army right after the Japanese attack on Pearl Harbor on December 7, 1941. But what really drove him to battle was his Jewish faith.[2]

"What Hitler was doing to the Jews, I knew he had to be killed and stopped," the then-ninety-five-year-old decorated veteran told me from his home in Jerusalem. "That was my motivation."

Nadel became an officer with the US Combat Engineers and landed in Normandy shortly after D-Day. He said that of the fifty-five men who hit the beach under his command only twelve survived. He credited his own miraculous survival to a Jewish amulet attached to his dog tags.

His home was filled with photo albums from that period and in his shaky voice he appeared to be reliving the stories as he told them, while donning his wartime cap and pins.

The only Jew in his outfit, Nadel went on to earn five battle stars while leading troops in the Battle of the Bulge and the liberation of France.

"You have no idea how miserable it was. It was the coldest winter on record. We didn't have enough clothes. Guys froze in their foxholes. Froze to death," he recalled.

However, his most harrowing experience came when, against Nadel's advice, General George S. Patton ordered him to lead an ill-advised assault across an ice-cold river in Belgium.

"We got halfway across the footbridge and the Germans threw up flares and threw everything at us. I had two company commanders with me, an 88-mm shell came directly at us. They didn't have helmets on. I did, and that saved my life," he recalled shakily. "The two of them were killed instantly, shrapnel in the brain. I didn't know if I was dead or alive. I was shell shocked but I came out of it with just a scratch. I will never forget that."

Later, he also found himself walking through a minefield when one of his soldiers, driving a jeep, rolled over a mine.

"He survived, but it blew half his ass off," Nadel recalled with a chuckle. "He wrote me a letter after saying 'Nadel, you used to call me a half-assed sergeant, well I am one now.'"

Throughout all the fighting, Nadel said he had no idea about the Nazi concentration camps and the scope of the Holocaust.

"We didn't know anything about it until we actually came across it and saw it with our own eyes," he said.

Eventually, though, he helped free his fellow Jews from them, speaking in Yiddish to emaciated survivors.

"You can't imagine what it was like. The stench, people walking around just like skeletons, just bones and skin, that's all. They went into our garbage bags and killed themselves ravaging our garbage," he recalled. "It was terrible. Our general, Patton, when he went into the camps, he puked."

After the war, his wife wanted to immigrate to Mandatory Palestine and help build up the Zionist armed forces. But Nadel said he'd seen enough fighting.

"I told her, honey, I just came from a war; I don't want to take a rifle in my hand ever again," he said.

They opted to stay in the United States, immigrating to Israel only in 1977.

There he became recognizable in his Jerusalem neighborhood for wearing a baseball cap that read "World War II veteran," and he ran the only club in Israel for American Jewish war veterans.

Another veteran I interviewed in Jerusalem was Norman Cohen,[3] a genteel ninety-one-year-old Brit with a thin, distinguished mustache. He withstood the Blitz in his hometown of Coventry before enlisting and then landed on Gold Beach in Normandy on D-Day, his ship reaching land only on its third attempt since the beaches were crammed with troops.

Cohen told me D-Day was a hectic hell on earth and the only realistic portrayal of it in film was the opening scene in *Saving Private Ryan*.

He disembarked into about six inches of water and then moved quickly to the fishing village of Ver-sur-Mer.

"The first 48 hours, we were hanging on by our fingertips," he said. "I had this silly grin on my face, and I said to myself, 'you've done it now, there is no going back.'"

He later swept through Europe as a radio operator with the 2nd Army under the command of General Miles Dempsey, eventually receiving the German transmission of surrender and even stumbling upon Nazi leader Heinrich

Himmler in Luneburg shortly before the SS chief killed himself.

Some of the most fascinating details Cohen shared with me didn't even make it into my Associated Press feature on May 29, 2015.[4] Such as when Cohen pulled out a dagger inside a sheath that he said he found in the Black Forest. The sheath was rusting but the stainless-steel spear was impeccable with its Nazi insignia and the engraved signature of its supposed owner, Heinrich Eichler. He also had a belt he said he found that belonged to a Nazi soldier, with a buckle featuring the German eagle and reading *Gott Mit Uns* – "God is with us."

Once, while in France, Cohen said that he repeatedly tried to exit his signal truck but encountered the ring of a bullet striking it every time he cracked open the door. He called in backup and the next time he opened the door, and a shot rang out once again, his comrades were there to unleash a hail of bullets on the source of fire.

They later discovered that the shooter was a young French woman who was having an affair with a German soldier and was sore at the Allies for disrupting their dalliance.

Another time he was struck by lightning while tending to radio gear on top of a truck. He said it flipped him into a double summersault, and he landed on a haystack.

But what he was most adamant about was dismissing the notion of heroism often associated with World War II battles.

"Just because you are in a certain time and place it doesn't make you a hero. You are just there," he said forcefully. "There were plenty of unsung heroes in the war. But nobody deliberately puts themselves into a position of being a hero.

Heroism just happens. And is it heroism or is it just bloody stupidity?"

I had hoped that the Associated Press story I wrote about the emerging museum, which had been published in dozens of outlets around the world, would move things along. Kan-Tor was inundated with responses, pleased with the attention and hopeful it would even generate some much-needed revenue.

But two years later, nothing had changed. My piece garnered plenty of interest but, unfortunately, no new major donations.

The Israeli government first committed to the museum in 2002 and vowed to match any funds raised from donors.[5] Successive governments had renewed the pledge and roughly $6 million had already poured into the project. The funds had gone toward collecting artifacts and testimonies and, of course, toward the building of a 2,200 square-meter (23,500-square-foot) structure inside the Armored Corps Memorial Site and Museum at Latrun, which was near the site of some of the most significant battles in Israel's 1948 War of Independence.

But an additional $10 million was needed to complete the museum.

I learned that despite Netanyahu's explicit promise to advance it, he had dumped the project on an underling who quickly sparred with the association behind the museum, accusing it of mismanagement. All the while, the government ignored the appeals of aging veterans pleading for a solution to be found. The government had refrained from renewing its matching funds agreement and the museum structure itself stood vacant like a white elephant in central Israel, eerily surrounded by one of the world's most diverse collections of battle-tested tanks. Inside the cavernous structure, all was silent but for the flapping wings of pigeons that had taken shelter.

There were no museums devoted solely to the Jews who fought the Nazis. Individual memorials existed in Israel, and Yad Vashem in Jerusalem also had exhibits devoted to the partisans and rebels in the various ghettos. But veterans bemoaned that these were just snippets, and the museum in Latrun was to be the one place that would serve as their legacy.

By 2017, Kan-Tor estimated there were no more than 5,000 veterans left and he provided me with written pleas from some of them to get the museum established while they were still alive to witness it.

He had embarked on this mission with his former wartime commander, Chaim Erez, and it had been their joint commander Ariel Sharon who first encouraged them to pursue the project when he was prime minister in 2002. Five years later, Ehud Olmert's government agreed to pay for its part of the establishment, and, in 2012, approval was given to begin building. But that's where the trouble began, with long years of government wavering and a cast of various characters getting involved and stunting the project.

Time was of the essence. Just like Holocaust survivors, these people were rapidly withering away. And as the museum's bureaucratic stalemate continued, more of them kept dying.

Dan Nadel, the American veteran who was my main character from the 2015 story, had since died. A brief phone conversation with Norman Cohen indicated that he had deteriorated considerably. He died shortly after. Another contact I got from Kan-Tor had died and two others did not respond. It was a stark reminder that, as with my Holocaust-related stories, there was no time like the present with these guys because they could be gone, or incapacitated, just like that.

The only veteran I managed to get a hold of this time who was able in mind and body was Peter Arton, a ninety-five-year-old Israeli from Czechoslovakia whose credentials immediately reminded me of someone I knew.[6]

Born on January 1, 1922, he was less than two months younger than Zaidy and he too was a navigator for the Royal Air Force in the war. He was stationed in Britain at the same time and seemed to have had a similar service, though it was unlikely they had crossed paths. The main difference between them was that Arton talked. He had written a memoir about his service in which he detailed a near-death crash landing and other adventures. He told me about how a third of his squadron was Jewish and what the museum would mean to him.

"This is also the story of the Jews. We participated massively," said Arton, who passed away in October 2021.

The museum was still going nowhere in 2017 when I published another story on Israel's annual Holocaust Remembrance Day about the frustration of these elderly veterans who helped establish Israel.[7]

Baruch Shub, who headed the now-defunct Organization of Partisans in Israel and coincidentally lived in a Kfar Saba retirement home right around the corner from me, fixed a menacing gaze as he accused the government of diverting away Holocaust compensation funds and neglecting survivors, veterans, and projects aimed at benefiting and memorializing them.

"They cheated us," said Shub, who was ninety-three at the time and died in December 2020. "I look in the mirror and say: 'What would my friends who died in the forest say about the behavior of the state of Israel that we fought to establish?'"

Shub's mother and three siblings were murdered by Nazis and their local collaborators in Lithuania. After a failed uprising in the Vilna Ghetto, he escaped to the forests to join the underground network led by famed resistance fighter Abba Kovner. Four battalions of Jewish fighters raided villages for food and supplies and hacked away at communication and electricity lines used by German forces, he said.

After the Red Army liberated the ghetto in 1944 in what is now called Vilnius, Shub returned to find all its Jews killed by Nazi SS troops. Among the bodies strewn on the street was that of his father. A blood-soaked note in his hand, written in Yiddish, said, "If anyone sees my son, tell him to take revenge."

Shub did his best to fulfill that dying wish, trying to undermine the Nazis by derailing trains, burning bridges, sabotaging communication lines, and killing the occasional collaborator.

"Whether or not it made a difference, I don't know. But it gave me a great sense of joy that at least I was doing something to get even with them," he said. "I want history to remember that Jews did not walk like cattle to their slaughter."

Yitzhak Arad, a longtime director of Yad Vashem whom I knew well from my Holocaust reporting, had similar motivations. He lost his parents and forty close relatives in the war. As a teenage resistance fighter in the Soviet forests, he blew up sixteen German supply trains during the war, part of the estimated 20,000–30,000 Jewish partisans who took part in guerilla warfare and sabotage across Europe.

Even in his nineties, he sported a boyish grin beneath curly gray hair and was still affectionately known to all by the nickname his fellow partisans randomly bestowed upon him as a teenager: Tolka (short for Anatoly).

"The picture is not complete if we don't understand that together with the 6 million victims, the Jewish people also had a decisive role in defeating the Nazis," he told me inside the hollow structure he hoped one day would house a museum.

Of the nearly 250,000 Lithuanian Jews before World War II, only a few thousand survived. Many of their murderers were fellow Lithuanians, a complicity the country has fought hard to reject.

Lithuanian authorities never charged any non-Jews for their slaughter of Jews. But in 2006 they did launch investigations into the partisans' wartime activities and accused Arad himself of killing Nazi collaborators who later came to be regarded as national heroes for opposing communism. Arad denied killing any civilians and the charges were dropped two years later. But it became part of a dangerous wave of Holocaust denial, distortion, and revisionism that swept through Eastern Europe and which Arad hoped the eventual museum would confront.

"There is a process of rewriting history in these places," said Arad, who died in May 2021. "We are fading away, so it will be up to the next generation to continue this battle."

I shared the article with Zaidy. His family had Lithuanian roots, and he was also pondering his mortality ahead of his high school's upcoming 125th anniversary. He was planning to attend and said that Harbord Collegiate alumni would be seated according to decades. Since he graduated in 1939, he would be among the youngest of the graduates of the 1930s – if there were even any others left.

"I don't know if there is going to be anyone there who I know," he confided.

He was also eager to discuss the upcoming enlistment of one of his great-grandchildren. Given that Zaidy's father had served in World War I, this marked a fifth-generation Heller to join the military.

Only in 2019 did Netanyahu's government renew its pledge to complete the museum.

Ultimately, it was a private donation that finally put the project over the top. The museum was to be named for former president Chaim Herzog, himself a World War II veteran who participated in the Normandy invasion with the

British military. He was later wounded in battle near Bremen, helped liberate Bergen-Belsen, and, as an intelligence officer, took part in Himmler's interrogation.

The high-powered Herzog family and the non-profit bearing their name helped with the fundraising and diplomatic muscle needed to get over the hump. President Isaac Herzog and his older brother Mike, who was then the Israeli ambassador to the United States, had been using their connections to close the deal to commemorate their father. With the government matching these funds, the project was finally underway. The museum's concept had been finalized, and construction crews were hard at work in 2022 to wrap everything up. It was just a matter of time before the exhibits themselves would be installed.

For Kan-Tor, it finally offered a heartening horizon after more than twenty years of frustration in which he struggled in vain to get the country, and the Jewish people, to take ownership of the project.

Adjacent to the Yad LaShiryon memorial now stood a fully built structure flanked by three World War II–era tanks representing the major Allies: the Soviet T-14, the British Cromwell, and the American Sherman.

A manicured garden featured a statue depicting an Israeli soldier carrying a wounded Machal volunteer on his back.

"Each one helped his fellow man and said to his brother: 'Courage,'" read the quote from the Book of Isaiah.

I helped in logging more Canadian names and stories in the database – Somer James, Willie Fisher, and others – and provided Kan-Tor with further expertise and input on the Canadian aspect of the museum.

The urgency was palpable as Kan-Tor and I checked off all the names of the people I had come across in my stories and realized they were all gone. It was incredibly frustrating. So many people had been waiting for this to happen, and they would never live to see it. At least now there was some hope for the few who remained.

Speaking to Kan-Tor also refreshed what got him into this project to begin with, how the mass immigration of Jewish Soviet war veterans in Israel in the 1990s changed his perception of the Jewish narrative of World War II.

"I just discovered I was ignorant about it all. No one in Israel talks about these men," he said in 2022. "Just like the Eichmann trial changed the perception of Holocaust victims, the Russian immigration changed the perception of Jewish veterans."

Even in pre-state Israel there were 40,000 Jews who joined the British military in World War II; 700 of them died in battle in Europe and North Africa, another 1,510 fell captive, most in Greece and on the island of Crete.[8]

"More people volunteered to fight with the British in World War II than against them here," Kan-Tor noted. "We've done a great disservice to all these Jews who fought in World War II. This museum will rectify that."[9]

For Kan-Tor, it was a chance to bring to life the legacy of people like Maurice Rose, the Jewish general who was the highest-ranking American officer killed by enemy fire in the European theater. Kan-Tor, a veteran Armor Corps man, considered Rose to be the second most significant American tank officer after Patton. To him, that the story of the son and grandson of rabbis was not more widely known among his own people was a travesty.

"This museum will convey the message to future students that we were not just victims. We stepped forward and took action," he said. "If there is one thing that unites the Jewish people, those in Zion and those in the Diaspora, it is the fight for survival. Jews from all over the world volunteered and fought for our survival. They fought for one joint cause: to rid themselves of the Nazi threat."

With Kan-Tor set to be the museum CEO, his old commander, Maj. Gen. (ret.) Chaim Erez would serve as chairman. One day, Erez handed me a copy of his biography, which laid out his astounding life story and clearly established his visceral connection to the project.

His life began as a Polish child who was separated from his mother at age four and had to flee the Nazis in 1939. It continued with trekking through Siberia, to becoming one of the orphaned "Tehran children" who made a famed circuitous journey to Israel via Iran, to his illustrious military career. Erez led a battalion in the Sinai in the 1967 war, then led the first tanks across the Suez Canal in 1973, and then as head of the Southern Command was the general responsible for the evacuation of the Yamit settlement in Sinai in 1982. Now, he was coming full circle by advocating for the World War II soldiers' commemoration.

"War has accompanied my entire life, so this museum is very personal to me," said Erez. "Jewish heroism did not start with the IDF (Israel Defense Forces). That is a great illusion that was created at the birth of Israel. Wherever there were people fighting Nazis there were also Jews. This museum is going to correct perceptions."

It had become a second joint mission for Erez and Kan-Tor, fifty years after their tanks crossed the Suez Canal together under Sharon's command in 1973. For Erez, it would mark the completion of a journey that began in bombed out Warsaw, continued in Siberia, Tehran, pre-state Israel, and throughout his lengthy military career. Erez called it his salute to the heroes of that war who fought, many of whom died as Jews with a weapon in their hand to liberate Europe and the entire world from German tyranny.[10]

For this pair of generals, the museum would serve as a fitting final piece to the World War II story of the Jewish people.

It had all become a reality by the spring of 2024. The ongoing Gaza war following the deadly Hamas attacks on October 7, 2023, had indefinitely postponed an official opening ceremony. But groups of soldiers, students, and guests from overseas – sometimes hundreds a day – were already taking tours of the museum and leaving with a renewed perspective on Jewish military history.

The museum's mantra was to complete the Jewish World War II experience by including an element of heroism to the Holocaust. The idea was to offer a flip side to the victimhood by adding the perspective of the victor to that of the vanquished. No doubt the genocide of European Jewry would forever be its defining aspect, but the fighting spirit of the Jews in World War II also needed to be recognized.

The museum sought to tell the whole story of the Jewish World War II fighters, in five interactive wings. This ranged from the early beleaguered battles of the Allied Powers for Western Europe, to the bloody Soviet front, to the American battlegrounds in the Pacific, in North Africa, and on

European soil. Additional wings were dedicated to the Jewish resistance fighters in the ghettos, the underground resistance and the partisans in the forests, and finally to the Jewish Brigade volunteers from the Holy Land and to the overseas World War II veterans who returned the favor and volunteered for Israel's War of Independence in 1948.

Featured throughout were artifacts, recordings, video accounts, and even holograms depicting the exploits of the Jewish warriors, including the 150,000 women who made up 10 percent of the fighting force.

"This is a unique museum whose presence has been missing, especially now when Jews are still fighting to defend themselves," Erez said. "Anyone who arrives for a visit feels a type of connection, and everyone leaves with broader shoulders."

It was indeed jarring to experience a museum devoted to the Jews who fought against the perpetrators of the Nazi-led genocide, when at the same time young Israeli soldiers were fighting, and dying, in Gaza, some thirty miles to the south. Even more unsettling was that the war was sparked by the massacre of October 7, 2023, which was the single deadliest day for Jews since the Holocaust.[11]

The very essence of Israel is the principle of "never again" – never again would Jews be left defenseless against those who sought to destroy them. The devastating attacks cut to the very heart of Israelis' sense of safety. And in their wake, the eruption of antisemitic attacks in the Western world made one wonder whether Jews would ever arrive at a true sense of refuge.

Until then, I'd mostly viewed the museum as an ode to the past. Now, Jewish vulnerability was suddenly being felt in a way that it hadn't been since the days of World War II.

Israel was experiencing perhaps its most agonizing moment, and this was compounded by the external forces calling its very legitimacy into question and by an extremist government that was exacerbating already deep internal strife. Altogether, it created a sense that the country was losing its way. What I internalized from all this was that Israel's well-being – perhaps even its existence – was not to be taken for granted. The Zionist project was still worth fighting for and preserving. And that was on us. It was our debt to those who sacrificed so much for Israel to come into being.

I'd always assumed that the wider Mideast conflict was mostly over Israel's post-1967 borders. But, in many ways, it now felt as if the 1948 War of Independence had never truly ended.

Against this backdrop, I'd also come full circle with the museum project itself, becoming a volunteer docent – for both Hebrew and English-language visitors – and the resident expert on the Jewish Canadian experience at a time when antisemitism was again rearing its ugly head in the country of my parents' birth.

The de facto seal of recognition came when Israel's Ministry of Immigration and Absorption decided to hold its annual Victory Day over Nazi Germany event at the museum.

Highlighting the ministry's Russian-centric bent, the event was held on May 9, 2024, to mark the Victory Day holiday favored by the Soviets rather than VE Day, which is typically marked a day earlier by the Western Allied nations. As such, it was a bilingual Hebrew-Russian affair that marked this 79th anniversary, featuring a Russian choir, a marching band playing Red Army tunes, and a youth dancing troupe made up of children of immigrants from the former Soviet Union.

A montage of video testimonies included those of Dan Nadel and others I'd interviewed who had passed away

Photo 11.1. Chaim Herzog Museum of the Jewish Soldier in World War II (Courtesy of Zvi Kan-Tor and the Chaim Herzog Museum of the Jewish Soldier in World War II.)

over the years. Another sad reminder of the long, lost years it took to reach this moment was that, according to the Ministry of Immigration and Absorption, only 165 World War II veterans and four partisan fighters remained. Just three of these exclusively Russian speakers were well enough to attend and none were able to speak.

Addressing these surviving few, President Herzog noted the significance of holding such an event at this specific time and place.

"This is not just 'another' museum. It is a site that should be mandatory for every Israeli and every Jew," he said.

"My father once said that under the uniform of every Jewish soldier who fought against the Nazis beat one Jewish heart," he continued. "Our fight against evil is not over. When I see you who fought the Nazis, and the testimony in this museum to that determined battle, I am filled not just with pride but also with hope that we will also know how to stand determinedly today against those that seek us harm."

CHAPTER TWELVE

Machal, the Foreign Volunteers

Israel was always close to Zaidy's heart, and he was always supportive – from a distance.

His first of more than a dozen trips came in 1969, to visit one of his children who was there on a leadership training program for Diaspora youth movements. The last came in 2008, for my wedding.

In between, he and Eunice visited regularly, traveled the land and spent time with family. They briefly considered buying a coastal apartment in Netanya for the winters but, deterred by the price, decided instead to invest in one in Florida. He similarly flirted with the idea of also doing some business in the Holy Land and setting up a partnership for his clothing line. But he was quickly disillusioned by the complexities of doing business in Israel and decided to keep his relationship strictly personal and philanthropic. He'd buy Israel bonds and give at shul and, of course, there was the KKL-JNF blue box in the kitchen where any extra change went to planting trees in Israel.

Even in Israel's notoriously raucous open-air markets he refused to haggle. "When I'm in Israel, I don't bargain," he once said.

He was proud of his sons and grandchildren who moved there and who served in the Israeli military. But serving there himself in 1948 was never on the table.

I secretly envied him. I too wished that I could be that strong supporter from afar, who stood up for the Jewish state without having to bear the full burden of daily life in the country.

Israel's romanticized version speaks of a magical land seeped in history, where Jews can freely live a life filled with meaning and solidarity. I've certainly absorbed much of that magic. But in practice, the heat is not the only thing that's oppressive in the Holy Land. Much like Willie Fisher's impressions in 1948, I've also experienced this element. Threats are abundant from every direction and that translates into an aggressive populace and a stressful existence.

Israel demands a lot from its citizens – taxes are high, traffic is terrible, prices are outrageous, and the public space is perpetually overcrowded. But most of all, you are expected to put your life on hold, and often on the line, in the never-ending quest for security.

Once my parents laid down their roots in Israel, I had to serve in the military. It wasn't voluntary, it was mandatory. And once you give three years of your life to the military, and twenty more years of annual weeks-long reserve duty, it does something to you. Whether you want it to or not, it ties you to the country. You are invested. It's very hard to explain to those who haven't served, but something about the Israeli military experience turns the country into a type of Hotel California. Once you've been through that you can check out anytime you like, but you can never truly leave. At least that's what happened to me, and that's what happened to most of the men I learned about who came as foreign volunteers in 1948 and whose sacrifice laid the groundwork for the country that has become so central to my identity.

Perhaps that's a fate my grandfather was trying to avoid after World War II?

One of the museum's primary missions was to link the Jewish participation in World War II to the establishment of Israel. The fifth and final wing of the museum was to be devoted to this theme.

About 40,000 Jews from pre-state Israel participated in World War II, some 10 percent of the Jewish population at the time. There were volunteer engineers in the Royal Pioneer Corps and infantrymen in the Royal East Kent Regiment (affectionately known as the "Buffs"). Later, the Jewish Brigade was established, an all-Jewish group of some 5,000 fighters who saw battle mostly in Italy. Overall, some 700 died.[1]

Their service was a symbol that the Jews in Mandatory Palestine were as committed as their brethren to defeating Nazi Germany, even as they resisted the British decrees in the Holy Land.

But for Israel to earn independence, it would ultimately need volunteers of a different kind – Jews with significant wartime experience who could wage war with the heavily backed surrounding Arab armies. Israel's locally grown warriors were ingenious and brave, but they didn't have the training or experience to command larger, newly established bodies in the fledgling Israeli military, such as armored and infantry brigades or airborne squadrons.

That's where Machal, the foreign volunteers, came in. These volunteers served in every branch of the new Israeli military, offering unparalleled combat experience from their World War II service. A compelling case can be made that young Israel would not have won its independence without their crucial contribution.[2]

So, it's puzzling and quite unfortunate how little they have been recognized, both in Israel and abroad. Some of the reasons are understandable.

With early Israel focused on nation building, it sought to champion local, not foreign, heroes. Many didn't even see the Machal volunteers as foreign saviors but rather as potential immigrants. Indeed, many of them chose to stay after the fighting ended and were absorbed into the new citizenry of the country. Those who returned home were of less concern.

Back in the United States and Canada, the Machalnikim had their own reasons for keeping a low profile, as they were potentially subject to severe punishment if prosecuted for fighting for a foreign army. It took years before anyone was comfortable enough to start detailing the stories and by then certain narratives had already taken hold.

"We were never 'forgotten,' because we were never known in the first place," wrote Ralph Lowenstein, an author and former dean of the College of Journalism and Communications at the University of Florida in Gainesville, who volunteered for the Israeli Defense Forces in his youth. "Yet, pound for pound, American and Canadian Jews contributed more to building the rock-solid foundation of the Israeli armed forces than any other volunteer group."[3]

Indeed, there was much of which to be proud.

Most renowned of the Machalnikim was David "Mickey" Marcus, who wrote the operational handbook of the Israel Defense Forces and oversaw the Burma Road Project – a massive engineering feat to create a bypass road that broke the siege of Jerusalem. He didn't speak Hebrew, though, and was accidentally shot dead when he failed to respond to an Israeli sentry's demand for a password. His story was memorialized in the 1966 Hollywood movie *Cast a Giant Shadow*, with Kirk Douglas playing the role of Marcus.

Paul Shulman of New York City fought in the Pacific before he helped establish the Israeli Navy and became the first commander to hold the equivalent rank of admiral.

Another foreign volunteer, Ben Dunkelman, was a highly decorated World War II veteran of the 3rd Canadian Infantry Division who led recruitment in Canada and then commanded Israel's legendary 7th Armor Brigade that captured the Upper Galilee. Only in 2015, in a report in the *Toronto Star*, would another part of his legacy be confirmed: that he refused his superiors' orders to expel the Arab residents of Nazareth in the 1948 war, essentially saving the residents of what is today Israel's largest Arab city.[4]

But by far their most significant impact was in Israel's nascent air force, where some 70 percent of the country's first flyers were foreigners.[5] Of those with World War II combat experience, more than 88 percent were foreigners, more than a third of whom were non-Jewish. So prominent was their role that long after Israel because a state, the working language of its air force remained English.

An American World War II vet, Lou Lenart, led Israel's first ever aerial attack, widely credited for saving Tel Aviv from being captured by Egyptian forces. On May 29, 1948, some 10,000 Egyptians were marching north at a bridge twenty-five miles south of Tel Aviv, seemingly on their way to victory, when Lenart and his crew – fellow volunteer Eddie Cohen from South Africa, Modi Alon, and Ezer Weizman, the future Israeli Air Force commander, defense minister, and president – appeared from the sky in their four Avia S-199 fighter planes and pummeled them with bombs. Cohen crashed to his death, but the others returned safely. That Israel even had planes was top secret, and the stunned Egyptians, fearing it was just the first of a larger assault, stopped cold in their tracks, never to advance further. To this day, a nearby major highway intersection is known as "Ad Halom," as in "up till here" is where the Egyptians reached.

"This was the air force of Israel. These four people and these four junk airplanes," Lenart, who died in 2015, recalled in *Above and Beyond*, a 2014 documentary produced by Nancy Spielberg. "'If you don't go now, they will be in Tel Aviv in the morning and there is no Israel,'" he said he was told.

Of the thirty-three fliers killed or missing in action in the War of Independence, nineteen were overseas volunteers – eight from the United States, six from Canada, three from Britain, and two from South Africa.

Most famous of them was George "Buzz" Beurling, Canada's top World War II ace, who was known as "The Falcon of Malta."

While others were out drinking in pubs, Beurling would stay in his room fiddling with model airplanes and devising new flying tactics. A flying fanatic and maverick by nature, Beurling relished nothing more than a good battle and rightfully earned a reputation as a lethal killing machine.

"I would give ten years of my life to live over again those six months I had in Malta in 1942," he once said. "Combat, it's the only thing I can do well; it's the only thing I ever did that I really liked."[6]

Alongside his legendary skills, Beurling was also known to have disciplinary issues and there were those who feared adding him to Machal.[7] Eventually though, his value far outweighed these concerns, and it was Canada's most highly decorated World War II Jewish serviceman, ace pilot Sydney Shulemson, who recruited Beurling and many of the nearly 300 Canadians who ultimately volunteered – more than a third of whom were air force men.[8]

Beurling, though, never got a piece of the action. He perished when the Norseman plane he was preparing to fly to Israel mysteriously burst into flames and crashed at a small airport near Rome in May 1948. It was never proven, but long suspected, that British forces nearing the end of their mandate were wary of the Jews recruiting such an asset and had sabotaged the plane. Beurling was buried at the military cemetery in Haifa, three plots over from Fred Stevenson.

That Israel had any planes at all is itself a miracle. As late as May 2, just two weeks before the war, they had none.

The first pair to arrive were those that Lenart and Coleman Goldstein flew from Italy over the Mediterranean Sea. The next morning, they were already dropping supplies to kibbutzim and that was the beginning of the Israel Air Force.

"It was the dumbest thing we ever did, flying eleven hours over water with a single-engine aircraft," Goldstein said in *Above and Beyond*. "The only person I ever know who did that was Lindbergh."

Lenart and Goldstein ultimately stayed in Israel and became El Al pilots.

Israel's unlikely air force took shape mostly thanks to the efforts of Al Schwimmer, who was indicted for violating the US Neutrality Acts and lost his citizenship. He stayed in Israel and founded Israel Aircraft Industries. Only in 2001 was he pardoned by President Bill Clinton.

Schwimmer smuggled various bombers and transport aircraft out of the United States just in time via a bogus Panamanian aviation company called Lineas Aereas de Panama. To get around a US arms embargo, and to avoid the British who still ruled Palestine, Schwimmer's pilots had to hop from New York, to Panama, to Brazil, to Morocco, to Italy, and finally to Czechoslovakia, which was the only country willing to break the embargo.

But even there they needed ingenuity for their junkyard planes to make the final leg to Israel. The Avia S-199 fighter planes were versions of the Messerschmitt ME-109s the Nazis flew in World War II; the flight suits were leftovers from the Luftwaffe and still had Nazi wings on them. The volunteers removed the swastika insignia, stripped the planes, and dismembered them in Czechoslovakia to be clandestinely shipped in pieces to Israel aboard larger transport planes, only to be reassembled in hangars in Israel.

The manual firing mechanism required shooting through the propellers, so if the timing was off, there was a danger of shooting oneself down and there is suspicion that's what happened with Eddie Cohen.

Still, to keep the element of surprise, the planes were put into immediate service, without 101 Squadron – Israel's first fighter squadron – ever having a chance for a single test flight.

The Egyptians had no idea what hit them, and it literally saved Israel.

CHAPTER THIRTEEN

Smoky Simon, the South African Witness

The Dakota crash was one of the first fatal aerial accidents in Israel's history. But it barely registered on the radar of a young Jewish state that was suffering daily casualties, and there was not even a reference to it in several newspapers over the following days.

In fact, the *Davar* newspaper reported on the one-year anniversary of the Israeli Air Force in its October 26, 1948 edition and noted with pride on its front page that not a single plane had been shot down in battle.[1] The following day it published a celebratory column by Prime Minister David Ben-Gurion marking the occasion.

The Dakota accident came right between the two major offensives that turned the tide on the battlefield: Operation Yoav, the October 15–22 campaign in the Negev during which Israel captured Beersheba, and Operation Hiram, the October 28–31 campaign during which Israel captured the Upper Galilee.

In terms of plane crashes, it was also considered negligible on the heels of the October 16 death of ace pilot Modi Alon, the commander of Israel's first fighter squadron and hero of its first aerial assault, who crashed his Avia S-199 upon return from a bombing sortie against Egyptian forces.

Even in the less glamorous 103 Squadron, known as the "Elephants Squadron" for the heavy transport loads it carried, the crash was overlooked. The squadron's fleet of Douglas C-47 Dakotas was mostly responsible for airlifting supplies nightly to Negev settlements that had been cut off by Egyptian forces. But some of its aircraft were also used for bombing missions.

In fact, one of the squadron's Bristol Beaufighters was shot down by anti-aircraft fire while attacking an Egyptian-held police fortress on October 20, just four days before Wilf Canter's Dakota went down. The Beaufighter's two Machal crewmembers were killed, Stan Andrews from California and Leonard Fitchett from Vancouver; Fitchett was one of fifteen non-Jewish Canadian pilots in the Israeli Air Force, and he too was buried in the Haifa cemetary in the same row as Fred Stevenson and Buzz Beurling.

All these years later, it was naturally quite difficult to find anyone well enough to remember Canter's crash and all that surrounded it.

Famed Israeli test pilot Dani Shapira told me he had no recollection. He was training in Czechoslovakia at the time and said news of the crash, unlike that of Modi Alon's just over a week earlier, did not even reach him until much later.

Alex Ziloni, an RAF veteran of World War II and one of the founders of the Israeli Air Force, was the first commander of the Tel Nof Air Force Base close to where the Dakota went down. But he too told me that at the age of 103, he had little memory of the night in question.

Even Tolkovsky, the former air force chief who according to military records was in the thick of things at the time of the accident, could not recall the event in detail.

There was one man, though, who had a firsthand connection to the Dakota crash and was still alive and well enough to put it all in context.

Harold "Smoky" Simon was the air force chief of air operations who was alerted on the night of the crash and dispatched a team to investigate it.[2] His life story embodied everything about the burgeoning museum, and he contrasted starkly with my still generally reclusive grandfather.

Getting Zaidy to talk about his wartime past was like squeezing blood from a stone. With "Smoky," all you had to do was open a vein and let it bleed. He needed no prodding. Whatever he remembered, he was ready to share. It was a type of candor to which I was unaccustomed, and which drew me in.

With Canter and his comrades long gone, and with my grandfather sticking to his long-standing silence, Simon had become the closest person I had to someone whose life experience resembled theirs. He was my last live link to the times of Zaidy and his band of brothers.

Sitting in the impeccably kept living room of his home in an exclusive housing complex near the Herzliya beachfront seventy years later, a then-ninety-eight-year-old Simon told me in 2018 that he too had fuzzy recollections of the night in question.

Just four days before the Dakota crash, Simon was dispatched in a twin-engine biplane to search the area of the Beaufighter crash near Isdud. He was looking for Andrews and Fitchett, his fellow foreign volunteers, and was carrying weapons and ammunition to toss down to them should he find them. All he found was the burning wreckage of their plane near the beach and a group of Egyptian soldiers who opened fire on him, forcing his biplane to withdraw.[3]

"It was just another night," Simon said about the Dakota crash, shaking his head. "History is just one damn thing after another. But so many things happened at that time."[4]

Simon couldn't recall ever meeting the four casualties on the flight who, like himself, were foreign volunteers. But the mention of Weimers put him in a reflective mood.

"There were these young Israelis, I just loved them," he said. "Their devotion and the efforts that they made and now that you mention his name, I haven't heard his name I think since those days: 'Michael, King of the Negev.' He was just one of the guys who was so great."

Simon said it was the defining period of his life, and he was full of insight about the foreign volunteers.

"It was a feeling of brotherhood," said Simon, who had headed World Machal, the volunteers' alumni organization, since its 1968 establishment. "You felt that your fellow Jews were in a desperate position, that a war was inevitable, the war clouds were gathering. There was no choice. We were going to do our best and we would fight till the bitter end."

The British were reluctant to let Jews living under their mandate become full-fledged World War II pilots, for fear of how they would use those skills after the war. But the policy changed in 1943, when men like Alon, Weizman, and Tolkovsky got their wings. Weizman, for example, trained in Rhodesia (known today as Zimbabwe), and Tolkovsky, another future Israeli Air Force commander, in South Africa. Tolkovsky became a Spitfire pilot and saw action in Italy, Greece, and France, and both amassed valuable flying hours.

But they were few and far between. Less than twenty-five had qualified as RAF pilots by the time the war ended, and maybe a handful of others had acquired other aircrew trades like navigators and air gunners.[5] When Israel declared independence on May 14, 1948, and found itself on the eve of war, outmatched and outgunned, very few were ready for aerial combat. Veteran World War II pilots like Wilf Canter and Fred Stevenson were invaluable as mentors to the neophyte Israeli airmen.

And there was something else driving them, perhaps still lingering from World War II, which gave Israel's War of Independence a magnetic pull for Jews and non-Jews alike. After helping beat the Nazis, the war in Israel offered them a sense of purpose they just couldn't recreate in routine civilian life.

"There were some guys who really came because of the adventure. They couldn't settle down after World War II," Simon said. "The transition was an enormous transition from serving for years in a war and then coming back to civilian life and you have to adjust to it. You have to rehabilitate yourself."

Either way, he said he could imagine what the crew of the Dakota went through together.

Photo 13.1. Smoky Simon (center) and others planning Israel's first B-17 attack in 1948
(Courtesy of Saul Simon.)

"This terrific union, different remote guys, objectives, backgrounds and here they come together and have an accident of this nature," he said, his voice trailing off.

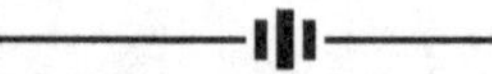

Even as Smoky approached 100, he had remained relatively spry, dashing his slouched, slender frame around his apartment to retrieve mementos to share. He loaned me the video of Nancy Spielberg's documentary *Above and Beyond* and we exchanged impressions. His slicked-back thinning hair and snow-white goatee gave off a debonair mystique even at his advanced age. And his memory was remarkably sharp.

Photo 13.2. Smoky Simon (second from the left) with General Amikam Norkin, the then–air force chief (second from the right), and other founders of the Israeli Air Force in 2020
(Courtesy of Saul Simon.)

Simon went on to establish a leading life insurance agency in Israel that was eventually folded into the giant Migdal corporation. He lived in Herzliya and kept active in Machal. He even took a flight on an old Tiger Moth aircraft for his 100th birthday.[6]

A native of South Africa, Simon served in two World War II commands, taking part in sixty missions overall. He served in Bomber Command in North Africa, participating in the battle of El-Alamein, and in the coastal command of flying boats in the United Kingdom, patrolling the Atlantic and the Indian oceans and chasing subs that were threatening commercial vessels.

He said he was driven to volunteer for World War II air force service for the same reason my Zaidy once gave: to get even with Hitler.

"I wanted to join up because I developed such a hatred for the Germans," he told me. "I felt that whatever I could do to kill Germans in the war would really be my whole mission."

He spent nearly five years in the air force as a navigator bombardier, from January 1941 until the end of November 1945. After returning, he started a business, married, and then – under the guise of a honeymoon to Europe – headed to the Holy Land, arriving on May 9, 1948, with the first batch of South African volunteers.[7]

There he became one of the founders of the Israeli Air Force. He flew twenty-four missions, including the first one ever of the Israeli Air Force, before he was appointed the air force's first chief of air operations in June 1948 and served in the role until 1950.

That first flight came even before the war officially started, a reconnaissance mission over Jordan to scope out their British-trained forces.

"This flight was at the very time that Ben-Gurion was declaring the State of Israel," he said. "When we got airborne, we were in Palestine and when we returned from the mission we were in Israel. It just happened that way."

He keenly recalled the strong sense of brotherhood that developed among the Machalniks. "There was an opportunity. None of us knew really what was involved," he said.

"I'm very sensitive to the loss of life, but you sort of come to terms with the reality. There is one factor that you can't define and that is fate."

Even so, he said he was fortunate to escape any real trauma from his various war experiences.

"I was terribly lucky. I said to myself, 'I am going to live through this experience,' and there are some guys who really used to worry like hell if they were going to make it," he said. "I just had this feeling – 'I'm going to get out of this. I'm going to see it through.' And thank God it worked out that way. I came out with no injuries and having lived through a terrific experience."

On March 1, 2022, on a pleasant, sunny day in Herzliya, just days after Russia invaded Ukraine and sparked warnings of a World War III, Harold "Smoky" Simon was laid to rest.[8] I had just written to him with a follow-up question about my research and had received no response.

On February 28, a note from his family informed me that he had passed away in his sleep the previous night, just short of his 102nd birthday. He left behind his wife, Myra, four children, fifteen grandchildren, and twenty-two great-grandchildren.

At the funeral, his children and grandchildren gave moving tributes, as did his best friend, noted entrepreneur Morris Kahn, an air force general, a former air force chief, and former president Reuven Rivlin, who called him a symbol of a "true Zionist."

"There is no higher test of courage than to put your life on the line and you did that several times," said his son Saul, himself a former pilot. "The chance of surviving the 1948 war was less than World War II. It was as close as you could get to a suicide mission."

Simon had once told me that he belonged to a "highly endangered species," and his passing felt like a chapter had truly ended. He was the most active of the Machalniks and with him now gone, it was questionable whether any actual veterans would be able to attend the official museum opening, if that would ever happen.

Zaidy would never be like Smoky Simon. He was just cut from a different cloth. Simon would have been a much more willing and captivating subject for a grandson's memoir.

But as each one of these veterans died, it highlighted how special it was to still have someone like Zaidy among us. I'd made my peace with his choices long ago and Simon's passing made me just feel so fortunate to have the chance to tell even a small part of Zaidy's story while he was still alive.

The Hellers

CHAPTER FOURTEEN

Samuel Heller, the World War I Veteran Father

In my quest to uncover any details about Zaidy's World War II past, I came across a new resource in 2015. The Canadian military attaché to Israel at the time pointed me toward all the open-source information available in Canada's online archive. There, I was confronted once again with the knowledge that as long as Zaidy was alive, I would need his written approval to access his military file. I knew it was a long shot, but I was determined to try. I prepared the paperwork for my parents to deliver to him during an upcoming visit.

In the meantime, I kept scouring and found that older files, such as those of World War I veterans, were open to the public. So, on a whim, I put in the name of Zaidy's father, Samuel Heller. In an instant, it was there – the man's attestation paper from October 1, 1915.

TRIPLICATE

ATTESTATION PAPER.

No. 348102

Folio.

CANADIAN OVER-SEAS EXPEDITIONARY FORCE.

QUESTIONS TO BE PUT BEFORE ATTESTATION.

(ANSWERS)

1. What is your name? — Samuel Heller.
2. In what Town, Township or Parish, and in what Country were you born? — Vladivostock. Russia.
3. What is the name of your next-of-kin? — (Father) Abram Heller.
4. What is the address of your next-of-kin? — 112 Parliament St. Toronto.
5. What is the date of your birth? — 11 Jany. 1882.
6. What is your Trade or Calling? — Merchant.
7. Are you married? — yes.
8. Are you willing to be vaccinated or re-vaccinated? or inoculated? — yes
9. Do you now belong to the Active Militia? — no
10. Have you ever served in any Military Force? If so, state particulars of former Service. — C Bty. RCHA
11. Do you understand the nature and terms of your engagement? — yes
12. Are you willing to be attested to serve in the Canadian Over-Seas Expeditionary Force? — yes

S. Heller (Signature of Man.)

H. W. Lean Br (Signature of Witness.)

DECLARATION TO BE MADE BY MAN ON ATTESTATION.

I, Samuel Heller, do solemnly declare that the above answers made by me to the above questions are true, and that I am willing to fulfil the engagements by me now made, and I hereby engage and agree to serve in the **Canadian Over-Seas Expeditionary Force,** and to be attached to any arm of the service therein, for the term of one year, or during the war now existing between Great Britain and Germany should that war last longer than one year, and for six months after the termination of that war provided His Majesty should so long require my services, or until legally discharged.

S. Heller (Signature of Recruit)

Date OCT 1915 191 H. W. Lean Br (Signature of Witness)

OATH TO BE TAKEN BY MAN ON ATTESTATION.

I, Samuel Heller, do make Oath, that I will be faithful and bear true Allegiance to His Majesty **King George the Fifth,** His Heirs and Successors, and that I will as in duty bound honestly and faithfully defend His Majesty, His Heirs and Successors, in Person, Crown and Dignity, against all enemies, and will observe and obey all orders of His Majesty, His Heirs and Successors, and of all the Generals and Officers set over me. So help me God.

S. Heller (Signature of Recruit)

Date OCT 1915 191 H. W. Lean Br (Signature of Witness)

CERTIFICATE OF MAGISTRATE.

The Recruit above-named was cautioned by me that if he made any false answer to any of the above questions he would be liable to be punished as provided in the Army Act.

The above questions were then read to the Recruit in my presence.

I have taken care that he understands each question, and that his answer to each question has been duly entered as replied to, and the said Recruit has made and signed the declaration and taken the oath before me, at Dauphin this 1st day of October 1915.

G Hunter Lieut-Col (Signature of Justice)

I certify that the above is a true copy of the Attestation of the above-named Recruit.

(Approving Officer)

M. F. W. 23.
200 M.—7-15.
H. Q. 1772-39-551.

Photo 14.1. Samuel Heller's World War I attestation paper (Courtesy of the Heller family)

It was fascinating to see it on my computer screen, my great-grandfather's century-old handwriting. I immediately noticed that he looped the "l" in Heller just like my father and I did. But beyond that curiosity, there was actual information in there of which neither Zaidy nor I had been aware.

Zaidy said his father arrived from Russia, near St. Petersburg, but in Samuel's statement his place of birth says Vladivostok, on the Pacific coast near the border with China and Korea.

That was likely a clerical error. Who knows what went on back then? Samuel followed in his older brother Morris's footsteps in migrating to Canada and they were the first to go by Heller after it was changed from the original Nachimovsky. Family lore has it that upon immigration to Canada, the border official quipped to Morris, "What the hell kind of a name is that?" and, voila, we became Hellers.

Samuel's paperwork listed his next of kin as his father Abram, though the man went by Efraim. Samuel said he was a merchant, 5'7" in height, with dark complexion, blue eyes and brown hair. His girth, when fully expanded, was 36 inches, and its range of expansion was three inches.

He identified himself as Jewish and attested that he was willing to serve in the Canadian Overseas Expeditionary Force. A doctor who examined him said he was "fit" to serve.

Samuel Heller is a mysterious figure in our family history, with stories circulated (mostly by my late great-aunt Jeanette) that something went wrong with him in World War I. He was even more tight-lipped about this world war than his youngest son eventually became about the second. The only evidence we had that he served were the pictures of

Photo 14.2. Samuel Heller as a member of the Royal Canadian Horse Artillery in World War I
(Courtesy of the Heller family.)

him in uniform: one where he posed with his young family and another where he was alone on horseback as a member of the Royal Canadian Horse Artillery in World War I.

Samuel later separated from his wife, an anomaly for a Jew at the time, and slowly distanced himself from the rest of the family. Not much was spoken about him, and he died alone in a nursing home in 1955.

When I shared these newly discovered details with Zaidy about his father, he got curious.

"I could just as easily get your record if you give me authorization," I finally blurted.

Zaidy demurred, saying it was a waste of time and he probably had it around somewhere anyway, if he didn't get rid of it in their spring 2014 move to a retirement community.

"We threw a lot of stuff away," he said.

That was unfortunate, but I wouldn't put it past him and especially Bubby. She was not the most sentimental type and once tossed away a treasured baseball card of my dad's – a Mickey Mantle rookie card – that if well preserved would today be worth millions of dollars. When they moved into a retirement home, we had to beg them to send to Israel a shipment of family items that they would have otherwise trashed in the downsizing operation.

Regardless, I hoped that the mention of his father would get Zaidy to play ball. All he had to do was sign on the dotted line of the form I had prepared. But it wasn't to be. Zaidy refrained from signing. He was going underground again.

It was five years later, amid a global pandemic, when the ghost of Samuel Heller reemerged in our life.

Zaidy and I had kept up in emails and phone conversations, and he gladly informed me that he had taught his devoted Filipina caregiver, Jojo, how to play Clubbyish during the frequent lockdowns in their complex.

We were back to our usual correspondences. We'd left most of the war talk behind. That chapter appeared to have passed. The one rule I set for myself throughout was that I would take him only as far as he was willing to go. Anytime he put on the brakes, I respected his wishes to "let it lie."

Yet somehow there was always something new that popped up and extended our exchange. This time it was the discovery of the comprehensive Library and Archives Canada website.[1] Years ago, I had obtained the attestation paper his father had filled out upon enlisting. But now I had something far more comprehensive: it was the full 176-page war record of Samuel Heller.[2]

I scoured through the document and shared my findings with Zaidy and other relatives.

Though filled with inaccuracies, it was fascinating just to see a scan of this century-old handwritten and typed document about our family patriarch. I noted to myself with irony how Zaidy's father's own military service was also shrouded in mystery.

The record was packed with information, particularly about Samuel's various medical ailments. Zaidy's father, it appears, was hospitalized frequently and eventually discharged for being medically unfit. Unbeknownst to any of his grandchildren, Samuel had served in France and

England but didn't appear to see much action as a member of the Royal Canadian Horse Artillery.

Already a father of six, Samuel Heller enlisted weighing 195 pounds and dropped to 145 pounds by the time he went home. His medical file detailed a series of stomach issues, neuralgia, myalgia, serious gland inflammations, and partial loss of his vision. He was diagnosed with a "high degree of hypermetropia" that granted him a 20 percent disability. It's unclear if he contracted syphilis, or another venereal disease, but he was given treatment for a grayish-pink gland the "size of a small walnut." A November 24, 1918, checkup revealed "swelling in left groin" and "small ulcer, left leg." There was also an inconclusive gonorrhea casesheet in his file.

Before his enlistment he could hoist heavy weights, but by 1918 he couldn't lift 150 pounds, and he tired after walking a mile. In France, he was hospitalized for six months because of his gastritis, and he frequently complained about heartburn that made it hard for him to eat. Overall, he was overseas in France for two years and his reason for returning home was "sick" on account of his lymphosarcoma, chronic gastritis, and loss of vision.

On June 26, 1919, Pte. Heller, no. 348102, was discharged as "medically unfit."

Other bits of information included that he was paid $45 a month throughout the war. Most of the forms show him aged thirty-two when he enlisted in 1915 but aged forty-five when he was discharged in 1919. However, according to our family records, he was born on January 11, 1882, which would have made him thirty-three upon enlistment.

Whichever was correct, it was an unusually old age to head off to war, and he was nearly forty by the time Zaidy was born in 1921.

I called Zaidy to ask what in the file was new to him.

"All of it. I didn't know anything about it," he replied. "He never told me, and I never asked him."

That wasn't going to happen with us. I was going to ask, and I hoped that he was eventually going to tell.

Discovering the background of Samuel Heller sparked a great deal of interest among Zaidy's children, with one of my uncles asking me if I could now get access to Zaidy's service file as well.

Sigh. That's what got me started on this journey in the first place. But, as I informed my uncle, this was not possible without Zaidy's written consent, and he'd made it clear to me several times that he wouldn't grant it.

Yes, it would be unfortunate for him to die without signing the consent, since that would mean that his service record would likely remain classified for an additional twenty years after his eventual death. But I was now far more at peace with the prospect of not acquiring his full record, having surmised from all our conversations and all my own lengthy research that there probably wasn't much there to discover in the first place.

Photo 14.3. Mickey Heller and his father, Samuel
(Courtesy of the Heller family.)

CHAPTER FIFTEEN

Mickey Heller, a Veteran's Journey Revealed

My Zaidy was a man of his generation. He wasn't a big conversationalist and it took a lot to get him to open up in general – and about the war in particular. Long-distance phone conversations were never going to cut it. They were typically brief, to the point, superficial and prone to end abruptly. For anything of significance to emerge, it would have to come in person, one-on-one, face-to-face, the way men used to talk, where dodging engagement was far more difficult.

There was a certain alchemy required for Zaidy to be in the state of mind where we could connect on that level. With me a half a world away, those opportunities were fleeting. But I made a point of at least trying to create it anytime we were together.

In September 2013, my third visit to Toronto in three years, this proved especially difficult. We were there for

Bubby, to celebrate her ninetieth birthday. The extended family had come together from Israel and my parents were staying with Bubby and Zaidy while my wife, nineteen-month-old daughter, and I were staying at my uncle's. We were only there for a few days, which were packed with large family gatherings. With my parents in the mix, a toddler on the move, preparations for the birthday party, and just plain jetlag throwing me off, the moment simply did not present itself.

In a quiet moment away from the crowd, I found an open letter lying on his meticulously kept desk. It was from the Jewish War Veterans of Canada, inviting him to a ceremony for Remembrance Day on November 11, 2013. The invitation said they would be honored to have him attend and a front row seat had been saved for him.

Just then, I was struck by a realization I should have noticed sooner. The reason he'd be such a distinguished guest is that, at ninety-two, he was likely among the last of the Canadian World War II veterans dispatched to Europe who were still around and in good health. Zaidy came back from the war in 1944 when he was twenty-three years old. How many others his age or older could still be alive, coherent, and involved in 2013?

In my Holocaust reporting I kept referring to the dwindling number of survivors who remained with real memories to share. The accepted number at the time was believed to be roughly 200,000 survivors in Israel and a similar number worldwide. But that included those who were too old and frail to access their memories and those who were too young to have had any memories of their own. Those with actual, life-lived stories to convey were far fewer, and this was even truer for World War II veterans who, by definition, had to be at least ninety years old at this stage.

I suppose my urgency to encourage Zaidy to speak derived from this realization that the passage of time had truly made him one of the "last of the Mohicans," as he was apt to call himself. He was one of those last live witnesses to the war. After him, we'd be entering a new era of history, one in which everything we learned about the war would come from books, recordings, and films. My grandparents were still doing well, but for how much longer?

Even with his continued reticence, Zaidy seemed to understand that too. Just as I was about to leave his apartment, he stopped me and gestured toward a painting that had been hanging on the wall for as long as I could remember. It was one of his favorites, depicting two boys in vibrant colors perched on a tree they had climbed. He said it reminded him of a childhood photograph of me and my cousin in a similar pose. He'd wedged that photo in the corner of the frame, along with a reproduction we choreographed some thirty years later.

"You want it?" he suddenly asked.

I was taken aback. "Why? Where are you going?" I responded.

"Well, I don't want to go anywhere, but your Bubby keeps talking about moving into a retirement home," he said. "I tell her she can go by herself. Get me a girl to cook and clean around here and I'll be fine," he added with a smirk.

"Keep it," I replied. "You aren't going anywhere."

But he insisted. One way or another, the day was nearing when this apartment would be emptied, he said, and

Photo 15.1. Lancaster bombers
(Photo credit: Aron Heller.)

their belongings dispersed. He wanted me to have it, and I reluctantly agreed. Instinctively, I then guided him back to his study. If he was already handing out early inheritances, there was something else I wanted.

"I'll take that too," I said, pointing to the framed photograph above his computer.

It was a wide-angle image of a pair of airborne Lancaster bombers. His late friend Sammy Greisman, in London, sent it to him years ago with an inscription on the back. It's the only personal war-related item Zaidy had ever displayed in his home, and I could sense it had a significance that he had yet to articulate. He hesitated for a moment.

"Once I'm gone, you can have that too," he said.

It was on my fourth visit to Toronto in this journey, in the summer of 2015, when I went in for broke. I had prepared a consent form for access to his war records that I had my parents deliver to him on a previous visit. He declined. But this was my project. I couldn't in good conscience not at least try on my own.

An intimate lunch with Bubby and Zaidy at their new retirement home was going to be my only solo time with them and perhaps the last pitch I'd be able to make in this personal journey that increasingly looked like it had run its course.

Bubby and Zaidy were doing remarkably well. They were both sharp, generally healthy, and still sporting witty senses of humor. The retirement home seemed to have done them good, and they managed to reinvent themselves among their fellow nonagenarians. But at the core they remained the same, and that rang true with Zaidy's still cagey back-and-forth with me about the war.

At the lunch hall, Zaidy introduced me to a fellow veteran who had provided me with a detailed list of Jewish Canadians who fought in Europe (I donated it to the burgeoning museum).

Zaidy showed me some old newspaper front pages he had saved from his wartime voyage to Europe. The November 1, 1942, edition of the *Elizabethan News* included headlines such as "Strong Japanese Fleet Unit Bombed" and "Rommel's Tank Attacks Held by Eighth Army." But when it came to him – still nothing.

With nothing to lose, I handed him a copy of his father's attestation paper. He studied it with interest.

And then I went for the ultimate Hail Mary. Casually sliding the consent form across the bridge table, I added: "I could get your military record too if you just sign this."

Deftly, he sidestepped it and once again we moved on, in what seemed like a fitting coda to the delicate dance we'd been having for years.

It felt like the closure I needed. I suppose some things were better left unsaid, and the bottom line is that if someone truly does not want to talk, they just can't be made.

I was content with giving it a good try. I'd laid out every opportunity before him and even did the legwork to make it possible. He chose otherwise. I could respect that and let it go with a clear conscience. I figured that I may seek out his record after he died, or I may not. It's a chapter of his life he seemed intent on keeping buried, just like so many of the stories of so many others who were literally buried with theirs.

And that's the way he seemed to want it.

It was Sunday morning, January 30, 2017, when I was awoken by a text message at 5:30 a.m. from my mother asking me to call right away.

Instinctively, I feared for Zaidy. But it wasn't him. I'm sure from his perspective, it was far worse.

An hour earlier, Bubby had gotten out of bed to go to the bathroom, and she'd collapsed on the way. Her heart just stopped. Zaidy called the medics but there was nothing they could do. She was gone.

As my parents scurried to find a flight, I called my grandparents' apartment. Zaidy quickly picked up.

"I'm holding up," he said, in a surprisingly calm voice. "They couldn't resuscitate her."

In a later call, he sounded shakier and on the verge of tears as he told me how much they were looking forward to seeing me and the kids in our planned visit later in the year. It was then that two things became clear to me. (A) I should go to the funeral to honor my Bubby. (B) For the first time in his ninety-five years, Zaidy was going to be alone.

That realization immediately took me to a story I had just written for International Holocaust Day. In dozens of features on survivors, I had focused on various themes of their unique existence. This one was apt since it dealt with aging nonagenarians, and that for those living out their final days the greatest concern was loneliness.

The focus of my story was Ernst Weiner, a blind, widowed survivor who was confined to a wheelchair and lived alone in an apartment south of Tel Aviv, and how a group of volunteers visited him frequently so that he had someone to talk to and share his life's story.[1]

"It's not pleasant to be alone," he told me shortly before a birthday party for him organized by concerned volunteers.

Zaidy's situation was much different. He was surrounded by people in his assisted living complex and still had two children and five grandchildren in Toronto. But he was now without his partner and best friend. I couldn't help but wonder whether this new status would make him more outgoing and ready to share, or, more likely, increasingly vulnerable and introverted.

Life with Bubby allowed Zaidy to maintain that quiet veneer. She was the dominant force in the family, the stereotypical Jewish matriarch. Her strongest attribute was her toughness, and she went out like she lived. When it was over, it was over. Even though she was ninety-three, I suppose her death caught us off guard because she was so tough.

Days later, I delivered a eulogy along that theme.

> You had to be tough when you were the youngest, and the only girl in a family of brothers. You had to be tough when your family fled Poland, twice, to flee antisemitism and start a new life in Canada. You had to be tough when your fiancé was off at war and when times were rough with your husband on the road and three little boys to take care of at home. And you had to be tough when you grew older, when illness struck and when friends, relatives and everyone else around started passing away.

On the plane ride over, I wrote the following passage as well.

> Her passing is not just the passing of the matriarch of this extended family of 4 children, 9 grandchildren and 8 great-grandchildren. It's also in a way the penultimate chapter of a generation – a generation some have coined the Greatest Generation. As the youngest and last survivors of their families, Bubby and Zaidy were our last link to that era.

Zaidy was now truly the last one left. When I arrived in Toronto, he looked good. His white goatee had grown out

Photo 15.2. Mickey and Eunice Heller dancing

to a full-fledged beard, and he smiled when I told him he looked a bit like Sean Connery.

When we had a moment alone, he said he hadn't been able to really cry yet. And then a tear appeared in the corner of his eye.

"It's a long time to be with someone," he said. "I'll be with her soon."

The following day was the funeral.

A pair of black limos took the extended family to Beth Tzedec synagogue, where the rabbi's sermon included the retelling of my grandfather's version of his engagement to my grandmother.

At the burial in the snowy cemetery, Zaidy was stoic. The frozen earth had already been shoveled out and before it was poured back atop Bubby's casket in the grave, Zaidy silently tossed in the same Valentine's Day card he had been annually giving her as a love letter for decades.

It was emotional, but in my five days in Toronto, even as a pallbearer, I found myself thinking very little about Bubby. My entire focus was directed toward Zaidy as we sat shiva together at his retirement home.

It's true that I was closer to him than to her, but the reason was purely practical: there was nothing more I could do for her now. Zaidy and I developed a ritual at mealtime: I'd push his chair in and strap a napkin around his neck with a chain he kept in his pocket. After the meal in a dining hall, I'd get his walker and then place a pillow on a chair in the corner of the room where I'd help him ease down and receive visitors. Then, after the visitors left, I would help him to the elevator and get him set up for a nap in his apartment.

Beyond the physical help, though, I was fascinated by the way he was coping. On the one hand, he was liberated. In intimate gatherings throughout the week, his wry sense of humor shined, and he regaled us with his outstanding memory, sharing stories that none of his children had ever heard before. There was the time he nearly died, skidding off the road in an Ontario winter in his years as a traveling salesman and how he parked the driver's side of the car by the curb for weeks after so that Bubby wouldn't discover the resulting dent.

He recalled the exact price and model of his first car and the names of long-gone relatives. He shared stories about his adventures on the road as he was trying to get his business going.

One of his best zingers came when I complimented the bedside manner of a young rabbi who came to comfort him and hear about his long life with Bubby.

"It's a tough job," Zaidy deadpanned. "It's no job for a Jewish boy."

Zaidy was holding court in a way our domineering grandmother would never have let him get away with if she were around.

For the most part, though, Zaidy was reserved and deeply appreciative of all of us who had arrived from as far away as Israel.

"I'm very proud of all of you this morning. Of all the grandkids, Bubby would have been so happy," he said, after my siblings and I were called to the Torah for the Thursday morning service. "People don't know what they are missing if they don't have a shiva. It helps you get through. It brings you back."

The best sign was that Zaidy appeared to want to come back. He still had a strong desire to live. He told me about a recent medical checkup when he asked the doctor how many of his prescribed pills he had to take, to which the doctor responded: "How long do you want to live?"

"So, what did you do?" I asked.

"I took the pills," he replied.

In spending so much time with him, I felt like we bonded in a way we never had before. It also reminded me of what I took away from my other encounters with elderly people. Most were beyond the nonsense of daily life and had a refreshing perspective on the big picture. At the end of the day, Zaidy said all that mattered was the people around you that you loved.

"You know, I loved her more at the end than I did at the beginning," he told me, his voice cracking. "It just grew."

"I don't know if she loved me back as much," he added, his voice trailing off.

"I have no regrets about anything. But I'll never forgive her for going first," he said.

"But then you'd be leaving her with grief. You did her a mitzvah by outliving her," I noted.

"Women handle this better," he concluded.

With all the newfound candor there was still one topic Zaidy was sparse about in detail. When a visitor paying her condolences noticed their wedding picture, with him in uniform, she tried to strike up a conversation about his service.

"Who won the war?" Zaidy asked jokingly.

"Thanks to you, we did," came the response. "Where were you?"

"Oh, I was all over the place," he said, bringing the exchange to an abrupt end.

When asked what his father, who died in 1955, had thought about his service and whether they had compared their experiences, Zaidy said, "We didn't talk much about stuff."

That seemed to be the model for men in our family. As Zaidy often said when asked to reflect upon the past: "What was, was."

Zaidy had mellowed and the week of shiva gave me a renewed appreciation of the man. I returned home to Israel intent on speaking to him more often. We set up a regular time for him to see my children and I promised to return with them later that year for an extended visit.

The shiva, and the intimate exchanges it spawned, helped me finally feel satisfied with just getting to know him better in his final years, regardless of what he had to say about his past.

It was late 2017 when our much-anticipated family visit to Toronto finally arrived. Everyone was excited: our youngest, a three-year-old, had mastered the family tree and was talking about her "Sabba's Abba." Her older sister, now nearly six, kept telling everyone how her great-grandfather was 100 years old, minus four, and she was eager to play cards with him and show off the Yiddish expressions I had taught her for just the occasion. And I was looking forward to just seeing him again, hearing how he had coped with a first year of widowhood. Though I was done with my probing, I still packed the consent form for his military record. Just in case.

It was great to see how our expected visit was filling him with excitement. Upon our arrival to my in-laws in Detroit twelve days earlier, he informed me that in addition to Shabbat dinner at my uncle's, he was going to take us out for lunch AND dinner, and we already had a brunch date set at his favorite place – United Bakers Dairy Restaurant at Lawrence Plaza. But as the day drew nearer, Zaidy seemed to be weakening. He'd been struggling with an earache that turned into a cold and in between coughs he jokingly promised me over the phone that he was going to try to "make it" till we got there. "You better," I replied in jest. But on the day of our departure from Detroit for Toronto, I got the following email that was far less jovial.

"It looks like I will have to cancel for United on Wednesday. I have developed a temperature and if I do not get any better it would also be for Friday night. What a bummer? Sorry – Zaidy. Please confirm."

Besides the novelty of a ninety-six-year-old man using the term "bummer," this really was a drag. The primary goal of the trip was to see him, and his illness was indeed a bad omen. In a follow-up phone call, I tried to cheer him up. But I had an ominous feeling as I made the four-hour drive to Toronto later that afternoon. The following morning, upon waking, I discovered that things had taken a turn for the worse overnight. He had passed out in the bathroom, fallen on his back, and been taken to hospital. Scans revealed he had pneumonia. They had him plugged into an antibiotic drip in an infectious room where you had to suit up to see him. He was coughing every few seconds – causing him great pain in his back. When I called, he could barely talk. All he could say was "sorry" about the inauspicious timing.

Our visit was suddenly upended. I rushed over to Sunnybrook hospital, suited up in a gown, gloves, and mask and tiptoed into his room. He was slumped in a chair, looking into space, his hair uncharacteristically disheveled. When he saw me, he audibly sighed "Aron" but then quickly shooed me when I tried to give him a hug. "I don't want you getting sick or taking anything back to your girls," he admonished me. He was more depressed than I had ever seen him, groaning after fits of coughing and seemingly tired of life. "I thought I was going to meet my maker," he said.

I got an update from his doctor and relayed the information to my parents in Israel, got to know the nursing staff and told them I was available. But there wasn't much else to do or even say. He was edgy and I was unsettled, and I mostly just waited for his cues, which didn't come. He told me not to visit again and definitely not to bring the kids. His only request, to which I gladly obliged, was to take a thin comb out of his bag, wet it with water, and comb his thin white hair back into place.

I called in frequently the following days. Sometimes he sounded stronger and sometimes he was struggling and just said, "Aron, I can't talk," and hung up. The medication was kicking in and he appeared to be out of immediate danger. But I had a creeping suspicion that he didn't want anyone seeing him the way he was.

Finally, after three restless days, I returned. He was no longer infectious, and I told him we were going to have dinner together one way or another – even if that meant sharing bland hospital food.

When I arrived a few hours later he was sleeping in his bed, his thin, pale legs sticking out from beneath the sheet. His silver watch slung on his wrist and the signature black masonic ring he wore on his finger lay on his chest. I just watched him for about forty-five minutes, which turned into the most calming and comforting moments of my turbulent Toronto stay. I just thought about him, the life he had lived, and how he could hold his head high if it was to end tomorrow.

He woke up, just before his dinner was served, and I helped him with his tray. He seemed to be improving, but our conversation was fitful. There just wasn't much to say. After finishing his banana, muffin, and tea, he said he needed to be alone so he could sleep. All I could muster as I put on my jacket was an "I love you, Zaidy." I left the room feeling like it was the last time I was going to see him.

"I love you too," he said, fighting back tears. "I love everybody."

Zaidy was discharged a few weeks later. After a few days at home, he was briefly hospitalized again. Eventually he settled back into his place with Jojo, his lovely live-in caregiver.

Soon after that, Efrat Gal and Tal Landman came into my life and the pursuit of Wilf Canter's story kicked into high gear. I had given up on the Zaidy "war project," but when it came to Canter, he proved to be a willing accomplice.

Delving so deeply into the lives of Canter, Stevenson, and Fisher naturally evoked the realization that by this point I knew a lot more about these Canadian veterans than I did about my own grandfather. We had talked a lot and yet he still hadn't shared anything of substance about his own service. I still had no military knowledge about him.

As was our custom, I would update Zaidy about my findings and he'd generally express interest. Now, under the guise of contributing research to the Canter story, he said he'd look to see if he still had anything hanging around. Since my parents were soon coming to visit him in Toronto, I asked if they could make a copy of any wartime mementos that he had.

"Who needs a copy?" he replied. "You can have it. What do I need all that stuff for anymore?"

My parents returned from Toronto with a brown manila envelope addressed to me from Zaidy. It was weighted, and I soon found out why. He had sent me his medals.

Photo 15.3. Mickey Heller's medals from World War II
(Photo credit: Aron Heller.)

Three were attached together, silver coins hanging from multicolored badges. One was for voluntary service, another was the "Defence Medal" bearing the image of King George VI, and the last one with Latin writing also featured the king with a crown on his head.

One of them had a pin attached to it with an image of a plane. Zaidy explained that it was for being a member of Bomber Command. And the others? "I don't know. I guess for coming back alive," he told me in a phone chat later that day.

A final, separate bronze medal of the Jewish War Veterans of Canada featured, on its back, an infantryman holding a Star of David.

Years of nagging felt like they had finally paid off. In my hands, I now had something tangible connecting me to his past. It was a memento I planned to treasure and hold close unless I was asked to contribute it to the future museum. Either way, I knew it was better in my hands than in his.

The rest of the package he sent included printed images of the memorial Zaidy dedicated in Toronto and a bland letter he received in the 1980s from his old comrade Sammy Greisman. Of interesting note was his RCAF identity card, number 160820, from June 9, 1944, with a picture of him back when he still had a full head of hair.

There was also his British RAF permanent pass from Dishforth, with permission to wear plain clothing within a twenty-five-meter radius of the base. The great reveal, from my perspective, was the name of his unit. It was the first real piece of evidence I had found relating to the details of his service. And there it was, handwritten in simple bold letters: 426 R.C.A.F. SQDN.

The 426 Squadron of the RCAF was known as the Thunderbird Squadron. It was established at Dishforth on October 15, 1942, as part of No. 4 Group and was later transferred to the more famous No. 6 Group and primarily flew Vickers Wellingtons on night bombing missions. (RAF personnel nicknamed the Wellington "Wimpy," after the portly J. Wellington Wimpy character from the *Popeye* cartoons.) In June 1943, it switched to Lancaster bombers, the kind of bombers that were featured in the photograph hanging in Zaidy's home office. In April 1944, the squadron began converting to Halifax bombers.[2]

Photo 15.4. Mickey Heller's RCAF ID card and permanent pass from the British RAF
(Photo credit: Aron Heller.)

The mythical thunderbird featured in the 426 Squadron crest originated from native North Americans. According to myth, the thunderbird signifies disaster and death to anyone on the ground who perceives it. The squadron motto read "on wings of fire." Adding to its mystique, 426 Squadron lost exactly 426 aircrew during World War II.

Overall, the squadron flew 261 operational missions that involved 3,213 sorties. It lost 88 aircraft before its last operation on April 25, 1945.[3] A month later it was rededicated as a transport squadron.

The squadron's most heroic moment likely happened on October 20, 1943, when bombers were dispatched to attack Leipzig. One aircraft was pelted with gunfire from German fighter jets that shattered the cockpit and gun turrets, poked holes in the fuel tanks, and destroyed hydraulics and navigation instruments. But the pilot, Frederick John Stuart, still managed to bomb his targets before guiding his crippled aircraft back to base.[4]

If my Zaidy had anything to do with this, I still had no idea.

The most powerful finding in Zaidy's package, however, was a copy of a letter he'd sent the *Globe and Mail* the previous year in response to a travel column a certain Catherine Dunphy had written about Scotland. In it, he disclosed to a stranger just the kind of tale I had always hoped he would share with me.

"I thought I was the only one in the world who knew where WIGTOWN was," he began his letter, before detailing how he ended up there.

Zaidy, it appears, first landed in Glasgow before spending the next six weeks in Bournemouth in southern England. In December 1942, he was shipped out to Wigtown for a six-week course in night flying. It's where he learned how to navigate at night using the stars.

Zaidy recalled how they would return from training to their base at 3 a.m. and be treated to a breakfast of porridge and kippers, with no milk and no brown sugar. "That was hard for my Canadian stomach to digest," he wrote.

It was cold and wet in Wigtown over New Year's, but Zaidy said RAF rules stipulated they were not allowed to wear their military-issued rubber boots unless it snowed. They were also only allowed one small scuttle of coal to heat their room. "This lasted only about one hour before we were freezing," he wrote. The solution my twenty-one-year-old grandfather and his buddies found was to climb the barbed wire surrounding the coal yard. "All well and good except at night I tripped and sprained my ankle very badly," he wrote.

Thanks to this prank, Zaidy ended up in the hospital, which he described as a blessing. "I spent five lovely warm days and nights there," he recounted. "The hospital was warm day and night. A bath was available every day, although only five inches of hot water."

Another memory he had of Wigtown was coming out of the local pub one night and hearing hobnailed boots on the cobblestones. "Expecting to see a brawny six-foot kilted Scotsman come in view, what I did see was a wee tyke wearing hobnailed boots carrying an empty pitcher to fill up at the pub and take home," he concluded.

The letter was so detailed and so colorful, even about a relatively benign part of his service, that it sparked my imagination about what he could have written or shared about the actual war. As usual, all I could do was keep imagining.

Zaidy had another brief hospital stay in the spring of 2019.

"They haven't got me yet. I keep dodging them," he told me. "I'm still winning the battle."

He said he was now looking forward to reading the story I just had published in the *New York Times Magazine* uncovering the story of Wilf Canter and exploring his relationship with Zaidy.[5]

Fittingly, it came out on Israel's annual Memorial Day. On the way to my office in Jerusalem that morning, I stopped at the Machal memorial for a ceremony with "Smoky" Simon and other remaining elderly volunteers and stood alongside them for the two-minute siren that honors Israel's war dead and brings the country to a standstill. I thought of Wilf Canter as the siren wailed and seeing his name on the stone tablet memorial gave me the sense that perhaps he was cosmically thanking me for keeping his memory alive.

I had learned so much on this journey, and met so many people, that I couldn't help but think back to where it all began – an innocent, adolescent curiosity about a mysterious grandfather that had evolved into all of this.

Still, I was nervous. Zaidy gave me his blessing to publish and patiently took a call from a *New York Times* fact-checker to confirm my findings. But he had yet to read the whole thing, and I was worried about how he would react to seeing his name, comments, and pictures in print.

I had considered waiting to publish it until after he had passed away to avoid this awkwardness but ultimately decided that I wanted him to read it. He deserved this tribute, and all the warm things that people had to say about him. Perhaps it would even help him get to the place where he would "open the vault" and let out the parts that still appeared to be locked inside him.

Later in the day I got Zaidy's initial response. He was urgently inquiring how he could properly print out the story. He couldn't quite conceptualize the importance of the online version of the *New York Times*. In his mind, something published was something you held that left ink marks on your fingers. This was a good sign, since it meant he was interested, and I didn't expect much more than that.

But once we found someone to properly operate his printer, he was genuinely excited, especially about the pictures. He shared it widely, proudly handing out copies to others in his assisted-living facility and glowing in the feedback.

The responses I got, online and in person, were overwhelming.

"Your Zaidy was a hero, whatever he did. From my perspective, they all were heroes. They showed up, did their duty, lived and died, endured and saved the world. For us," wrote John McNicholas of Santa Cruz, California.

Others responded with stories about their own veteran relatives and the similar dynamics they encountered with those who steadfastly kept quiet throughout the years. Others recommended further research options and commemoration sites. While nearly all praised the article and recognized the love in my endeavor, there was one comment that cut deep, since it touched on my greatest fear throughout the process.

"The war years are never good years, Mr. Heller. Your grandfather learned that as a young man. He doesn't want to relive his days as a warrior, separating fact from fiction, reality from the gentle memories re-created over time," wrote a woman identified as Midway. "Would you accept some advice from a woman, and a non-Jew at that? Let your grandfather be. He's lived a long life. Don't focus on those years that make you, as his young grandson 'proud.' Listen to what he is telling you about letting those years, and those deeds of great glory long, long ago simply go. You helped research some of his memories and found details about long-lost friends. Enough."

It's a sentiment that had been conveyed to me for years, even from within my own family, and one that I was still incredibly sensitive about. I felt as though I had always insisted that my love and curiosity of Zaidy be balanced with respect for his privacy. That's why I refrained from including anything that could shame or embarrass him in my article, even though with time I was growing more convinced that shame and embarrassment were what had driven his prolonged silence.

Three weeks later, a longer version was published in *Tablet* magazine.[6] It expanded on my exchanges with Zaidy and on Canter's wartime heroics, diving deeper into his service as a foreign volunteer in Israel. It also branched out to include the biographies of Canter's fellow crewmates on the doomed Dakota flight and the overall contributions of the Machal volunteers.

And with that, I thought I was done. I did my part. I told Zaidy's story, and its various tentacles, and we could both move on with our lives.

But there was something about this journey that just would not die. The genie was out of the bottle, and various acquaintances, and strangers, kept approaching me with further threads to follow.

Among the new contacts that reached out after the stories were published was Brian Ferstman. A retired lawyer then living in Victoria, British Columbia, he had exhaustively researched his father Abe's service as a navigator who survived thirty-three missions in Bomber Command, and Ferstman had become somewhat of an expert sleuth in the process.

Ferstman had already been through the process and generously offered to help with my research too. I mentioned, once again, how I did not have Zaidy's consent for the full record. Ferstman explained, however, that through the Canadian Freedom of Information Act, one could apply for a partial record that would at least provide some details I could cross check.

Now this was a real dilemma, one that encapsulated years of conflicting feelings. Do I finally abandon this quest, as that astute *New York Times* reader suggested and Zaidy had insinuated I should, or do I follow up a lead that had come my way and see it through?

Ferstman solved the initial quandary for me by requesting the file from the National Archives out of his own curiosity, and I ultimately decided that whatever he got, I should see as well. I had vowed never to pursue classified material without Zaidy's consent, but if this was an open source, I figured it was fair game. Besides, I was heading back to Toronto that summer and, as always, it would be a waste not to have the information handy if Zaidy suddenly decided he was ready to talk. If I had learned anything, it was that he could be unpredictable. And I won't lie, I was curious to see how he would react. The mission, though, would remain the same, to be ready to offer him the option if he chose it.

Shortly after, I received a large brown envelope in the mail from Ferstman with selected documents from Zaidy's official war record. I doubted there would be a great mystery in there to uncover. Still, I opened the manila folder with a fair share of trepidation.

Inspecting these eighty-year-old, partially redacted documents felt momentous. In practice, they offered the first real glimpse into Zaidy's actual service and provided the best indication yet of his longtime assertion that he "didn't do much."

Zaidy enlisted on March 10, 1941; the same day that Admiral Isoroku Yamamoto received a draft of the Pearl Harbor attack plan.

Zaidy's standard attestation paper, in which he described himself as a "male stenographer" and "clerk," lists various other qualifications like "signaling, wireless, first aid, fencing, Boy Scouts." He stated that he worked for Sanitary Products Co. as a stenographer, clerk and shipper for a year before joining the RCAF in 1941, and that he engaged in hockey, swimming, baseball, tennis, and rugby.

SPECIAL RESER...

1/10 OK. (6)

AIR FORCE No. R.97329 POSTED TO #1 Manning Depot, Toronto TRADE Clerk (Steno) "Std"

ROYAL CANADIAN AIR FORCE

(ATTESTATION PAPER)

(Pages one and two, only, are to be completed in Applicant's own Handwriting)

1. Surname ~~Heller~~ Heller FULL Christian Names ~~Mervin (Mickey)~~ Mervin ~~(Mickey)~~
2. Present Address 168 Robert Street, Toronto Telephone Ra. 8736
3. Permanent Address 168 Robert Street, Toronto, Ontario
4. Place of Birth Toronto, Ontario, Canada Citizenship Canadian
5. Date of Birth [redacted] 1921 Married, Single, Widower, Separated, Divorced Single
6. Particulars of Children

Name	Date of birth	Name	Date of birth
Not applicable			

7. Occupation Male Stenographer, Clerk 8. Religion [redacted] State denomination
9. Languages English
10. Next of Kin (Full Name) Mrs. ~~[illegible]~~ Lena Heller Relationship Mother
 " Address 168 Robert Street Toronto Ont
11. Father (Full Name) Heller, Samuel Birthplace Russia
 " Address 168 Robert Street Toronto Citizenship Canadian (Nat.)
 " Occupation Pensioner
12. Mother (Full Maiden Name) Davis, Lena Birthplace Canada
 " Address 168 Robert Street Toronto Citizenship Canadian
13. Details of any Naval, Military or Air Force Service:

Unit	Place	Rank	Trade	Date From	Date To	Reason for discharge
Nil						

R.C.A.F. Records Office
Rec'd MAR 13 1941
O. K. C. B.
R. C. N.
S. L. R.

14. Honours, Awards, Mentions Nil

Photo 15.5. Mickey Heller's RCAF attestation paper
(Courtesy of the Heller family.)

When asked which air force duties he wished to enlist for, he crossed out "Flying Duties" and instead opted for "Ground Duties," saying he could contribute as a clerk or stenographer.

His first posting was at No. 1 Manning Depot in the colosseum of the Toronto Exhibition Grounds, where all the new recruits enlisted, did their basic training, and often had to sleep in stalls that smelled like cows and horses. In a letter to his parents on March 26, 1941 – a date when Zaidy was likely experiencing the same thing – future pilot Frank Sorensen described the daily routine during his ten-day security guard training. It included an early rise, the shining of shoes and buttons, marching drills, and physical training in 10-degree weather.[7]

By May 1941, Zaidy had completed his clerk stenographer composite training school in Trenton, Ontario. I found a picture of the class, with Zaidy standing in the second row, among the few pictures he kept in family albums. There was also a brief stint at the bombing and gunnery school in Mountain View, Ontario.

Yet somehow, along the way, he transferred over to aircrew, earning the distinctions of "aircraftman first class" and "leading aircraftman." In April 1942, he completed Instrument Flying School in Belleville, Ontario, and then trained as a navigator at Air Observer School in Malton, Ontario, earning his navigator's badge on October 9, 1942, less than three weeks before he was dispatched overseas from Halifax on October 28.

A 2001 form Zaidy filled out with the Jewish Canadian Military Museum Archives confirmed this chronology. For

Photo 15.6. Mickey Heller's navigating class in Malton, Ontario. He is seated seventh from the left in the front row.
(Courtesy of the Heller family.)

the record, he detailed that his reason for enlisting was "to serve." When asked how the military affected his life, he responded that he "matured and broadened."

Yet his official record sheet revealed just how little action he saw in Europe.

After brief stays in Bournemouth and then in the advanced flying unit in Wigtown, Zaidy learned to fly in a bomber crew at the No. 22 operational training unit in Wellesbourne before he was finally deployed in 426 Squadron on April 4, 1943. For some reason, he only lasted there for two weeks before being reassigned to administrative work in the English town of Topcliffe and then to another advanced flying unit in Dumfries, Scotland, for most of the rest of 1943.

It was during this period that he apparently served alongside David Smith, another Jewish Canadian friend and fellow navigator. Smith's daughter Miriam told me that her grandmother saved all of Smith's wartime letters home, some of which included mentions of my Zaidy. Nearly eighty years later, Zaidy had no recollection of the man, but Miriam thankfully was able to decipher her father's "chicken scratches" and shared them with me to offer another newfound glimpse at Zaidy's past.

One letter was dated May 11, 1943: "I just had a letter from Mickey Heller & he writes that his mother tells him more about me than I do. Gee I feel lonesome. All the boys I know here have been posted out."

The second letter was dated May 23, 1943, while her dad was stationed in Bournemouth, in the south of England: "Around the beginning of April Mickey Heller came down to Bournemouth on leave. He has finished operational training (O.T.U.) & has been posted to a squadron. We went dancing on Saturday night. On Sunday I went cycling & on Monday he left along with an Australian boy I'd been chumming around with. So once again I was left alone."

Later in the same letter he describes a visit to London, returning to Bournemouth sixteen hours late: "I reported immediately to the postings officer & found that I'd been taken off a draft to an A.F.U. (Advanced Flying Unit). That is, I was on reserve posting instead of definite posting. All the boys in my flight went. So, I was kinda left behind. Oh well. Mickey Heller was at that A.F.U. & he said it was an awful place. So, I didn't miss much."

On October 9, 1943, Zaidy was promoted to the rank of Warrant Officer Class II, the only promotion of his service.

In early December, he was finally reassigned to the newly established No. 433 Squadron that mostly flew the Halifax and began its night bombing and mine-laying missions over Europe in early 1944. Known as the Porcupine Squadron to symbolize its potency, the squadron brandished an equally imposing motto: *Qui s'y frotte s'y pique* ("Who opposes it gets hurt"). In just over a year and three months of operation, 433 Squadron dropped nearly 7,500 tons of bombs and took over 250 casualties.[8]

Zaidy lasted longer in the 433 than he did in the 426, but not by much. His record indicated just a two-month stint, from December 4, 1943, until February 15, 1944, before being transferred out to operational training again, first in Pershore and then again in Wellesbourne.[9] Finally, in July, he was sent to the Repatriation Depot at Warrington, near Liverpool. It was a place notorious for serving some of the war's worst military meals, which were passed out one at a time through a single narrow opening with a guillotine door that would quickly descend on your hand if you didn't move quickly enough.[10] Zaidy stayed there until he was ultimately sent home to Canada in September.

Ferstman suggested there were likely one of two reasons for the short deployments. The first was that his crew may have lost its pilot when he was training on a "Second Dickie" flight, which was when a pilot joined a more experienced crew to gain operational experience before taking his own crew into action. This would have left the rest of the crew as "odd bods" without a pilot and thus reassigned to training. The second explanation was that there was some physical or emotional issue that made him unfit to fly.

Though he said it was more likely to be the first reason, there were several other indications that it could be the second. In section 4 – character and trade proficiency – Zaidy got high marks for his conduct. But he was also passed up several times for promotion and ended as a Warrant Officer Class II (WOII,) which was the lowest possible rank given his time served. He didn't receive any citations above the bare minimum and was officially discharged "having become unsuited for the special duties for which [he had been] trained."

Ferstman said that was telling, and a "very unusual statement for a discharge certificate."[11]

The fact that he didn't get promoted also indicated a modest service since promotions tended to follow combat experience. The more operations an airman flew, for instance, the more likely he was to get promoted. An airman who flew very little, whatever the reason, would not get promoted, with the only exception being POWs, which we know Zaidy was not.

In all, the paperwork suggests his most impressive feat was to have endured.

"He certainly did not complete a tour of duty. There is no way he could have done his thirty flights in that time," Ferstman suggested. "It sounds like he did his best, but it wasn't quite enough."

Only in 2019 did Zaidy reluctantly acknowledge that while he trained as a navigator, he never actually completed any missions. The explanation he provided was that he simply threw up too much and was so airsick that they sent him home in 1944. It was along the lines of what I long suspected, but something I suppose he never quite felt comfortable enough to share.

Ferstman said this too was unusual, as airsickness and vomiting were common reasons for prospective bomber crew members to be removed from the training pipeline. Ferstman speculated that Zaidy lasted as long as he did because of his determination to overcome the problem, and possibly because he showed promise at his job and his superiors hoped that it would resolve itself eventually.[12]

Regardless, it appears that at the end, the great mystery was not so great after all.

The other main finding was that Zaidy's travel dates did not align with those of Canter's. Zaidy embarked from Canada on October 28, 1942, and arrived in the UK on November 4, 1942, after a weeklong passage across the Atlantic on the *Queen Elizabeth*, the converted luxury liner. While Zaidy was at sea, a German submarine sank a British passenger ship near the Azores, killing 362 people, the RCAF sank a pair of German subs near Newfoundland, and thirty Luftwaffe planes bombed Canterbury in one of the heaviest raids on England since the Blitz.

Canter's record, however, showed him traveling from August 21, 1942, till September 1, 1942, an eleven-day journey more likely to have been on one of the slower convoys. There's no doubt the two were friends, but it doesn't appear they sailed over together. The friendship must have been cemented elsewhere. It was just another reminder of how human memory could be such a tricky thing to rely upon after so many years.

The bottom line from the files is that Zaidy likely had very little airtime and may have been unable to cope with the rigors of war. The findings affected nothing about how I felt about him or his service. If anything, it generated more empathy for him and the burden he'd been carrying all these years. I, too, struggled emotionally in my military service in Israel, was unsure of my contribution, and was eager to move on when it was over. I can't even imagine how much more draining it must have been to endure all that while being deployed for two years in a war overseas.

"It sounds like, regardless of what he did or didn't achieve during the war, that he was a good man who lived a good life, and was a good father and grandfather," Ferstman concluded. "Much for him to be proud of."

My feelings exactly.

A solo visit to Toronto in August 2019 was my seventh since 2011, and it felt like a redemptive experience given that the last one was so trying for us both and felt at the time like a final farewell. It was also perhaps my last chance to present to Zaidy what I had discovered.

Over lunch at his place, he put in the hearing aids he'd been provided as part of his veteran health benefits so that we could converse more comfortably, though it took a while to get them to work properly. I helped lift Zaidy up from his reclining chair so he could show me some emails on his computer. Then we sat down for the traditional game of Clubbyish. I occasionally had to remind him of the trump suit, but he still had it and beat me handily.

Finally, when the time felt right, I pulled out the wartime records I had brought with me from Israel and placed them on the bridge table.

He studied them closely, impressed with the findings. He smiled as he keenly recalled the names of the references he gave: his dentist, his previous employer, and his Boy Scout instructor. If any of the dates or acronyms rang a bell, he didn't show it. He acknowledged the data but deflected any follow-up questions by sheepishly saying he just couldn't remember anymore.

"That's what happens to your memory," he said, flipping through the papers and the small handwritten notes. "Can't read it, can't see it, can't remember it."

Zaidy did remember being in England on D-Day and hearing the reports from there. He said it was exciting because it meant that after that significant turning point they would start sending some excess people home. But when I tried to steer him toward his own details, such as his flight log, he replied, "Who can remember?" and he suddenly lost his train of thought. He said he was tired and that he was having trouble hearing.

His interest seemed genuine, though, so, seizing the moment, and for the sake of my conscience, I went in for yet another, final, pitch. With a simple signature, I told him gently, I could get a full record to help him remember all those things he said he had forgotten.

"It's too late for that now," he said, sighing. "Just let it lie."

We celebrated Zaidy's ninety-ninth birthday on November 3, 2020, on a Zoom call with all his children, grandchildren, great-grandchildren, and some nieces and great-nephews. Zaidy was obviously thrilled to see everyone together marking the milestone and we all expressed hope that, God willing and pandemic permitting, we'd make it to Toronto the next year to celebrate the big 100. Zaidy seemed to be on a good track. He was in good hands with Jojo, in good spirits, and in good humor.

But just a few weeks later we got the troubling news that he, and Jojo, had contracted the coronavirus from a nurse visiting his apartment. Despite the initial and obvious concern, Zaidy had a very nonchalant approach. He said he felt well, had no fever or any other symptoms, and we joked that with Jojo quarantined with him, they were going to enjoy a two-week sleepover party.

"*Que sera, sera,*" he said. "I just take it one day at a time."

However, a few days later, his oxygen levels dropped, he became uncharacteristically disoriented and repeated himself constantly. The management of his assisted living home suggested he go to the hospital.

To this, he adamantly refused. "That's where sick people go," he used to tell me, and after the 2017 scare he seemed intent on never going back. Eventually, after pressure from his children, an oxygen tank was brought to his room, and soon his vital signs and oxygen levels stabilized.

His spirits took longer to rebound. Overcome with emotion, he reached out to everyone with instructions and comments that seemed like he was saying goodbye. My dad said he knew it was serious when Zaidy told him he loved him, words his father had mouthed to him only a handful of times in his seventy-four years.

When I called Zaidy, the exchange was brief.

"How are you doing?" I asked.

"Not good, Aron," he said. "I love you. Take care of the family."

Once again, Zaidy eventually recovered and by New Year's 2021, 100 years since the year he was born, Zaidy was all better. That a ninety-nine-year-old could bounce back from the coronavirus so impressively offered the rest of us some valued perspective on a pandemic that was still deeply upending our lives.

After Zaidy's brief, emotional response to his brush with death, he returned to his typical, casual approach to it all. New inquiries about his well-being were answered with his usual refrain: "Can't complain. I'm still here."

The episode, though, revived my own consciousness about his mortality. As the year wore on, he seemed to acknowledge it as well, eagerly awaiting his 100th birthday and a letter from Queen Elizabeth II.

But the dispatch he was most proud of was the certificate he received from the Canadian Minister of Veteran Affairs, Laurence MacAulay, marking his upcoming birthday: "On behalf of a grateful nation, we present this Certificate of Recognition to *Mervin Heller* as a tribute to your selfless acts of service and sacrifice during the Second World War, in defence of Canada and our shared values of freedom, democracy and the rule of law."

The big day had arrived: it was Zaidy's 100th birthday party. Not only did he make it, but he made it well. I arrived

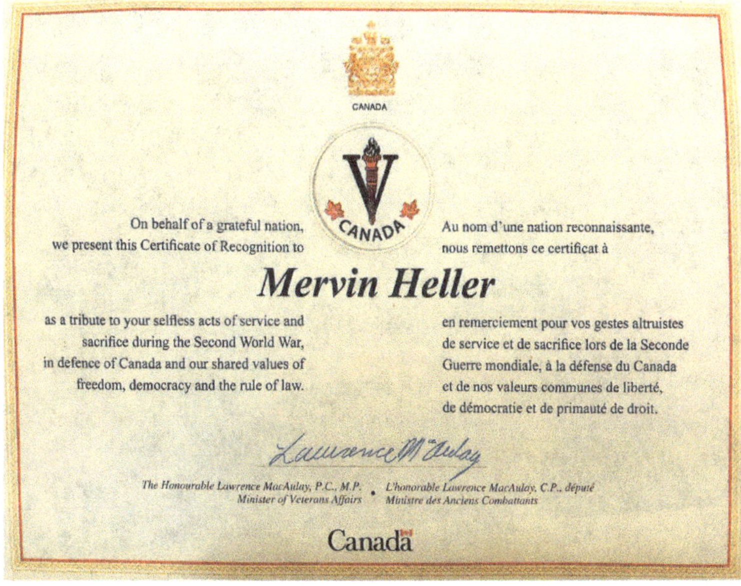

CANADA

CANADA

On behalf of a grateful nation,
we present this Certificate of Recognition to

Au nom d'une nation reconnaissante,
nous remettons ce certificat à

Mervin Heller

as a tribute to your selfless acts of service and
sacrifice during the Second World War,
in defence of Canada and our shared values of
freedom, democracy and the rule of law.

en remerciement pour vos gestes altruistes
de service et de sacrifice lors de la Seconde
Guerre mondiale, à la défense du Canada
et de nos valeurs communes de liberté,
de démocratie et de primauté de droit.

The Honourable Lawrence MacAulay, P.C., M.P.
Minister of Veterans Affairs

L'honorable Lawrence MacAulay, C.P., député
Ministre des Anciens Combattants

Canada

Photo 15.7. Mickey Heller's Certificate of Recognition
(Courtesy of the Heller family.)

in Toronto with my siblings and my dad to join the celebration. We all decided to make the trip, and it felt far more fitting to go for such a momentous celebration than for an eventual funeral.

We weren't alone. In a rare reunion, his four children and nine grandchildren had all arrived to join his closest surviving friends and relatives in Toronto. From afar, his twelve great-grandchildren watched parts of the party on Zoom.

Zaidy had been very excited about the upcoming event. He'd been handing out invitations left and right, essentially to everyone he knew who was still alive. He himself had insinuated that the party had given him something to look

Photo 15.8. Mickey Heller surrounded by his grandchildren at his 100th birthday party
(Courtesy of the Heller family.)

forward to, and an underlying refrain in the family had been that, once that passed, he may be ready to as well.

In preparing comments for the party, I tried to put his longevity in perspective.

When Zaidy was born, the world was still recovering from World War I and the Spanish Flu pandemic. Women had just been given the right to vote in the United States.

In 1921, Hitler became leader of the Nazi party in Germany, the Communist Party was formed in China, and Ireland gained independence. In America, alcohol was illegal, films were silent and headlines were shouted from street corners.

That year, the first Miss America pageant was held, and the first baseball game was broadcast on the radio. There was no TV, no internet, no smartphones. There were no electric guitars, no nuclear weapons, no penicillin.

I joked about an expression Zaidy often used to describe something being "the best thing since sliced bread." Well, there wasn't even sliced bread when Zaidy was born since it was only invented in 1928.

The math was staggering. Zaidy had been alive for more than 876,000 hours. That's 52.5 million minutes. He was born the same day as Charles Bronson and had outlived the ultimate Hollywood tough guy by nearly twenty years.

The US president at the time was Warren Harding, meaning Zaidy had lived under eighteen presidents. The pope was Pope Benedict XV, meaning Zaidy had lived under nine popes.

I also cited a quote from the certificate he had received from Lawrence MacAulay, Canada's Minister of Veterans Affairs, congratulating him on his 100th birthday: "It is my honour to commend you for your dedicated service during the Second World War. The bravery and determination of those who served Canada helped ensure a safer, more peaceful world."

That was all the war talk I was going to initiate. But I felt compelled to add the following:

> As someone who has spoken to you quite a bit about that period of your life, I can't help but feel that your ultimate service is the one that followed it. Your service to your family.

Minister
of Veterans Affairs

CANADA

Ministre
des Anciens Combattants

Mervin (Mickey) Heller

Please accept my warmest congratulations on the occasion of your 100th birthday on November 3, 2021.

It is my honour to commend you for your dedicated service during the Second World War. The bravery and determination of those who served Canada helped ensure a safer, more peaceful world.

Best wishes for happiness.

Minister of Veterans Affairs and Associate Minister of National Defence
The Honourable Lawrence MacAulay, PC

Ministre des Anciens Combattants et ministre associé de la Défense nationale
L'honorable Lawrence MacAulay, CP

Veterans Affairs Canada | Anciens Combattants Canada

Canada

Photo 15.9. Mickey Heller's 100th birthday certificate
(Courtesy of the Heller family.)

> Your unending dedication to your wife, your hard work to raise a young family when things were tough, and your continued love and support to all that have followed you since. You served your country with dignity. But your true legacy is right in front of you: your four children, your nine grandchildren and, from afar, your twelve great-grandchildren.

During our visit, though, Zaidy shocked me once again by using the occasion of his birthday to initiate the most detailed and carefree recounting I had heard of his military past. It was enough to inspire me to publish another article about him, this time in *The Canadian Jewish News*.[13]

It was telling, I noted in my first-person column, that after so many years of silence, my Zaidy decided to devote his 100th birthday celebration to the theme of commemorating the wartime service of Jewish Canadian veterans like himself.

Now largely confined to a wheelchair, he trekked out of his assisted living facility on a chilly autumn morning to take his visiting children and grandchildren from Israel to visit the memorial he contributed to outside the Prosserman Jewish Community Centre on Bathurst Street. The granite slab was flanked by the Canadian and Israeli flags that he had dedicated on behalf of the servicemen and women in his extended family.

Looking at the hundreds of engraved names of the Canadian Jewish soldiers, those who made it back and those who didn't, Zaidy glowed with pride. Pointing at the various names, he regaled us with stories about his old high school friends from Harbord Collegiate who died in action and noted the successes of those who went on to live nearly as long as he had. The names came to him easily: his brother Joe, his brother-in-law Morris, his good friends Wilfred Canter and Somer James.

Energized, he told me to roll him into the Community Centre so he could speak to a manager to share his memories, the kind he had refrained from for years.

"I'm the only one still here who knew all those guys out there," he told the stunned receptionist.

She said she would look for the appropriate person. "Well, you better do it quick because I don't know how long I'm going to last," he quipped. "This may be my last time here."

It sure didn't feel that way. Zaidy was more vibrant, witty, and downright funny than he had been in a decade.

Most surprisingly, he was not only willing to finally engage in stories about his World War II service but even initiated them. He shared many of them with me and my visiting siblings, telling us about his voyage overseas in the stern of the *Queen Elizabeth* and showing us mementos from that journey.

At the birthday party itself, where he was surrounded by his family and longtime friends, Zaidy held court alongside the framed certificate he received from MacAulay.

Always a man of few words, Zaidy kept his own comments brief, devoting them almost exclusively to the visit we paid to the war memorial. His voice cracking, he asked his guests to make the pilgrimage to honor "all the Jewish boys who sacrificed their lives."

"If you get a chance, it's real history," he added.

In one of his more candid moments of our five-day visit, Zaidy pulled out his wallet to reveal the two pictures he always carried with him. The first was his favorite of his wife and children. The second was of himself and three other Canadian Jewish wartime buddies – Sammy Greisman, Harold Wolfman, and Ralph Goldman – posing in uniform at Trafalgar Square in October 1943, exactly seventy-eight years earlier.

Over a deli lunch, I asked Zaidy why he kept these two photos so close. "Because they are small enough to fit in my wallet," he quipped.

But they obviously meant more. It was yet another reminder of how momentous that period remained for Zaidy, even through his years of prolonged silence.

Photo 15.10. Mickey Heller with wartime friends in Trafalgar Square, London, October 1943. From left to right: Mickey Heller, Ralph Goldman, Harold Wolfman, and Sammy Greisman.
(Courtesy of the Heller family.)

The kicker was that the man Zaidy is seen hugging in the picture, Ralph Goldman, was still alive and he made it to the party, where the two centenarians warmly embraced once again.

It was a thrill to meet another piece of living history, even more so one with such a firm handshake and the same flowing locks of hair as he had in the old black-and-white photo. He was a flight mechanic, a "grease monkey," he said, and told me about once emerging from his base near London to see a "light show" of bombs exploding from above. He also said he used to go swimming in the English Channel even though it was heavily mined. He figured it would take more

Photo 15.11. Ralph Goldman at 100
(Courtesy of Ralph Goldman.)

than his mere frame to set one off. But he acknowledged that that was the closest he got to the action, nothing like the boys in Bomber Command with Zaidy.

Details aside, it was just very touching to meet someone who knew Zaidy way back then and to see how they had maintained this special connection so long after.

Watching the two men together was a stirring reminder of how, for better or for worse, World War II will always define their Greatest Generation. About 17,000 Jewish Canadians served in World War II. Mickey and Ralph, now both 100, were truly among the last of their kind.

The good vibes lasted several days longer.

Jojo said Zaidy was "happy and proud" to read my article. It was the best birthday present I could have given him.

The same day that story was published, November 11, Zaidy gave a Remembrance Day talk in the lobby of his building to some forty residents. It was the first time I know of that he'd done anything of the sort. Seated in his wheelchair, with one of his signature flat caps, he wore a jacket bearing a poppy and war insignia as he recalled his days in World War II.

Naturally, it focused more on others, in particular a recently deceased fellow resident that he played bridge with and who had helped liberate Holland.

He also mentioned his father Samuel, who had served for five years in World War I, in the Royal Canadian Horse Artillery. "It was the 'war to end all wars,' and then I ended up in another war," Zaidy said with a chuckle.

He concluded by reciting "In Flanders Fields," the famous World War I–era poem written by Canadian Lieutenant-Colonel John McCrae, that introduced the red poppy as a memorial symbol for soldiers who died in conflict.

In Flanders fields the poppies blow
Between the crosses, row on row,
That mark our place; and in the sky
The larks, still bravely singing, fly
Scarce heard amid the guns below.

We are the Dead. Short days ago
We lived, felt dawn, saw sunset glow,
Loved and were loved, and now we lie,
In Flanders fields.

Take up our quarrel with the foe:
To you from failing hands we throw
The torch; be yours to hold it high.
If ye break faith with us who die
We shall not sleep, though poppies grow
In Flanders fields.

Judging by the video clip Jojo sent me, it seemed as if a weight had been lifted, and Zaidy had finally made peace with his past. It only took his 100th birthday to get there.

It was right around this time that funding had finally been secured for the establishment of the museum in Israel and what had for years been a pipe dream was becoming a reality. Even Zaidy was excited to hear that news.

"I hope I'm still here to see it," he said.

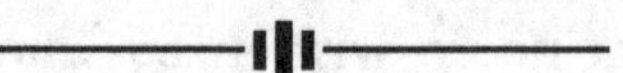

For several years, Scott Masters, a high school history teacher at Crestwood Preparatory College in Toronto, had been building a vast database of the testimonies of hundreds of World War II veterans and Holocaust survivors. As the director of the Crestwood Oral History Project, Masters, along with his students, digitized their photos, mementos and video interviews to create an impressive collection of personalized historical documents.[14]

Some 1.1 million Canadians served in uniform in World War II. As of 2022, only about 20,000 remained.[15] At such a stage, recording any testimony was doubly significant.

Masters's latest subject was Ralph Goldman. In conducting his research, he discovered the connection to Zaidy from my column about their recent meeting for Zaidy's 100th birthday. Eager to expand his collection, Masters reached out and I played matchmaker. Zaidy, with his newfound openness, quickly agreed to take part in the project.

They met in May 2022 and the result, I soon discovered from video clips Masters shared with me, was the most candid account I believe Zaidy had ever given about his life and service. Nothing was exceptionally surprising, but it was still moving to see Zaidy dig up old memories and share them freely and at ease for posterity, on camera, once again with a relative stranger.

The legwork I did in previous years likely led him to this point where he finally felt liberated enough to do so and it gave me great satisfaction to see where he had landed and where our joint journey likely concluded. Zaidy capped the experience by signing a historic logbook in which he wrote "it was my honour to serve."[16]

Seated in his room in a black leather reclining chair and wearing a plain gray sweatshirt, Zaidy casually answered all the questions Masters asked him. He often had to pause to recall details and would easily get sidetracked. He closed his eyes when he struggled to remember something, and he stopped several times to request a drink of water. But he didn't appear to hold anything back, and what he said was the closest to a full biography that he had ever laid out.

Whatever he still remembered, Zaidy seemed willing to share with Masters.

Zaidy acknowledged that one of his motivations for volunteering for the RCAF was to avoid the harsh conditions of the army. "We all wanted a good bed to sleep in," he said.

His early military basic training experiences reinforced that choice.

"They gave us all a gun. I dropped mine on my foot, and they said: 'This is not for you,'" he recalled, grinning.

The RCAF, though nowhere nearly as antisemitic as the navy, was also not always a welcoming home for Jews. Most were prevented from becoming pilots and instead were channeled into the navigator track based on the prevailing stereotype that brainy Jews were good at math and would likely be able to figure out where they were going.

Zaidy noted that, unlike his friend Mark Charness,[17] he was no math whiz and had no idea how he ended up in navigator's school.

"He [Charness] was on the Pathfinders because he was a good student. He told me he came back with 70 percent of his crew, that's how good a navigator he was," Zaidy said. "I say how lucky he was."

Zaidy said it took two years for him to become a navigator because of what he claimed was an aversion to having Jews in aircrews.

"They wouldn't take any Jewish boys at the beginning. So, we went in whenever we could to get out of having to go into the army," he said with a chuckle, explaining that Jewish boys preferred to sleep in a bed indoors rather than roughing it out in the cold. "I was drafted to the army on my way overseas. That's how they found me."

By the time he was sailing over on the *Queen Elizabeth*, he was fully trained and ready for action. "We got on in Halifax. My hammock was right in the back of the ship, and it went like this, every three minutes," he said, waving his hand back and forth. "That I remember. We ate two meals a day because it took hours to get served."

He said that German U-Boats were of little concern at this stage of the war because the *Queen Elizabeth* was too fast for them and traveled in a zigzag pattern across the ocean.

"They never bothered because they couldn't keep up," he said, of the U-Boats. "It [the zigzagging] didn't bother you too much unless you were lying in your hammock. Otherwise, you were in line for meals or entertainment or something."

Surprisingly, Zaidy said he got his sea legs quickly. "That's the interesting part. I used to get seasick in a street-car," he said, laughing. "I don't know how or why. I have no idea because they didn't ask us if you were seasick when you went in. It didn't matter. You went."[18]

He said the ship landed in Greenock, Scotland. From there they took a train down to Bournemouth and stayed there for quite a few months until they figured out where to dispatch the airmen. Zaidy was sent to flight school in Wigtown, in southern Scotland.

At this point Masters popped the million-dollar question that had been skirted around for so long. And Zaidy at long last confessed that, despite all his training, he never actually partook in any air missions.

"You see, you are assuming. Do you know how many people it took to keep an airplane in the air? I don't know whether it was sixty or 600. But that was the story. Everybody assumed because you were in the air force that you were a pilot or something," he said. "I flew in them, but I didn't get anywhere. I saw my combat when I came home."

He said his only wisp of battle came when he was in London during bombing raids and had to hustle underground like everyone else.

"I didn't fly any missions; I was training all the time," he concluded.

Without combat stories to share, his main memories were social. Most revolved around the Balfour Services Club in London, a popular hangout for Canadian Jewish soldiers on leave. It was a place where they could rent a room, have a haircut, take a dance, and attend religious ceremonies.[19]

Zaidy also had distant family in Leeds and elsewhere in England he could visit. He was not a big drinker and, with his mind firmly focused on Eunice back in Canada, he wasn't interested in chasing girls around London either. So, he mostly spent his downtime drinking tea (not coffee) with friends.

"I remember once, in camp, my girlfriend [Eunice] sent me ketchup inside a rye bread that was scooped out. We put it on a big wooden table with six guys around it. Some other guy came over and asked if he could borrow the ketchup. We almost killed him," he said smiling. "All food was in short supply. We put the ketchup on whatever they gave us."

Another longtime mystery that Zaidy touched upon was his early return home in 1944.

"For some reason, they shuffle you around. I got shuffled around. I didn't know where I was going or what I was doing. Finally, they sent me to a place called Warrington, a repatriation depot, and when they sent me to the R depot that's when I went out to the east end and I bought a ring for my wife with the 30 pounds that I won in a craps game," he recalled. "Once you got there you knew you were going to go home. When? You didn't know."

He also didn't know why he was going home. But he didn't ask any questions. Within two weeks of returning, he was married and then bided his time in local administrative jobs until his formal release the following February.

Zaidy was now tiring, so Masters concluded by asking him whether he enjoyed any of his service.

"There was no such thing," Zaidy replied. "You went, you did it."

The detailed interview left me with both a sense of closure and yet a few loopholes that I sought to close. Seizing on the moment, and knowing Zaidy's limited patience for phone calls, I composed a list of questions and emailed them to Zaidy and Jojo. She said he was reviewing them, and they had begun to work on a response draft together. Jojo spent more time with Zaidy than anyone else after Bubby died, and though he seemed to confide everything in her, she said that war talk never came up between them and this was the first time he had enlisted her help on the matter.

But first I tried to fill in some blanks of my own in an hour-long conversation with Masters on June 8. He needed me to explain some of the pictures he saw at Zaidy's and to share my observations from years of trying to decipher his military past. But it was a two-way conversation. Masters gave me much insight from the wide variety of interviews he had conducted with World War II veterans and Holocaust survivors – more than 1,000 in all.

We agreed that Zaidy likely had a mundane service, like that of most soldiers. He did what he was told, did his best, didn't ask questions, and when he was done, he moved on.

I had always been wary of projecting anything more than that since, over time, it had become abundantly clear that Zaidy's humility was merely the plain truth. There likely were no heroics, no major trauma, or anything of that dramatic nature. Perhaps it was this sense that it was all so insignificant compared to what everyone else expected to hear that drove his prolonged silence. Whatever it was, it was honorable, and I've come to believe that that ordinariness was more reflective of daily reality than most published accounts. It helped convince me that this whole project I had undertaken was a valuable exercise after all.

Still, there remained these various suspicious signals along the way that something was awry. It wasn't that Zaidy was merely bashful or dismissive of the various inquiries that had been asked of him. There was always something cagey about the way he deflected the questions that kept arousing doubt that there was something else lurking.

At the conclusion of the journey, I had managed to synthesize these suspicions down to three main gaps I was eager to resolve about the whole saga.

The first related to Zaidy's training. His attestation paper said he wanted to join "Ground Duties," and he listed his civilian occupation as a stenographer and clerk and expressed a desire to do those roles in the military. Zaidy openly stated that he executed these roles while stationed in Canada. And yet, he ended up training for flight duties, earned his navigator badge, and completed various flight training courses.

There are pictures of him in flight suits, in front of bomber planes. Masters said this was highly unusual. Of the 450 vets he interviewed, he said he never heard of anyone transferring mid-service from ground duties to flight duties. What happened there?

The second suspicion related to Zaidy's operational experience. Even after all the training he only spent a brief time in a pair of operational squadrons. Now, after eighty years, he also finally admits that he never actually flew any missions. Why?

Finally, he came back to Canada early, in September 1944, while fighting still raged in Europe. Servicemen usually only did that after completing a full tour of thirty missions. He obviously didn't. So why was he sent back?

Did any of these questions contain the answer to this mystery?

Just as Zaidy had made strides, so had I. We were at the stage of our relationship where I finally felt I was ready to ask him these questions head on and accept any explanation he offered. But it wasn't going to happen today. He had just become a great-grandfather again – twice. Both my brother and a cousin had just had children on that same day so the only relevant exchange to be had was a quick phone chat in which I congratulated Zaidy on the arrival of his thirteenth and fourteenth great-grandchildren.

Two days later, though, Jojo wrote to say Zaidy wanted to talk. We hopped on a video chat on June 10, and he filled in the blanks about his siblings and about his godmother, whose son he'd frequently visited in London during the war.

Then, fearlessly, I unleashed the three questions. This time he didn't duck. For the first time, I felt it was the God-honest answer. And that answer was essentially the same one that guided him throughout his entire life: he didn't know, he didn't ask, he didn't care.

"Everyone wanted to be aircrew," he said of his early placement as a stenographer. "You get bounced around and they don't tell you why. They don't tell you anything."

He repeated that Jews were kept out of the aircrew for a while until there was a need for them and that is how he transitioned in his service. Regarding his lack of operational experience, he merely said that it just didn't work out and he never had a desire to push for it.

He said that once the D-Day invasion got underway, there was less need for personnel and that's why he thinks he was sent home early. "They never tell you what they want to do with you," he said.

I asked once more if he had reflected on any of this at the time or since, about whether the service gave him any satisfaction, pride, or happiness.

"There was nothing to think about – you did as you were told," he shot back. "And when you were over there you were always busy with all these other things. You didn't have time to think about much."

It all added up to what I had assumed more than a decade earlier when I set out on this journey. The only difference was the conclusion I had reached after digging as deeply as I consciously could: none of it mattered. What he did or didn't do was irrelevant. The bottom line is that he did his duty, and he returned whole, both physically and mentally, and our whole family owed its existence to that.

At the end of the day, I think the main thing I discovered was that while Zaidy may not have completed any air bombing operations, he did ace his own single-minded wartime mission: to get back to Eunice.

Shortly before my last Toronto visit, I stumbled upon some of Zaidy's wartime letters. They were tender and intimate handwritten love letters to my grandmother that I had never seen before, and which confirmed this thesis.

The first was a letter to his then-girlfriend Eunice marking Halloween in 1942, an odd time transport to exactly seventy-nine years earlier. It was sent from England yet written aboard the *Queen Elizabeth* on his journey over the Atlantic. He described it as a "beautiful ship" with plenty of room yet apologized for his shaky handwriting, blaming it on the shaking of the engines in the stern – as he was bunked in the back of the ship.

"I am writing on my suitcase and sitting on my kitbag," he reported.

(In a fitting coda, Bubby and Zaidy celebrated their 25th anniversary in 1969 with a cruise on the same *Queen Elizabeth*, now once again a luxury liner. After confiding his history to the captain of the ship, Zaidy discovered that they had in fact sailed over together as young men. Bubby and Zaidy were invited to a private cocktail party in the captain's cabin.)

The longing grew stronger over the coming two months. In another letter home, dated December 21, 1942, Zaidy reports that he heard she had been "putting on a little weight and that it becomes you."

"As long as you still fit into my arms, I am not worried," he wrote. "I'll bet you look pretty good. What I wouldn't give to be home now."

In another undated letter, he was even more emotional, writing how he hoped that by the age of twenty she would be an "old married woman ... to me I mean."

"My roommate just asked me who I was writing to and when I told him he said he never saw anyone so interested in all his life," he wrote. "There, that's how much I think of you."

(I would later joke with Zaidy that I too had a "wartime romance" when I met my future wife just a week before heading off to cover the 2006 Israel-Lebanon War, and I corresponded with her through email for the next month while on a journalistic assignment that brought me far closer to battle than anything I'd ever encountered in my actual military service.)

Against the backdrop of war, Zaidy was jotting down his vision for the future. How satisfying it is to know that it all came true.

"All we have now are our dreams and wishes but if we dream long enough and wish hard enough, I know they will all come true," he wrote. "If I hold my breath much more while I try to think up words to tell you how much I love you there just wouldn't be any writing done. Bye for now dear. Love ever yours. Mickey."

And so, the great reveal was ultimately simple and poignant: Mickey Heller was one of millions who wanted out of World War II and to return to his beloved.

Photo 15.12. Mickey Heller in London
(Courtesy of the Heller family.)

Epilogue: The Grandson, Me

In covering the Eichmann trial, Hannah Arendt famously coined the controversial phrase "the banality of evil." Its conventional interpretation was that even monsters like Eichmann who abetted the worst crimes imaginable were ultimately cogs in a machine.

I'm not sure that I agree, and I wish I had a better point of comparison, but the main phrase I can come up with in summarizing Zaidy's military experience is "the banality of war." For most soldiers, there was little heroism or drama in World War II. It was a mundane experience that they drudged through. Few considered a legacy or how they were impacting the war's outcome. They were there to offer their meager contribution to a larger, noble cause. In practice, they were ants in a massive army. Mostly they were there to do a job, get home safely, and move on. They just happened to be of service age when this historic war broke out.

Some, like Alfred Brenner and Somer James, found themselves in extreme situations and responded heroically. Others, like Al Glazer and Lorne Winer, participated in historic battles. Someone like Wilfred Canter encountered even more dramatic circumstances and dodged death several times before it eventually caught up with him when he sought out another war. And for some, like Michael Weimers, their war was the one they found in Israel.

And then there were the majority, like Zaidy, who didn't have much to say and didn't seek to say it. There's a reason they never wrote memoirs or gave speeches. Their stories weren't sexy. They didn't fit into a neat narrative. But without this silent majority there was no larger story. I'm proud to present what I've discovered about just one of these men – and the band that surrounded him.

World War II affected everyone in different ways, but it left its mark on all. It not only altered world history, it also altered personal and family trajectories. The Jewish war effort helped defeat Nazism and, as a byproduct, its veterans played a key role in establishing Israel and solidifying its ties with the Jewish Diaspora for decades to come.

On a personal level, my Zaidy's war lesson was to keep his head down, never look back, and get on with it.

My takeaway is that there is heroism in that path too. I didn't need to discover an epic war saga or a life-altering trauma to have a greater appreciation of the arc of his life. I spent my lengthy journalism career searching for that narrative, for that headline, for that climax that drove home a story. Ironically, I'm glad I never found one with my grandfather.

Or am I?

I tried very hard not to turn this project into a romantic quest of discovery into how Zaidy's service affected the greater meaning of his life. Still, I must have projected and assumed, even pined for him to fit into some preconceived notion of what it must have been like to live and fight through World War II.

He was in Bomber Command after all, where nearly half of its wartime personnel perished. I must have yearned to discover something similar, like the personal diaries of airman Joey Jacobson that his cousin Peter Usher turned into the book *Joey Jacobson's War: A Jewish Canadian Airman in the Second World War.* I was also inspired by British journalist Thomas Harding's attempt to find out whether his long-dead great-uncle Hanns Alexander helped bring Auschwitz commander Rudolf Hess to justice in his book *Hanns and Rudolf.*

After all, what Jewish kid wouldn't want his grandfather to emerge as a bona fide hero? Who wouldn't want to be associated with such an icon?

If I am being honest with myself, I probably looked to ascribe a greater significance to my grandfather's service and life that he never sought and never wished to express.

If I have done so, Zaidy, I apologize.

With age, comes wisdom. The older we get the more we realize how mundane life often can be. The same goes for war and military service. To relate Zaidy's ordinary service to World War II in many ways feels more genuine than the dramatic stories we often read in books, see in films, or conjure in our imaginations.

In a more profound way, Zaidy's wartime experiences and conclusions echoed those of his father in World War I and, to a far lesser degree, my own as a soldier in the Israeli military in the mid-1990s.

Like my grandfather, I also struggled to find my role in what I largely felt was an inconsequential service buried amid extraordinary times. I too shared an aversion to combat and a frustration with a bureaucratic behemoth that seemed to meaninglessly shuffle you around. I too wanted to get it over with and get on with my life.

But like my grandfather before me, what I experienced in the military also shaped my future path. I had a unique vantage point to years of bloody battles against Hezbollah guerillas in southern Lebanon, to tense interactions with Palestinians in Israel's expanding control of the West Bank, to the hopeful prospect of the Oslo peace accords, and to the assassination of Yitzhak Rabin and the massive wave of suicide bombings that eventually contributed to their unraveling. It all deeply affected my worldview and molded my various identities as a Zionist, Israeli, and Jew.

Mostly, though, it made me a writer. I started observing how all the things around me represented this shaky bridge between Israel's early, pioneering spirit to its powerful, yet often idealistically compromised, present.

My American and Canadian upbringing was clashing with this Israeli reality, and I started to see my life experiences as just a small slice of this bigger geopolitical puzzle. I too was a cog in the system and my mundane service was also representative of what for most people was the banality of the modern-day Israeli experience.

I evolved from someone with a distaste for the army to someone with a fascination with military history; from someone with an ambivalent take on life in Israel to someone who would henceforth have a permanent, more visceral, link to the country and the land, even as I began to increasingly question some of its truisms that we were raised upon.

My coping mechanism in the military was to channel all this angst and range of conflicting emotions into dozens of pocketbook journals in which I meticulously documented everything I was seeing and feeling. It not only provided sanctuary amid turbulent times, but it also sparked a fascination with the written word that set me on a journey toward becoming a reporter, a writer, and eventually the author of this book about my grandfather and his times.

When I served, I had yet to be exposed to Joseph Heller's (no relation) epic novel, *Catch-22*, about the insanity of military service. As an anxious, overthinking eighteen-year-old who was prone to bouts of depression, I questioned everything. I figured all the craziness had to mean something. As we all know now, it doesn't. Basic training and beyond are aimed at breaking down the independent-thinking civilian in you and inserting an order-following military mindset so that you are physically and psychologically primed for the rest of your service when, hopefully, a healthier balance between the two can be restored.

But I didn't know that at the time. In the absence of a real war to fight, I waged war with the institution itself in a stubborn battle to get out of my initial, ill-fitting posting in military police in favor of what later became a more rewarding role as a liaison to foreign forces in the region. That I somehow emerged victorious and went on to have a generally satisfying service taught me a toughness I never knew I had and likely left more of an impression on the course of my life than any other battle. It built up a steeliness I had previously lacked and taught me about the world I would later cover as a journalist.

I once naively thought that my own turbulent service could be the basis of a coming-of-age memoir about the mandatory military service in Israel. But the questions that period generated about identity, struggle and sacrifice, and which swirled around in my head for the next thirty years, were ultimately addressed in this book.

Neither my grandfather nor I had the full answers I sought. But it turns out that, despite our differences, we had far more in common than I thought. We certainly had more in common with each other than we did with the boys in the Dakota, or with Zaidy's Canadian veteran friends, or with the super soldiers depicted in the museum in Latrun who better fit the prototype of the fearless Jewish warrior.

In the end, what I have to offer is the story of one of those who remained torn between pride and regret, those who just wanted to move on, those who preferred to be left alone. To quote the title of Aaron Copland's famous 1942 musical composition, this is a "Fanfare for the Common Man."

For most people of Zaidy's generation, the historic times in which they lived were merely a backdrop to their routine existence. One day, my future grandchildren may look back at me and my times the same way.

To them, I can recommend the following:

> Don't seek the legend or try to fulfill fantasies of long-ago eras that preceded your time. Instead, just get to know your

Photo E.1. Mickey Heller and Aron, 2019
(Courtesy of the Heller family.)

> grandparents better in any way you can. If you are as fortunate as I have been to have one who lived past the age of 100, appreciate the intergenerational interactions, however brief and superficial they may seem at the time. Because one day they will surely be gone.

Ultimately, I've come to appreciate my Zaidy for how unextraordinary he perceived himself to be. He was just like most of those around him back then. That didn't make him any less special. It just made him *him*. He refused to let the war define the rest of his life. In that, he succeeded in a big way. That he lived so long was an added gift.

Photo E.2. Mickey Heller with bomber plane during World War II
(Courtesy of the Heller family.)

And improbably, after all, he was able to find comfort as a centenarian in his role as one of the last surviving World War II veterans able to bear witness to those historic times.

Mervin (Mickey) Heller died in Toronto on Friday, July 8, 2022, four months shy of turning 101.[1] It also marked fifty years to the day that he first became a grandfather and one month to the day that he became a great-grandfather for the fourteenth time.

Photo E.3. Mickey Heller visiting the memorial at the Prosserman Jewish Community Centre in 2021
(Courtesy of the Heller family.)

Even more symbolically for me it came the same day I completed the initial manuscript of this book, exactly four weeks after we had our last war chat. The initial outline of this epilogue was typed as he took his final breaths.

Acknowledgments

This book has essentially been the culmination of a lifelong project, so naturally there are plenty of people along the way who helped me get here.

The first order of thanks goes to my grandfather, Zaidy Mickey. His mysterious wartime past was the genesis of this whole ordeal. Trying to learn about his backstory was the engine that drove me throughout and it led to all the other discoveries I would eventually make. His reticence at times was frustrating, and it look him a long time to start opening even a small crack of the window into his life. But it sparked a passion that burned for decades and, without even trying, he ultimately became the connecting thread for all the stories in this book. Our joint journey brought us closer than we'd even been before. For that alone, I deeply thank him. To him this book is dedicated.

The next words of gratitude go to all the veterans and survivors that I've interviewed over the years and whose stories are included here. Nearly all are no longer with us: Shmuel Amid, Yitzhak Arad, Peter Arton, Norman Cohen, Ralph Goldman, Joseph Harmatz, Yehuda Maimon, Dan Nadel, Gerry Rosenberg, Baruch Shub, Smoky Simon, Samuel Willenberg, Lorne Winer, and many more. I'm indebted to them all for their time and patience and for recalling with me some of the most consequential moments of their lives.

I'm similarly thankful for the cooperation of the descendants of the major characters in this book, the families and friends of Wilfred Canter, Fred Stevenson, William Fisher, Leon Lightman, Michael Weimers, Somer James, Al Glazer, Ralph Oren, David Smith, and so many others. I hope I have provided you with even a small, well-deserved dose of pride.

These stories would never have come to life if not for the selfless effort and dedication of Efrat Gal and Tal Landman. They introduced me to the other forgotten airmen of the 1948 Dakota transport aircraft and triggered in me a desire to publish the first of several articles about their exploits, which eventually evolved into the first section of this book. I'd also like to thank Zvi Kan-Tor for connecting me with the last remaining Jewish World War II veterans in Israel and for confiding in me throughout the extended and challenging process of finally dedicating a museum in their honor.

Given my grandfather's hesitance to engage openly about World War II, much of the initial insight into his service came from the assistance of outsiders. Brian Ferstman was crucial in providing information that Zaidy either couldn't remember or had no interest in trying to. Scott Masters got Zaidy on camera and on record in a way that I never could have, and he proved to be the impartial outlet I needed to take Zaidy down the path he had to go but refused to with any of his family members.

Jojo was also an excellent conduit, and I'm indebted to her for aiding Zaidy in conveying his stories – and, of course, even more so for her dedicated and loving care of Zaidy in his final years.

The greatest assistance, though, came from Ellin Bessner, my mentor on all Jewish Canadian World War II things. Ellin also visited with Zaidy and helped jot his memory. To me, she was an endless source of information, support and encouragement, a trusted sounding board throughout this whole journey. Along with Anna Shternshis, she also provided invaluable feedback on this manuscript.

I'd also like to thank the good people at the *New York Times Magazine, Tablet, and The Canadian Jewish News* for publishing my various features throughout this journey. Your commitment to telling this story, and the touching responses the articles generated, reinforced my conviction that this was a book that needed to be written. A special word of gratitude goes to those friends and colleagues who reviewed and endorsed this work and especially to those who encouraged me to keep at it, even when it appeared doubtful that this full narrative would ever be published. You know who you are.

A huge thank you goes out to Natalie Fingerhut, my literary editor at the University of Toronto Press, who took a chance on an unconventional project, believed in it throughout, made it better and helped shepherd it across the finish line. Thanks also to Mary Lui and Vesna Micic for their care and attention to the project, and to freelance editor Beth McAuley for her meticulous copyediting and sourcing prowess.

Despite some initial reservations, my extended family got on board with this pursuit and cooperated in digging up pictures and memories. I hope I did everyone proud in bringing Zaidy's story to life.

Photo A.1. Aron Heller's immediate family, including Bubby and Zaidy, at his 2008 wedding in Israel
(Courtesy of the Heller family.)

The most special thanks are reserved to my immediate family for their steadfast support in this and in everything in my life: my father Mark, my sister Miriam, my brother Daniel, and, above all, my wife Jerrin, and my daughters Lia, Dafna, and Gaia.

Finally, this book is also dedicated to my mother, Barbi. Ima was always my greatest supporter and the earliest advocate of my writing. In addition to being the quintessential mother, she was also, at various stages, my teacher, mentor, coach, therapist, emotional barometer, and best friend. No one appreciated me more or understood me better. In a life full of challenges and change, she was my anchor. I miss her dearly.

I'm so grateful that even at an advanced stage of her illness, she was able to read my initial manuscript and find joy in it. She always believed I had a book in me, and I know how proud and happy she would have been to finally see this dream come true.

Notes

1. Mickey Heller, My Grandfather

1 Stuart Schoenfeld, "Jewish Canadians," *The Canadian Encyclopedia.* Historica Canada, December 3, 2012; last edited July 26, 2024, https://www.thecanadianencyclopedia.ca/en/article/jewish-canadians.
2 Scott Masters, interview with Mickey Heller, Toronto, Forest Hill Place retirement home, May 29, 2022.
3 Masters, interview.
4 "Knocked Off Cycle," *The Toronto Daily Star*, June 27, 1936.
5 Masters, interview.
6 Jamie Michaels, "Christie Pits Riot," *The Canadian Encyclopedia. Historica Canada,* December 16, 2020; last edited December 16, 2020, https://www.thecanadianencyclopedia.ca/en/article/christie-pits-riot.
7 Ellin Bessner, interview with Mickey Heller, Toronto, Forest Hill Place retirement home, March 29, 2019.
8 For King and Country, "Secondary Schools: G to M: Harbord Collegiate Institute (HRB-SS),"accessed March 3, 2025, https://torontofamilyhistory.org/kingandcountry/tdsb/secondary-g-m.
9 Martha Jackson, "School for an Immigrant Neighbourhood: Harbord Collegiate's Happy Ghosts," For King and Country, November 17, 2022, https://torontofamilyhistory.org/kingandcountry/archives/2268.
10 Ellin Bessner, *Double Threat: Canadian Jews, the Military and World War II* (Toronto: New Jewish Press, 2018), 247.

11 Yad Vashem, "About the Central Database of Shoah Victims' Names," accessed March 3, 2025, https://www.yadvashem.org/archive/hall-of-names/database.html. A search there will list more than 150 entries for the Buch family of Mosciska. Author also has in his possession a physical printout from the old Museum of the Jewish Diaspora before it closed.

12 Elinor Florence, *The German Jew Who Bombed Berlin* (blog), April 23, 2014, https://www.elinorflorence.com/blog/jewish-pilot.

13 Aron Heller, "Israel Honors GI Who Told the Nazis, 'We are all Jews,'" *Times of Israel*, December 2, 2015, https:// www.timesofisrael.com/israel-honors-us-gi-who-told-the-nazis-we-are-all-jews.

14 Aron Heller, "Last-Known Treblinka Survivor's Death Signals Looming Post-Witness Era," *Globe and Mail*, February 22, 2016, https://www.theglobeandmail.com/news/world/last-known-treblinka-survivors-death-signals-looming-post-witness-era/article28843330/.

15 Aron Heller and Randy Herschaft, "Jewish Avengers Unapologetic for Targeting Nazis after WWII," *APNews.com*, August 31, 2016, https://apnews.com/article/6bc424c8a39743d1a43ad9518c5481a5.

16 Aron Heller, "Jewish WWII 'Avenger' Joseph Harmatz Dead at 91," *New Jersey Herald*, September 26, 2016, https://www.njherald.com/story/news/nation-world/2016/09/26/jewish-wwii-avenger-joseph-harmatz/3038567007.

17 Aron Heller, "My Aunt Jeanette – The World's Oldest Rockette," Aron Heller Journalist, September 15, 2007, https://www.aronheller.com/articles/my-aunt-jeanette/.

18 Sandra Martin, "Canada's Original Rockette 'Did Everything but the Circus,'" *Globe and Mail*, October 17, 2008, https://aronheller.com/wp/wp-content/uploads/2011/09/Aunt-Jeanette.pdf.

19 Mosaic Lodge, "Historical Sketch of Palestine Lodge," accessed March 3, 2025, https://www.mosaiclodge.com/home.

2. Wilf Canter, the Great Escapist

1 David Grossman, "Jewish War Memorial Unveiled on 11-11-11," *The Canadian Jewish News*, November 17, 2011, https://thecjn.ca/news/canada/jewish-war-memorial-unveiled-11-11-11.

2 Veterans Affairs Canada, "Jewish War Veterans of Canada Memorial," accessed March 3, 2025, https://www.veterans.gc.ca/eng/remembrance/memorials/national-inventory-canadian-memorials/details/8880.

3 Canter citation quoted in David Rome, ed., *Canadian Jews in World War II, Part 1, Decorations* (Montreal: Canadian Jewish Congress, 1947), 57.

4 Ted Barris, *The Great Escape: A Canadian Story* (Toronto: Dundurn Press, 2013), 3.

5 Government of Israel, "Zeev (Wilfred) Canter" [in Hebrew], Izkor: The Commemoration Site of Fallen Defense and Security Forces of Israel, accessed March 3, 2025, https://www.izkor.gov.il/%D7%96%D7%90%D7%91%20%D7%A7%D7%A0%D7%98%D7%A8/en_9da7e863fd31f6cd85feca5f35fe1ad7.

6 "The Long March," Stalag Luft III, accessed September 7, 2025, https://stalagluft3.com/long-march/.
7 World Machal, "Wilfred (Zeev) Canter," translated by Joe Woolf, accessed March 3, 2025, https://www.machal.org.il/personal-stories/wilfred-zeev-canter.
8 Barris, *The Great Escape*, 108.
9 Avi Cohen, *The History of the Israeli Air Force in the War of Independence*, vol. 3 (Jerusalem: Israeli Ministry of Defense, 2004), 73.
10 Cohen, *The History of the Israeli Air Force*, vol. 3, 74.
11 Cohen, *The History of the Israeli Air Force*, vol. 3, 75.
12 Cohen, *The History of the Israeli Air Force*, vol. 3, 72.
13 Shmuel Amid, interview with author, Kfar Saba, Israel, Bayit Bakfar retirement home, March 27, 2019.
14 Cohen, *The History of the Israeli Air Force*, vol. 3, 77.
15 Cohen, *The History of the Israeli Air Force*, vol. 3, 441.

3. Fred Stevenson, the Devoted Wingman

1 Eddie Kaplansky, *The First Fliers: Aircrew Personnel in the War of Independence* (Jerusalem: Israel Defense Forces, The Air Force History Branch, 1993), 41.
2 World Machal, "Fred Stevenson," accessed March 3, 2025, https://www.machal.org.il/personal-stories/fred-stevenson.

4. Willie Fisher, the Zionist Navigator

1 World Machal, "William Fisher," accessed March 3, 2025, https://www.machal.org.il/personal-stories/william-fisher.
2 Leon Tessler, phone interview from Toronto with author in Israel, October 8, 2018.
3 Leon Tessler, *A Glimpse of the Passing Scene: An Autobiography* (Toronto: AMA Graphics, 2013), 130–2.
4 Allan Chapnick, phone interview from Winnipeg with author in Israel, October 4, 2018.
5 Yaacov Markovitzky, *Machal Overseas Volunteers in Israel's War of Independence*, translated from the Hebrew by Moshe Kohn (Tel Aviv: World Machal, 2007), https://www.machal.org.il/wp-content/uploads/attachments/Machal.pdf.
6 Bomber Command Museum of Canada, "Bomber Command Losses," accessed March 3, 2025, https://www.bombercommandmuseumarchives.ca/commandlosses.html.
7 Peter J. Usher, *Joey Jacobson's War: A Jewish Canadian Airman in the Second World War* (Waterloo, ON: Wilfrid Laurier University Press, 2018), xiii.
8 Bomber Command Museum of Canada, "Bomber Command's Losses."
9 Imperial War Museums, "Who's Who in an RAF Bomber Crew," accessed March 3, 2025, https://www.iwm.org.uk/history/whos-who-in-an-raf-bomber-crew. See the "Navigator" section.

5. Leon Lightman, the Idealistic Airman

1 There are varying figures about the number of Machal volunteers who arrived in Israel in 1948. This is the one commonly cited by Smoky Simon, who headed World Machal from its 1968 establishment.
2 World Machal, "Rabin Speech," accessed March 3, 2025, https://www.machal.org.il/machal-memorial/rabin-speech/.
3 World Machal, "Jerome Lightman," https://www.machal.org.il/personal-stories/jerome-lightman.
4 Taken from a eulogy that Reines delivered in 1957, a copy of which a daughter of Reines, Rachel Ginat, provided the author.
5 Government of Israel, "Aryeh-Yehuda (Leon) Lightman" [in Hebrew], Izkor: The Commemoration Site of Fallen Defense and Security Forces of Israel, accessed March 3, 2025, https://www.izkor.gov.il/%D7%90%D7%A8%D7%99%D7%94-%D7%99%D7%94%D7%95%D7%93%D7%94%20%D7%9C%D7%99%D7%98%D7%9E%D7%9F/en_5272f9eeba51aec8dc5c9661ed616ce4.
6 Comments drawn from a speech by Rachel Avidor, circa 2000. Rachel Ginat provided the author with a copy of the speech.
7 Meir Reines, phone interview with author, in Israel, February 29, 2024.

6. Michael Weimers, the King of the Negev

1 Tal Landman, phone interview with author, in Israel, January 27, 2022.
2 Hans-Jörg Greimel, "Anna Essinger" [in German], Anna Essinger Gymnasium, accessed March 3, 2025, https://www.anna-essinger-gymnasium.de/schule/anna-essinger/.
3 Harold Jackson, "Anna's Children," *The Guardian*, July 18, 2003, https://www.theguardian.com/education/2003/jul/18/schools.uk1.
4 From documents that Noa Schendar provided the author in 2022.
5 From Noa Schendar documents.
6 Yoel de-Malach, *From the Hills of Tuscany to the Plains of the Negev: Memories 1924–2006* [in Hebrew] (Jerusalem: Ariel Publishing House, 2007), 174.
7 Revivim Kibbutz, "Michael Weimers" [in Hebrew], accessed March 3, 2025, https://revivim.kibbutz.org.il/cgi-webaxy/sal/sal.pl?lang=he&ID=213588_revivim_degem&act=show&dbid=pages&dataid=revivim_420192_revivim_32.
8 de-Malach, *From the Hills of Tuscany*, 175.
9 de-Malach, *From the Hills of Tuscany*, 175.
10 Uri Dromi, phone interview with author in Israel, January 28, 2022.
11 According to the account of his brother, Yoav Tsur, in an interview with Raffi Kaufman that appeared in an edition of the Association of Israelis of Central European Origin newsletter (n.d.).
12 Dan Tolkovsky, phone interview with author in Israel, May 13, 2021.
13 Cohen, *The History of the Israeli Air Force*, vol. 1, 563.

14 Information gleaned from Avi Cohen, *An Aerial Bridge to Independence* [in Hebrew] (Jerusalem: Israeli Ministry of Defense, 1997).
15 Cohen, *An Aerial Bridge to Independence*, 335.
16 Uri Dromi, "Operation Dust Bowl 1948: Achievement and Missed Opportunity," *Ma'archot* magazine, July 1984, 92.
17 Cohen, *An Aerial Bridge to Independence*, 335.
18 Dromi, "Operation Dust Bowl 1948," 96.
19 Dromi, phone interview.
20 Drawn from documents that Noa Schendar provided the author in 2022.
21 Cohen, *The History of the Israeli Air Force*, vol. 2, 255.
22 Cohen, *The History of the Israeli Air Force*, vol. 3, 464.
23 Cohen, *The History of the Israeli Air Force*, vol. 3, 75.
24 de-Malach, *From the Hills of Tuscany*, 176.
25 Tolkovsky, phone interview.
26 Cohen, *The History of the Israeli Air Force*, vol. 3, 676.
27 According to Margalit Tsur's account in an interview published in the Association of Israelis of Central European Origin newsletter (n.d.).
28 Michael Tsur, phone interview with author in Israel, January 28, 2022.

7. The Dakota Revisited

1 Aron Heller, "King of the Negev," *Tablet* magazine, May 3, 2022, https://www.tabletmag.com/sections/community/articles/king-of-the-negev.
2 Aron Heller, "The Day That Changed Me Forever," Aron Heller Journalist, January 22, 2005, https://www.aronheller.com/articles/the-day-that-changed-me-forever/.

8. Somer James, the Reluctant War Hero

1 Aron Heller, "WWII Veteran Died as He Lived: Serving," Aron Heller Journalist, April 11, 2005, https://www.aronheller.com/articles/wwii-veteran-died-as-he-lived-serving.
2 Heller, "WWII Veteran Died as He Lived." See also Bernie M. Farber, "'If That's Not Bob Metcalfe, It's His Twin': The Mystery of the Veteran on the Canadian $10 Bill," *National Post*, November 10, 2020, https://nationalpost.com/news/the-mystery-of-the-veteran-on-the-10-bill.
3 Martin Sugarman, *Jews in the Merchant Navy in the Second World War: Last Voices* (Ellstree: Vallentine Mitchell, 2018), xiii.
4 Bessner, *Double Threat*, 99.
5 Wendy James, phone interview from Ottawa with author in Israel, February 4, 2024.
6 Canadian War Museum, "Somer Oscar James Merchant Navy," Second World War Discovery Box Personal Stories, accessed March 5, 2025, https://www.warmuseum.ca/s3/supplyline/assets/swwteacherresources/personalstories/T2.3.4-PS-Eng-James.pdf.

7 Family video testimony of Somer James on April 11, 2004. Private collection.
8 Keith James, phone interview from Winnipeg with author in Israel, November 26, 2023.
9 Royal Canadian Navy Volunteer Reserve, Canadian Merchant Navy, "James, Somer Oscar, Ordinary Seaman," Honours and Awards to Canadian Merchant Seamen for WW2, accessed March 5, 2025, https://web.archive.org/web/20170925123929/www.rcnvr.com/Merchant Seaman in WW2.php.
10 "A Hero – Somer James," *The Canadian Jewish News*, October 18, 2012, 16.
11 Ayah McKhail, Special to the *Globe and Mail*, May 4, 2005, S7.

9. Alfred Brenner, the Man in the Flying Suitcase

1 Canadian Jewish Congress, *Jewish War Heroes* (Ottawa: Canadian Jewish Congress, 1944), https://www.jwmww2.org/Jewish_War_Heros.
2 Bernie M. Farber, "Alfred Brenner, the Man in the Flying Suitcase," *National Post*, November 11, 2011, https://nationalpost.com/opinion/bernie-m-farber-alfred-brenner-the-man-in-the-flying-suitcase.
3 Veterans Affairs Canada, "Alfred Brenner," accessed March 5, 2025, https://www.veterans.gc.ca/eng/remembrance/people-and-stories/alfred-brenner.
4 Veterans Affairs Canada, "Alfred Brenner."
5 Prime Minister of Canada Justin Trudeau, "Prime Minister's Remarks Marking the Start of Veterans' Week," November 5, 2020, https://pm.gc.ca/en/news/speeches/2020/11/05/prime-ministers-remarks-marking-start-veterans-week.

10. Zaidy's Band of Brothers, the Jewish Canadian Soldiers

1 "Canada's Ultimate Story," *Legion Magazine*, Spring 2025, 8, 85.
2 Barris, *The Great Escape*, 116.
3 Canadian War Museum, "The Royal Canadian Air Force, 1939–1945," accessed March 7, 2025, https:// www.warmuseum.ca/cwm/exhibitions/chrono/1931rcaf_e.html.
4 The Chaim Herzog Museum of the Jewish Soldier in World War II, "Canada," accessed March 7, 2025, https:// www.jwmww2.org/Canada.
5 Bessner, *Double Threat*, 84.
6 Bessner, *Double Threat*, 92.
7 Bessner, *Double Threat*, 114.
8 Scott Masters, interview with Mickey Heller.
9 Ellin Bessner, interview with Mickey Heller.
10 Bomber Command, "No. 6 Group and the Canadian Squadrons," accessed March 7, 2025, https:// www.bombercommandmuseumarchives.ca/contribution.html.

11 Albert Glazer quoted in his obituary by James McCready, "A Hero of the Siege of Malta," *Globe and Mail*, September 7, 2004.
12 Albert Glazer citation in Rome, *Canadian Jews in World War II, Part 1, Decorations*, 27.
13 Bessner, *Double Threat*, 97.
14 Aron Heller, "These Jewish World War II Veterans Would Be Legends, if People Knew Their Stories," *New York Times Magazine*, May 8, 2019, https://www.nytimes.com/2019/05/08/magazine/canadian-jewish-veterans-world-war-ii.html.
15 Veterans Affairs Canada, "In Memory of Flying Officer Lou Warren Somers, June 25, 1943," accessed March 7, 2025, https://www.veterans.gc.ca/eng/remembrance/memorials/canadian-virtual-war-memorial/detail/2964960.
16 Oral History Project, "Winer, Lorne," accessed March 7, 2025, https://crestwood.on.ca/ohp/lorne-winer.
17 Catherine Porter, "History Lessons from Survivors, WWII Veterans," *Toronto Star*, May 9, 2015, https://www.thestar.com/news/gta/history-lessons-from-survivors-wwii-veterans/article_ad30139b-f6f9-5c7a-ac28-f55cfc8199a1.html.
18 Bessner, *Double Threat*, 229.
19 Bessner, *Double Threat*, 200.
20 Veterans Affairs Canada, "Jewish Canadian Service in the Second World War," accessed March 7, 2025, https://www.veterans.gc.ca/en/remembrance/people-and-stories/jewish-canadian-service.
21 David Rome, ed., *Canadian Jews in World War II, Part 1,* Casualties (Montreal: Canadian Jewish Congress, 1947).
22 Veterans Affairs Canada, "Sydney Shulemson," accessed March 7, 2025, https://www.veterans.gc.ca/eng/remembrance/people-and-stories/sydney-shulemson.
23 Ontario Jewish Archives, "Toronto's Jewish War Heroes," accessed March 7, 2025, https://www.ontariojewisharchives.org/Exhibitions/Online/For-King-and-Country/Toronto-s-Jewish-War-Heroes.
24 Canadian Military Engineers Association, "Lt Albert Hanson, 1st Field Company, Military Cross," accessed March 7, 2025, https://cmea-agmc.ca/award/gallantry/lt-albert-hanson-1st-field-company-military-cross.
25 They Were Soldiers, "Excursions in Jewish Military History and Jewish Genealogy: William Weiser," accessed March 7, 2025, http://theyweresoldiers.com/index.php/tag/wing-commander-william-weiser.
26 Ontario Jewish Archives, "Two Decorated Brothers: Leo and David Heaps at the OJA," February 9, 2015, https://www.ontariojewisharchives.org/Blog/Two-Decorated-Brothers-Leo-and-David-Heaps.
27 They Were Soldiers, "Excursions in Jewish Military History and Jewish Genealogy: Philip Goldstein," accessed March 7, 2025, http://theyweresoldiers.com/index.php/tag/philip-m-goldstein.

28 Noteh Glogauer, "Inspiration, Courage, Leadership: Canadian Jewish Heritage Month," Government of Canada, May 4, 2023, https://www.canada.ca/en/department-national-defence/maple-leaf/defence/2023/05/inspiration-courage-leadership-canadian-jewish-heritage-month.html.

11. Zvi Kan-Tor, the General on a Mission

1 The Chaim Herzog Museum of the Jewish Soldier in World War II, "Mervin (Mickey) Heller," accessed March 10, 2025, https://www.jwmww2.org/soldier.aspx?id=9560.
2 Dan Nadel interview with author in Jerusalem, May 25, 2015.
3 Norman Cohen, interview with author in Jerusalem, May 25, 2015.
4 Aron Heller, "Israeli Recognition, at Last, for Jews Who Fought the Nazis," *Times of Israel*, May 29, 2015, https://www.timesofisrael.com/israeli-recognition-at-last-for-jews-who-fought-the-nazis.
5 The Chaim Herzog Museum of the Jewish Soldier in World War II, "Government's Decision on the Establishment of the Jewish Soldier Museum in World War II," accessed March 10, 2025, https://www.jwmww2.org/Governments_decision_on_the_establishment_of_the_Jewish_Soldier_Museum_in_World_War_II.
6 The Chaim Herzog Museum of the Jewish Soldier in World War II, "Peter Arton," accessed March 10, 2025, https://www.jwmww2.org/soldier.aspx?id=10542.
7 Aron Heller, "Jewish War Veterans Bemoan Stalling of Israel's WWII Museum," *APNews.com,* April 24, 2017, https://apnews.com/article/bf32ca65a7d64043a0ce71dd1eab3b26.
8 Ilan Kfir and Danny Dor, *Chaim Erez: A Journey of Life* [in Hebrew] (Tel Aviv: Kinneret Zmora-Bitan Dvir, 2017), 313.
9 Zvi Kan-Tor, interview with author, Latrun, Israel, February 8, 2022.
10 Kfir and Dor, *Chaim Erez*, 318.
11 Aron Heller, "An Unprecedented Attack that Conjures Images of the Holocaust," *Times of Israel*, October 11, 2023, https://blogs.timesofisrael.com/an-unprecedented-attack-that-conjures-images-of-the-holocaust/.

12. Machal, the Foreign Volunteers

1 The Chaim Herzog Museum of the Jewish Soldier in World War II, "Eretz Israel," accessed March 10, 2025, https://www.jwmww2.org/Eretz_Israel_Volunteers.
2 Markovitzky, *Machal Overseas Volunteers.*
3 Ralph Lowenstein, "Why the Experiences of North American Volunteers Are Largely Unknown," Aliyah Bet & Machal Virtual Museum: North American Volunteers In Israel's War of Independence, accessed March 10, 2025, https://www.israelvets.com/essay.php.
4 Mitch Potter, "The Toronto Man Who Saved Nazareth," *Toronto Star*, December 20, 2015, https://www.thestar.com/news/insight/the-toronto-man-who-saved-nazareth/article_d07daec6-4159-5b2c-81be-68850de4b35e.html.

5 Kaplansky, *The First Fliers*.
6 Robert Gandt, *Angels in the Sky* (New York, W.W. Norton, 2017), 33.
7 Cohen, *The History of the Israeli Air Force*, vol. 1, 54.
8 According to statistics provided by World Machal, "USA Canada Machal," accessed April 15, 2025, https://www.machal.org.il/volunteer-database/usa-canada-machal/.

13. Smoky Simon, the South African Witness

1 "The Israeli Air Force Is a Year Old," *Davar*, October 26, 1948.
2 Cohen, *The History of the Israeli Air Force*, vol. 3, 74.
3 Gandt, *Angels in the Sky*, 286.
4 Smoky Simon, interview with author, Herzliya, Israel, July 20, 2018.
5 From Kaplansky, *The First Fliers*.
6 Saul Simon, "Flight of the Century – Smoky Simon," YouTube, September 14, 2020, video, 5:38, https://www.youtube.com/watch?v=uscN4a4ePcI.
7 "Smoky Simon's Story – The Birth of the Israeli Air Force," YouTube, n.d., video, 52:00, https://www.youtube.com/watch?v=-cuULmBJg84.
8 The Chaim Herzog Museum of the Jewish Soldier in World War II, "Harold Simon," accessed March 10, 2025, https://www.jwmww2.org/soldier.aspx?id=4787.

14. Samuel Heller, the World War I Veteran Father

1 Library and Archives Canada, "Collection Search," https://library-archives.canada.ca/eng.
2 Samuel Heller, Attestation Paper, October 1, 1915, Library and Archives Canada, https://central.bac-lac.gc.ca/.item/?op=pdf&app=CEF&id=B4237-S036.

15. Mickey Heller, a Veteran's Journey Revealed

1 Aron Heller, "Israelis Seek to Comfort Holocaust Survivors," *Santa Fe New Mexican*, January 27, 2017, https://www.santafenewmexican.com/news/israelis-seek-to-comfort-holocaust-survivors/article_7599835e-30ef-53ee-acaa-9b942ff87678.html.
2 Bomber Command Museum of Canada, "426 Squadron," https://www.bombercommandmuseumarchives.ca/squadron_426.html.
3 Bomber Command Museum of Canada, "No. 426 Squadron RCAF," archived February 1, 2008, at the Wayback Machine, accessed March 12, 2025, https://web.archive.org/web/20080201011612/www.raf.mod.uk/bombercommand/h426.html.
4 "Conspicuous Gallantry Medal (Flying)," *Supplement to the London Gazette*, November 19, 1943, 5076, https://www.thegazette.co.uk/London/issue/36254/supplement/5076.
5 Heller, "These Jewish World War II Veterans."

6 Aron Heller, "The Lost Dakota Fighters of Israel's War of Independence," *Tablet* magazine, May 28, 2019, https://www.tabletmag.com/sections/community/articles/dakota-fighters-of-israels-war-of-independence.
7 Pierre Lagacé, "Chapter Two – No. 1 Manning Depot," *Flight Lieutenant Frank Sorensen* (blog), October 20, 2019, https://colinfranksorensen.wordpress.com/2019/10/20/chapter-two-march-26-1941-the-fourth-letter/.
8 RCAF Association, "No. 433 Squadron," accessed March 12, 2025, https://www.rcafassociation.ca/heritage/history/rcaf-and-the-crucible-of-war/433-squadron/.
9 Air of Authority – A History of RAF Organisation, "Operational Training Units," accessed March 12, 2025, https://www.rafweb.org/Organsation/OTU_1.htm.
10 Bill McRae, "Bed and Breakfast: A Canadian Airman Reflects on the Food and Quarters during the Second World War," *Canadian Military History* 9, no. 1 (2000): 69, https://scholars.wlu.ca/cgi/viewcontent.cgi?article=1281&context=cmh.
11 Brian Ferstman, phone interview from Victoria, BC, with author in Israel, July 10, 2019.
12 This is an observation that Brian Ferstman shared with the author in an email on March 7, 2025.
13 Aron Heller, "Even as He Turns 100, RCAF Veteran Mickey Heller Goes Back to Memories of the Second World War," *The Canadian Jewish News*, November 11, 2021, https://thecjn.ca/perspectives/even-as-he-turns-100-rcaf-veteran-mickey-heller-goes-back-to-memories-of-the-second-world-war/.
14 Crestwood, "Oral History Project," accessed March 12, 2025, https://crestwood.on.ca/ohp.
15 Michael Petrou, "Echoes of War Live On in Our Veterans in Ways We Must Understand," *Globe2Go*, accessed March 12, 2025, https://globe2go.pressreader.com/article/282437057831781.
16 Log Book Project is available at https://thelogbookproject.com.
17 Oral History Project, "Mark Charness," accessed March 12, 2025, https://crestwood.on.ca/ohp/charness-mark.
18 Oral History Project, "Mickey Heller," accessed March 12, 2025, https://crestwood.on.ca/ohp/heller-mickey/.
19 Bessner, *Double Threat*, 188.

Epilogue: The Grandson, Me

1 Benjamin's Park Memorial Chapel, "Mervin (Mickey) Heller," accessed March 12, 2025, https://www.benjaminsparkmemorialchapel.ca/ServiceDetails.aspx?snum=116108&fg=0.

Bibliography

Air of Authority – A History of RAF Organisation. "Operational Training Units." Accessed March 12, 2025. https://www.rafweb.org/Organsation/OTU_1.htm.

Barris, Ted. *The Great Escape: A Canadian Story*. Toronto: Dundurn Press, 2013.

Benjamin's Park Memorial Chapel. "Mervin (Mickey) Heller." Accessed March 12, 2025. https://www.benjaminsparkmemorialchapel.ca/ServiceDetails.aspx?snum=116108&fg=0.

Bessner, Ellin. *Double Threat: Canadian Jews, the Military and World War II*. Toronto: New Jewish Press, 2018.

Bomber Command Museum of Canada. "Bomber Command Losses." Accessed March 3, 2025. https://www.bombercommandmuseumarchives.ca/commandlosses.html.

– "426 Squadron." Accessed March 12, 2025. https://www.bombercommandmuseumarchives.ca/squadron_426.html.

– "No. 6 Group and the Canadian Squadrons." Accessed March 7, 2025. https://www.bombercommandmuseumarchives.ca/contribution.html.

– "No. 426 Squadron RCAF." Archived February 1, 2008, at the Wayback Machine. Accessed March 12, 2025. https://web.archive.org/web/20080201011612/www.raf.mod.uk/bombercommand/h426.html.

"Canada's Ultimate Story," *Legion Magazine*, Spring 2025.

Canadian Jewish Congress. *Jewish War Heroes*. Ottawa: Canadian Jewish Congress, 1944. https://www.jwmww2.org/Jewish_War_Heros.

Canadian Military Engineers Association. "Lt Albert Hanson, 1st Field Company, Military Cross." Accessed March 7, 2025. https://cmea-agmc.ca/award/gallantry/lt-albert-hanson-1st-field-company-military-cross.

Canadian War Museum. "The Royal Canadian Air Force, 1939–1945." Accessed March 7, 2025. https://www.warmuseum.ca/cwm/exhibitions/chrono/1931rcaf_e.html.

Chaim Herzog Museum of the Jewish Soldier in World War II. "Eretz Israel." Accessed March 10, 2025. https://www.jwmww2.org/Eretz_Israel_Volunteers.

– "Government's Decision on the Establishment of the Jewish Soldier Museum in World War II." Accessed March 10, 2025. https://www.jwmww2.org/Governments_decision_on_the_establishment_of_the_Jewish_Soldier_Museum_in_World_War_II.

– "Harold Simon." Accessed March 10, 2025. https://www.jwmww2.org/soldier.aspx?id=4787.

– "Mervin Heller." Accessed March 10, 2025. https://www.jwmww2.org/soldier.aspx?id=9560.

– "Peter Arton." Accessed March 10, 2025. https://www.jwmww2.org/soldier.aspx?id=10542.

Cohen, Avi. *An Aerial Bridge to Independence* [in Hebrew]. Jerusalem: Israeli Ministry of Defense, 1997.

– *The History of the Israeli Air Force in the War of Independence* [in Hebrew]. Vols. 1–3. Jerusalem: Israeli Ministry of Defense, 2004.

"Conspicuous Gallantry Medal (Flying)." *Supplement to the London Gazette*, November 19, 1943, 5076. https://www.thegazette.co.uk/London/issue/36254/supplement/5076.

de-Malach, Yoel. *From the Hills of Tuscany to the Plains of the Negev: Memories 1924–2006* [in Hebrew]. Jerusalem: Ariel Publishing House, 2007.

Dromi, Uri. "Operation Dust Bowl 1948: Achievement and Missed Opportunity." *Ma'archot* magazine, July 1984, 92.

Farber, Bernie M. "Alfred Brenner, the Man in the Flying Suitcase." *National Post*, November 11, 2011. https://nationalpost.com/opinion/bernie-m-farber-alfred-brenner-the-man-in-the-flying-suitcase.

– "'If That's Not Bob Metcalfe, It's His Twin': The Mystery of the Veteran on the Canadian $10 Bill." *National Post*, November 10, 2020. https://nationalpost.com/news/the-mystery-of-the-veteran-on-the-10-bill.

Florence, Elinor. *The German Jew Who Bombed Berlin* (blog). April 23, 2014. https://www.elinorflorence.com/blog/jewish-pilot.

For King and Country. "Secondary Schools: G to M: Harbord Collegiate Institute (HRB-SS)." Accessed March 3, 2025. https://torontofamilyhistory.org/kingandcountry/tdsb/secondary-g-m.

Gandt, Robert. *Angels in the Sky*. New York, W.W. Norton, 2017.

Glogauer, Noteh. "Inspiration, Courage, Leadership: Canadian Jewish Heritage Month." Government of Canada, May 4, 2023. https://www.canada.ca/en/department-national-defence/maple-leaf/defence/2023/05/inspiration-courage-leadership-canadian-jewish-heritage-month.html.

Government of Israel. "Aryeh-Yehuda (Leon) Lightman" [in Hebrew], Izkor: The Commemoration Site of Fallen Defense and Security Forces of Israel. Accessed March 3, 2025. https://www.izkor.gov.il/%D7%90%D7%A8%D7%99%D7%94-%D7%99%D7%94%D7%95%D7%93%D7%94%20%D7%9C%D7%99%D7%98%D7%9E%D7%9F/en_5272f9eeba51aec8dc5c9661ed616ce4.

– "Zeev (Wilfred) Canter" [in Hebrew]. Izkor: The Commemoration Site of Fallen Defense and Security Forces of Israel. Accessed March 3, 2025. https://www.izkor.gov.il/%D7%96%D7%90%D7%91%20%D7%95%D7%99%D7%9C%D7%A4%D7%A8%D7%99%D7%93%20%D7%A7%D7%A0%D7%98%D7%A8/en_9da7e863fd31f6cd85feca5f35fe1ad7.

Greimel, Hans-Jörg. "Anna Essinger" [in German]. Anna Essinger Gymnasium. Accessed March 3, 2025. https://www.anna-essinger-gymnasium.de/schule/anna-essinger/.

Grossman, David. "Jewish War Memorial Unveiled on 11-11-11." *The Canadian Jewish News*, November 17, 2011. https://thecjn.ca/news/canada/jewish-war-memorial-unveiled-11-11-11.

Grossman, Roberta, dir. *Above and Beyond*. Produced by Nancy Spielberg. Hollywood: Paramount Productions, 2014. [Documentary about Machal]

Heller, Aron. "The Day That Changed Me Forever." Aron Heller Journalist. January 22, 2005. https://www.aronheller.com/articles/the-day-that-changed-me-forever/.

– "Even as He Turns 100, RCAF Veteran Mickey Heller Goes Back to Memories of the Second World War." *The Canadian Jewish News*, November 11, 2021. https://thecjn.ca/perspectives/even-as-he-turns-100-rcaf-veteran-mickey-heller-goes-back-to-memories-of-the-second-world-war/.
– "Israel Honors GI Who Told the Nazis, 'We are all Jews.'" *Times of Israel*, December 2, 2015. https://www.timesofisrael.com/israel-honors-us-gi-who-told-the-nazis-we-are-all-jews.
– "Israeli Recognition, at Last, for Jews Who Fought the Nazis." *Times of Israel*, May 29, 2015. https://www.timesofisrael.com/israeli-recognition-at-last-for-jews-who-fought-the-nazis.
– "Israelis Seek to Comfort Holocaust Survivors." *Santa Fe New Mexican*, January 27, 2017. https://www.santafenewmexican.com/news/israelis-seek-to-comfort-holocaust-survivors/article_7599835e-30ef-53ee-acaa-9b942ff87678.html.
– "Jewish War Veterans Bemoan Stalling of Israel's WWII Museum." *APNews.com*, April 24, 2017. https://apnews.com/article/bf32ca65a7d64043a0ce71dd1eab3b26.
– "Jewish WWII 'Avenger' Joseph Harmatz Dead at 91." *New Jersey Herald*, September 26, 2016. https://www.njherald.com/story/news/nation-world/2016/09/26/jewish-wwii-avenger-joseph-harmatz/3038567007.
– "King of the Negev." *Tablet* magazine, May 3, 2022. https://www.tabletmag.com/sections/community/articles/king-of-the-negev.
– "Last-Known Treblinka Survivor's Death Signals Looming Post-Witness Era." *Globe and Mail*, February 22, 2016. https://www.theglobeandmail.com/news/world/last-known-treblinka-survivors-death-signals-looming-post-witness-era/article28843330/.
– "The Lost Dakota Fighters of Israel's War of Independence." *Tablet* magazine, May 28, 2019. https://www.tabletmag.com/sections/community/articles/dakota-fighters-of-israels-war-of-independence.
– "My Aunt Jeanette – The World's Oldest Rockette." Aron Heller Journalist. September 15, 2007. https://www.aronheller.com/articles/my-aunt-jeanette/.
– "These Jewish World War II Veterans Would Be Legends, if People Knew Their Stories." *New York Times Magazine*, May 8, 2019. https://www.nytimes.com/2019/05/08/magazine/canadian-jewish-veterans-world-war-ii.html.

– "An Unprecedented Attack that Conjures Images of the Holocaust." *Times of Israel*, October 11, 2023. https://blogs.timesofisrael.com/an-unprecedented-attack-that-conjures-images-of-the-holocaust/.

– "WWII Veteran Died as He Lived: Serving." Aron Heller Journalist. April 11, 2005. https://www.aronheller.com/articles/wwii-veteran-died-as-he-lived-serving.

Heller, Aron, and Randy Herschaft. "Jewish Avengers Unapologetic for Targeting Nazis after WWII." *APNews.com*, August 31, 2016. https://apnews.com/article/6bc424c8a39743d1a43ad9518c5481a5.

Imperial War Museums. "Who's Who in an RAF Bomber Crew." Accessed March 3, 2025. https://www.iwm.org.uk/history/whos-who-in-an-raf-bomber-crew.

Jackson, Harold. "Anna's Children." *The Guardian*, July 18, 2003. https://www.theguardian.com/education/2003/jul/18/schools.uk1.

Jackson, Martha. "School for an Immigrant Neighbourhood: Harbord Collegiate's Happy Ghosts." For King and Country, November 17, 2022. https://torontofamilyhistory.org/kingandcountry/archives/2268.

Kaplansky, Eddie. *The First Fliers: Aircrew Personnel in the War of Independence*. Jerusalem: Israel Defense Forces, The Air Force History Branch, 1993.

Kfir, Ilan, and Danny Dor. *Chaim Erez: A Journey of Life* [in Hebrew]. Tel Aviv: Kinneret Zmora-Bitan Dvir, 2017.

Lagacé, Pierre. "Chapter Two – No. 1 Manning Depot." *Flight Lieutenant Frank Sorensen* (blog). October 20, 2019. https://colinfranksorensen.wordpress.com/2019/10/20/chapter-two-march-26-1941-the-fourth-letter/.

"The Long March." Stalag Luft III. Accessed September 7, 2025. https://stalagluft3.com/long-march/.

Lowenstein, Ralph. "Why the Experiences of North American Volunteers Are Largely Unknown." Aliyah Bet & Machal Virtual Museum: North American Volunteers in Israel's War of Independence. Accessed March 10, 2025. https://www.israelvets.com/essay.php.

Markovitzky, Yaacov. *Machal Overseas Volunteers in Israel's War of Independence*. Translated from the Hebrew by Moshe Kohn. Tel Aviv: World Machal, 2007. https://www.machal.org.il/wp-content/uploads/attachments/Machal.pdf.

Martin, Sandra. "Canada's Original Rockette 'Did Everything but the Circus.'" *Globe and Mail*, October 17, 2008. https://aronheller.com/wp/wp-content/uploads/2011/09/Aunt-Jeanette.pdf.

McRae, Bill. "Bed and Breakfast: A Canadian Airman Reflects on the Food and Quarters during the Second World War." *Canadian Military History* 9, no. 1 (2000): 61–70. https://scholars.wlu.ca/cgi/viewcontent.cgi?article=1281&context=cmh.

Michaels, Jamie. "Christie Pits Riot." *The Canadian Encyclopedia. Historica Canada*, December 16, 2020; last edited December 16, 2020. https://www.thecanadianencyclopedia.ca/en/article/christie-pits-riot.

Mosaic Lodge. "Historical Sketch of Palestine Lodge." Accessed March 3, 2025. https://www.mosaiclodge.com/home.

Ontario Jewish Archives. "Toronto's Jewish War Heroes." Accessed March 7, 2025. https://www.ontariojewisharchives.org/Exhibitions/Online/For-King-and-Country/Toronto-s-Jewish-War-Heroes.

– "Two Decorated Brothers: Leo and David Heaps at the OJA." February 9, 2015. https://www.ontariojewisharchives.org/Blog/Two-Decorated-Brothers-Leo-and-David-Heaps.

Oral History Project. "Mark Charness." Accessed March 12, 2025. https://crestwood.on.ca/ohp/charness-mark.

– "Mickey Heller." Accessed March 12, 2025. https://crestwood.on.ca/ohp/heller-mickey/.

Petrou, Michael. "Echoes of War Live On in Our Veterans in Ways We Must Understand." *Globe2Go*. Accessed March 12, 2025. https://globe2go.pressreader.com/article/282437057831781.

Porter, Catherine. "History Lessons from Survivors, WWII Veterans." *Toronto Star*, May 9, 2015. https://www.thestar.com/news/gta/history-lessons-from-survivors-wwii-veterans/article_ad30139b-f6f9-5c7a-ac28-f55cfc8199a1.html.

Potter, Mitch. "The Toronto Man Who Saved Nazareth." *Toronto Star*, December 20, 2015. https://www.thestar.com/news/insight/the-toronto-man-who-saved-nazareth/article_d07daec6-4159-5b2c-81be-68850de4b35e.html.

RCAF Association. "No. 433 Squadron." Accessed March 12, 2025. https://www.rcafassociation.ca/heritage/history/rcaf-and-the-crucible-of-war/433-squadron/.

Revivim Kibbutz. "Michael Weimers" [in Hebrew]. Accessed March 3, 2025. https://revivim.kibbutz.org.il/cgi-webaxy/sal/sal.pl?lang=he&ID=213588_revivim_degem&act=show&dbid=pages&dataid=revivim_420192_revivim_32.

Rome, David, ed. *Canadian Jews in World War II, Part 1, Decorations*. Montreal: Canadian Jewish Congress, 1947.

–, ed. *Canadian Jews in World War II, Part 2, Casualties*, Montreal: Canadian Jewish Congress, 1947.

Schoenfeld, Stuart. "Jewish Canadians." *The Canadian Encyclopedia. Historica Canada*, December 3, 2012; last edited July 26, 2024. https://www.thecanadianencyclopedia.ca/en/article/jewish-canadians.

Simon, Saul. "Flight of the Century – Smoky Simon." YouTube, September 14, 2020, video, 5:38. https://www.youtube.com/watch?v=uscN4a4ePcI.

"Smoky Simon's Story – The Birth of the Israeli Air Force." YouTube, n.d., video, 52:00. https://www.youtube.com/watch?v=-cuULmBJg84.

Sugarman, Martin. *Jews in the Merchant Navy in the Second World War: Last Voices*. Ellstree: Vallentine Mitchell, 2018.

Tessler, Leon. *A Glimpse of the Passing Scene: An Autobiography*. Toronto: AMA Graphics, 2013.

They Were Soldiers. "Excursions in Jewish Military History and Jewish Genealogy: Philip Goldstein." Accessed March 7, 2025. http://theyweresoldiers.com/index.php/tag/philip-m-goldstein.

– "Excursions in Jewish Military History and Jewish Genealogy: William Weiser." Accessed March 7, 2025. http://theyweresoldiers.com/index.php/tag/wing-commander-william-weiser.

Usher, Peter J. *Joey Jacobson's War: A Jewish Canadian Airman in the Second World War*. Waterloo, ON: Wilfrid Laurier University Press, 2018. https://doi.org/10.51644/9781771123433.

Veterans Affairs Canada. "Alfred Brenner." Accessed March 5, 2025. https://www.veterans.gc.ca/eng/remembrance/people-and-stories/alfred-brenner.

– "In Memory of Flying Officer Lou Warren Somers, June 25, 1943." Accessed March 7, 2025. https://www.veterans.gc.ca/eng/remembrance/memorials/canadian-virtual-war-memorial/detail/2964960.

– "Jewish Canadian Service in the Second World War." Accessed March 7, 2025. https://www.veterans.gc.ca/en/remembrance/people-and-stories/jewish-canadian-service.

– "Jewish War Veterans of Canada Memorial." Accessed March 3, 2025. https://www.veterans.gc.ca/eng/remembrance/memorials/national-inventory-canadian-memorials/details/8880.

World Machal. "Fred Stevenson." Accessed March 3, 2025. https://www.machal.org.il/personal-stories/fred-stevenson.

– "Jerome Lightman." Accessed March 3, 2025. https://www.machal.org.il/personal-stories/jerome-lightman.
– "Rabin Speech." Accessed March 3, 2025. https://www.machal.org.il/machal-memorial/rabin-speech/.
– "Wilfred (Zeev) Canter." Translated by Joe Woolf. Accessed March 3, 2025. https://www.machal.org.il/personal-stories/wilfred-zeev-canter.
– "William Fisher." Accessed March 3, 2025. https://www.machal.org.il/personal-stories/william-fisher.

Website Resources

Air of Authority – a History of the RAF Organisation: https://www.rafweb.org/
Bomber Command Museum of Canada: https://www.bombercommandmuseum.ca/
Canadian Military Engineers Association: https://cmea-agmc.ca/
Canadian War Museum: https://www.warmuseum.ca/
Chaim Herzog Museum of the Jewish Soldier in World War II: https://www.jwmww2.org/en
Imperial War Museums: https://www.iwm.org.uk/
Izkor, the Commemoration Site of Fallen Defense and Security Forces of Israel: https://www.izkor.gov.il/en/
National Library of Israel: https://www.nli.org.il/en
Ontario Genealogical Society, Toronto Branch: https://torontofamilyhistory.org/
Ontario Jewish Archives: https://ontariojewisharchives.org/
Oral History Project: https://crestwood.on.ca/ohp/
Royal Canadian Air Force Association: https://www.rcafassociation.ca/
They Were Soldiers, Excursions in Jewish Military History and Jewish Genealogy: https://theyweresoldiers.com/
Veterans Affairs Canada: https://www.veterans.gc.ca/eng
World Machal: https://www.machal.org.il/